ANDERL HECKMAIR My Life

ANDERL HECKMAIR

My Life

Eiger North Face, Grandes Jorasses, and other adventures

FOREWORD BY
REINHOLD MESSNER

Translated by Tim Carruthers

Bâton Wicks

Published by
The Mountaineers Books
1001 SW Klickitat Way, Suite 201
Seattle, WA 98134

© 2002 English translation by The Mountaineers Books

First North American and British editions, 2002

German Title: *Eigernordwand, Grandes Jorasses und andere Abenteuer*
© AS Verlag & Buchkonzept AG, Zürich, 1999

Published simultaneously in Great Britain by Bâton Wicks, London
Distributed by Cordee, 3a DeMontfort Street, Leicester LEI 7HD

Manufactured in the United States of America

Translation: Tim Carruthers
Project Editor: Laura Drury
Editor: Brenda Pittsley
Cover and Book Design: Ani Rucki
Layout: Amy Winchester

British Library Cataloguing-in-Publication Data
ISBN 1-898573-55-7
A catalogue record for this book can be obtained from the British Library

 Printed on recycled paper

Contents

Introduction

Anderl Heckmair: An Independent Man

"We were lying in a suffocating guesthouse in the north of Pakistan waiting for the morning. It was hot, but the whirring of the ceiling fan was so aggravating that I got up and switched it off. Then Anderl got up and immediately put it back on. So I switched it off again. And he put it back on."

Without uttering a single word they carried on like this for the rest of the night. This episode was told to me by Hias Rebitsch who set off for the Karakorum with Anderl Heckmair a few years after World War II. Neither man had the slightest desire to give in to the other. They had no interest in subordination or strict regulation—their whole lives long they belonged to the independents, and that by itself was enough to make me like them.

Anderl Heckmair is one of a dozen or so mountaineers of the twentieth century who achieved celebrity status yet remained independent. During his best years Heckmair was neither a loner nor a pal. He was an unmistakable character. Consider the efforts that he and other "mountain vagabonds" of the 1930s took upon themselves merely to get to the Alps in the first place! Because these young men, who ruled the scene in those days, were unemployed and did not want to fit in, they discovered minimalism in mountaineering. Silently, they agreed upon a few unspoken rules. They practiced tolerance even in rivalry, and voluntary self-restraint was the code.

Reinhold Messner and Anderl Heckmair at Castle Juval, Vinschgau, summer 1997

Thus they climbed the walls of the Civetta, the Grandes Jorasses, and the Eiger in a style that commands respect even today. They took great risks while mountaineering—and they had fun doing it. Anderl Heckmair is the prototype of the mountain vagabond. He found his path between the battle and the fun, between world economic crises and the Nazi era, between the Karakorum and the Andes, and in 1938 he was the one to find the way and lead his team off the Eigerwand. The way he lead the rope of four through the Traverse of the Gods, the Spider, and the Exit Cracks, dependable and determined, responsible to the point of self-sacrifice, is one of the glory hours of alpine mountaineering.

An idol in his time, Heckmair remained a mountain guide and a citizen of the world. He was a pilgrim; a seeker who wanted to know where the boundaries lay and which of them should be respected. He always set an example of how fun and achievement in mountaineering are not mutually exclusive, that the one is a precondition for the other. Because danger is part of mountaineering, he advocated solidarity in the team as more important than great words, at least during the climb.

Why is the Heckmair Route on the North Face of the Eiger one of the greatest climbs, indeed even a work of art? Because it is an expression of the serious and playful self-realization of four mountaineers who, trusting the strongest in the team, in fair partnership, managed a unique achievement, an achievement that signified a personal increase in experience. Is there anything more?

Anderl Heckmair did not hoist flag on the summit of the Eiger. True, he did not assume a contradictory stance in the triumphal celebrations that others around him launched for a country, an ideology, and a race. His dangerous game between the Hinterstoisser Traverse and the summit ice field was borne of his ability and his desire to achieve his own objectives. He succeeded in the greatest achievement of his life, but the prestige linked to this victory was never intended to enhance the reputation of the Third Reich. He remained true to his path throughout, a path epitomized by the Heckmair Route on the North Face of the Eiger.

To be sure, the North Face of the Eiger is, thanks to the Helicopter Rescue Service and the copious information now available, no longer the climb it once was. The era of the mountain vagabonds is also long gone, never to be repeated. We should not glorify it. Yet we shouldn't forget it either, as the independence with which Heckmair and those like him braved the dangers and mastered extreme difficulties on the great walls of the Alps is an expression of the values that set mountaineering apart. They are still valid today; let us hope they remain so tomorrow.

Reinhold Messner

Anderl Heckmair,
age 11, at the
Munich
orphanage

1. Going Up!

As an infant, I was something of a problem child, according to my mother. Sickly and unable to eat properly, from the day I was born on October 12, 1906, almost to my second birthday I survived by being packed, quite literally, in cotton bindings. On escaping from my cocoon I became very lively. I was sent to a kindergarten where I proceeded to unleash my zest for life that had been so long constrained. The place was thrown into disarray, and after a few days they sent me home again.

My father was from Bad Aibling, where generations of his family had owned and operated a gardening business. He was employed by the City of Munich as a master gardener and died at the age of 42 in the First World War. After his death, my mother, born in the "Au" and therefore a true Munich lass, could not afford to feed my older brother Hans and me on her tiny war pension, so we were sent to the Munich orphanage as "semi-orphans." I was ten. I spent four years there, attending school at the same time.

The mother: Magdalena Heckmair, (1876-1962), age 80

My memories of those years are mostly of the endless praying of the sisters of the convent that operated the orphanage, and of hunger, which was a constant companion. We used to sneak into the pigsty to steal boiled potatoes from the pigs. We never saw any pork; instead every evening there was a thin soup made of pearl barley, which, strangely enough, I could never get enough of. I like it even today when I think about how hungry we were then. At school, I was not a brilliant student by any stretch. Lessons began to interest me only in my last year, particularly anything to do with natural science and geography, and my grades improved noticeably.

In 1918, during the First World War, I had the luck to be sent to Switzerland for the summer holidays. I was one of forty kids looked after by two nuns who took us for walks in the neighborhood of Stans. Hand in hand, as befitted orphans, we walked up the paths of the Bürgenstock until a sister clapped her hands and said, "Now, children, you may run around and play." Immediately, we'd tear off up a steep gully interrupted here

The father: André Heckmair (1874-1916). Photo taken after 1900

and there with short vertical rock steps, scrabbling off loose stones without out a thought for anyone following behind. Before long there came a scream of terror. An orphan had been hit by a stone and fallen down the gully. The rest of us were not allowed move until local people arrived to escort us down one by one. The boy who had been hit lay dead in the grass. I was instructed to remain beside him with one of his sisters. This was my first introduction to the seriousness of the mountains. It seemed natural to me—in no way did it prevent my thoughts and desires from inclining toward mountaineering.

In 1920 my time at the school was over and the orphanage arranged for me to be apprenticed to a Munich gardening firm. My boss was a slave driver. After a year in his employ, I had done little except mow grass. I did not have days off, because, I was told, plants need attention even on weekends. Then one Sunday I seized my freedom and left without asking to go sledding with my brother. This led to an argument and I left the firm in a rage.

Luckily, I soon found another company where I could complete my apprenticeship. I felt at home there. I was not exploited and my new boss taught me the names of all the plants, something his predecessor had never troubled to do. However, one day I forgot to water a rare plant that stood at the entrance to the greenhouse. This was an oversight that my otherwise good-natured boss sought to punish by thumping me. Unfortunately for him, when he went to belt me he was standing next to a wooden lean-to where he did the bookkeeping. As he drew back his arm, I ducked and he hit the edge of the hut, breaking his arm. At the same moment his dog, a large schnauzer, leapt up and bit him on the other arm. To the huge amusement of his friends, this left my boss with one arm in plaster and the other thickly bound with bandages. I escaped scot-free and, plagued by my conscience, redoubled my efforts at work.

With brother Hans at their first communion, around 1913

No one is born a mountain climber. Despite the hard physical labor of gardening during my years of apprenticeship, I pursued all kinds of sports—gymnastics, track and field, swimming, and the like. My older brother was my role model in athletics, but every time I attained his level and began to surpass him, he would switch to a different sport and I would feel bound to switch too. Following his lead, this period is when

Age 20 in lederhosen

I made my first attempts at climbing the local Munich crags, the Kampenwand, the Ruschenköpfen, and the Plankenstein. But then I moved away to Stuttgart, where I had been offered a position in a landscape gardening company.

After a while in Stuttgart I received a postcard from my brother, who still lived up in the mountains, and a longing for the mountains flared immediately. Now I could think of nothing but how to move closer to them. Then by coincidence I was offered a grant to attend the Advanced Horticultural College at Weihenstephan near Freising. I seized the opportunity, and somehow I managed to study, live, and spend almost every weekend in the mountains on 30 marks a month.

I quickly found a circle of friends. It was wintertime, so one of them found a pair of skis for me and took me up to a hut. I had never worn skis before and knew about these planks of wood only from hearsay. It was also the first time I experienced the atmosphere of a mountain hut, and I felt proud and happy to be asked along. We carried the skis up an icy goat track in the dark. These skis were long, ugly things with a comical binding of leather thongs. Early the next morning we strapped them on and set off up the Brünstein. I grasped the idea of kick turning at once, and the uphill plodding and trailbreaking was a real pleasure to me, so I was always a couple hundred meters ahead of the others. I reached the summit in great shape and wasn't at all worried about the descent; I presumed it would be like a standing sleigh ride. There seemed no point

With this postcard of a Whitsuntide trip to the Zillertal Alps, Hans Heckmair lured his brother Anderl away from Stuttgart back to the mountains

in waiting, so I attacked straight away. Aha! So that's how it's done! All I had to do was to pick out a spot to head for, and land on it in a heap. I thought it was great and applied this technique all the way down to Bayrischzell.

But later I felt so exhausted I could not even eat, and the others, who at least had known how to do a snowplow turn, did not seem much better off. Our enthusiasm was undiminished, however, since no one in those times really knew how to ski anyway. Many winters went by before I picked up the proper technique by trial and error after experimenting with various styles. When I took my ski instructor's test in 1932, an onlooker remarked pointedly, "Never seen so many bad skiers on one slope at the same time."

By now my thoughts and desires were entirely directed toward the mountains. This passion comes from deep in the soul and cannot be explained. It can lead to supreme heights, but also to deepest ruin.

While I had sat idle in school, my brother developed into a real mountain climber, at least in my eyes. Knowing my uncontrollable nature, he had no intention of letting me come with him. However, one weekend he and his friends were going up to the Meilerhütte in the Wettersteingebirge above Garmisch. I accompanied him to the train station in the secret hope that he would ask me along, but the thought never entered his head. Sadly, I slouched homeward. But there was one more train to Garmisch, scheduled to arrive there at 11:30 P.M. Why shouldn't I just turn around and catch up with them? No sooner thought than I was on my way. From Garmisch I groped my way up through the night as best I could, and at dawn I slumped down on the bench in front of the hut. The first to appear through the door were my brother and his friend. "How the hell did you get here?" they asked. They could not very well chase me away, so they took me along with them to the Musterstein.

When the next excursion came a few weeks later they knew that there was no point in not taking me along to the Kopftörlgrat in

"I had never worn skis before and knew about these planks of wood only from hearsay."

Rappeling in the Wilder Kaiser Mountains in the 1920s

the Wilder Kaiser. Modest and well behaved, I trotted behind them on the way up from Hinterbärenbad to the Törl, where the end of the rope was solemnly passed over to me with the words, "There! That's so that you can become a great mountain climber." I thought, "They're crazy, but it must be a custom."

Surprised and slightly apprehensive I followed my leader as he worked his way panting and snorting up the cracks and grooves. When it was my turn to climb I thought, "What was with all that panting and snorting?" But I only thought it and said nothing until we reached the summit, where I asked, "Is that all there is to it?" Upon this, my brother Hans, who always took great interest in my upbringing, gave me a resounding box on the ears.

That same year my brother and his friends arranged to meet at the Stripsenjochhaus in the Kaisergebirge. It was pouring rain, so Hans volunteered to pay my fare if I took his place. In this way he avoided making a journey in vain and at the same time did not let his friends down. That

was all right by me, as I did not give two hoots about the weather. I knew the way as far as Hinterbärenbad, but there it began to grow dark. Naturally, I had no light. Night and mist combined to create darkness as impenetrable as the legendary Stygian gloom. I literally could not see my hand held up before my eyes. It seemed wise to sit it out until morning. But the rain continued and I grew so wet and cold that I had to move at all costs. I groped my way up the path on my backside, none too sure if I was still on the right track. After I had been sliding around in the wet on my bottom for hours, it began to grow lighter at last, and I was able to rise to my feet and make upright progress. By the time I reached the hut, the rain had turned to snow. I knocked half-heartedly on the closed door, not expecting anyone to open up, when suddenly the hinges turned and a sleepy but kindly girl ushered me into the warm parlor. She gave me some dry clothes and I curled up on the bench before the stove, safe and secure. I woke at about 6:00 A.M. as the first climbers began to appear out of the dormitories.

In the Wilder Kaiser Mountains

Outside, everything was sugared white and the sky was a radiant blue. I loitered around waiting for my brother's friends to appear, but they were nowhere to be seen.

A climber sat down next to me and began to sort out his pitons and carabiners. I had heard of these things. Fascinated, I looked on with great respect. Presently he directed a question my way. "Are you on your own too? We could do something together if you like." I would have gone with him on any face without another thought. He suggested the north arête of the Predigstuhl and I agreed with enthusiasm.

The gullies and chimneys leading to the foot of the climb were wet and icy. The first pitch begins with a traverse. I watched with rapt attention to see how he would tackle it. After he had slipped a couple of times he announced, "It's no good, it won't go today." I asked him to let me try. Somewhat derisively, he agreed. I stepped down, used the holds on which he had been standing as handholds, and suddenly there I was in the cracks above, so I continued and finished the pitch. When his turn came to follow, he was complimentary and took over the lead until the next difficult pitch, where the lead was passed to me again. So it went on until we came to the summit tower.

Failing to find the normal route (the Opelband), we climbed straight on. That was when it happened. I was on a small but good stance belaying over a spike of rock when he skidded off an icy slab and swung to and fro on the rope below me, wailing "Slack! Slack!" in a distressed manner. Centimeter by centimeter so that the rope should not run out too fast, I lowered him down to a ledge where he could stand. What next? He had the hammer and all our pegs and carabiners. "Rappel down to me!" he called. "Yes? How?" I had absolutely no idea how one went about doing this, and anyway I wanted to go up, not down.

After a prolonged exchange he hit upon the idea of tying the ironmongery to the rope, and I hauled it up. I then drove in the first piton of my life, though not without a few powerful blows on my own fingers. Luckily my companion was no more than ten meters below me, so I was able to double the rope. I fixed one strand so that he could haul himself up on it while I kept him tight on the other. When he reached me he was as white as cheese; there was no question of going on. Back then.

I had to tell him exactly where to go, like a schoolboy. As afternoon dimmed into twilight he wanted to call for help, but that was not to my taste and we almost started arguing. Somehow or other we reached the foot of the arête in pitch-blackness. As for groping our way back to the hut, I already had plenty of practice. I then found my way down to Kufstein alone so as at least to catch the first train back to Munich. In the station in Munich I ran into my brother, all suited up to come find me. I was touched by his concern.

Now the climbing bug really bit me. The holidays arrived, and I took a job in Munich to earn pocket money. Each evening after work I cycled up the Isar valley to the training crag where the "experts" could be seen swinging from hold to hold like monkeys. To climb like them became my goal. For the time being, however, I contented myself with the Fingertip Traverse, which is close to the ground.

My skills improved after a few evenings, and I struck up friendships with others of about the same ability. The local matadors paid no attention to us beginners. For our part, we observed them closely to learn how to tie on and above all how to distribute our own weight so as to climb and rappel cleanly. I did not possess a rope of my own, but a pair of *kletterschuhe* or proper climbing shoes were my pride and joy.

Somehow we are drawn to those neither worse nor better off than ourselves, and so it was that I teamed up with another climber who possessed nothing at all, not even a rope. No matter. We resolved to try the east face of the Lamsenspitz in the Karwendel.

After my dubious success on the north arête of the Predigtstuhl, my self-assurance advanced rapidly. I already felt myself to be in the position of leader, albeit still without a rope. Anytime my companion was in difficulty, I lowered him my anorak, and he pulled up on that. It seemed

like the most natural thing in the world. We cycled home feeling profoundly pleased with our successful climb.

Eight days later my friend fell to his death on the east face of the Watzmann. That is often the fate of climbers, but it shouldn't have happened so soon. Just one week later, another friend from the training crag was killed by a fall in the Karwendel. It began to dawn on me that mere rock-climbing technique is not all that a mountaineer needs. However, this realization did not inhibit me from trying to climb one of the most notorious faces. Once again my partner for the climb, the east face of the Fleischbank in the Kaisergebirge, was an acquaintance from the local crag, this time a dentist's son who possessed a rope.

My brother already knew that he was not going to keep up with my rapid development as a climber—he was always the more reasonable brother—but nevertheless he wanted to be somewhere nearby. Therefore, he teamed up with Hans Ertl to do the west face of the Predigtstuhl, directly opposite the Fleischbank.

On the east face of the Fleischbank, 1927

My partner and I gained height rapidly, having already learned and practiced various tricks for getting up the harder bits and doing tension traverses at the training crag. Now I wanted to see what "exceptionally severe" pitches were like. I was disappointed. Even those pitches that had been so described seemed no harder that what I had already done elsewhere. And they were certainly far from extreme. As a climber, the play of balance that affords such a marvelous feeling of freedom came naturally to me. I was never extravagant in my demands, being quite happy to make do with small holds. Yet the death of my two comrades had been a salutary and painful lesson. Even if you are lucky enough to have a kind of sixth sense for the mountains, it still needs to be exercised, developed, and sharpened. The early, impetuous years are the most dangerous for a climber. That was especially true in those days to a far greater extent than now.

As we climbed that day, shouts of encouragement echoed back and forth from one wall to the other between the climbing parties. Then suddenly there was a curious noise and the other party became very quiet. Not until we were sitting together on the "Strips" after successfully completing our respective climbs did the dentist's son and I learn that a solo climber following behind us had fallen to his death. The faces of Hans Ertl and my brother, who had had a clear view of the fall, still bore the shock. Later the same year, my companion on the Fleischbank fell off the Vajolet Towers.

Next I teamed up with Hans Ertl to do a few nice routes in the Kaisergebirge, the Karwendel, and the Wetterstein. One of those climbs remains etched in my memory because, through no wish of my own, it became my first first ascent.

Hans wanted to do the east face of the Oberreintalturm. However, we could not even find the start. "If we just climb straight up," I suggested, "we're bound to reach the summit." Hans was not exactly delighted with the idea, but when he emerged on the top, covered in blood as a result of my dropping a stone on his head shortly before, his pride at making a first ascent couldn't be restrained. I was less happy, since I was embarrassed at having to admit that the first ascent came about only because we failed to find the proper route. I felt even worse when, as a result of the inadequate description we gave him, Franz Singer, a most likeable member of our circle and an excellent climber, was killed trying to make the second ascent.

The eventful year of 1928 ended with us finding favor in the eyes of the great mountaineers whom we had admired at the training crag. We were elected members of a group of "extremists" called the Hochempor. The qualifications were to have done a number of extreme climbs and be able to play the game of schafkopf. At the weekly gathering, each member would give an account of the route he had done the previous weekend, then everyone got down to playing cards. Anyone who could not play did not belong. For us, membership represented not only a great honor, but also a great advantage, as the club had two huts for its roughly thirty members, the Bockhütte in the Wetterstein and a ski hut on the Spitzing. The latter was particularly beneficial, as I was desperate to improve my miserable abilities on skis. The other members were already hot skiers and racers with little patience for my problems as a beginner.

Bayrischzell traditionally held a ski-jumping competition at New Year's. One of those registered to compete, Leo Rittler, broke a leg while training the day before the event. "You'll have to go down there instead

of him," I was informed; and when I objected, "But I don't know how to ski," no one was interested. Leo's jumping skis were passed over to me, and we were towed behind a car from Neuhaus to Bayrischzell, arriving just in time for the competition. My knees were still knocking from the ski *jöring* when I looked at the ramp and began to shake inwardly as well. Suddenly it was my turn, or at least the turn of my number, as I was jumping for Leo. Well, I thought, if I make a mess of it, he is the one who will get the blame, not me. The thought comforted me and gave me confidence. As I jumped, an appalling void yawned before me, then the next moment I thudded onto the steep landing slope. Applause broke out, but no one was more surprised than me at my success. Feeling quite the star, I climbed back up the tower. This time I fell heavily, but that was normal. Successful jumps were very infrequent. That was just a little artistic bad luck, I thought, this time I'll show them. Show them I did. I landed so heavily that pieces of ski flew in all directions and I had to be carried away on a stretcher. My grateful public took up a collection, which raised so much money I was able to replace Leo's old skis and buy a pair of jumping skis for myself.

By spring my broken leg was healed. I could ski again and was eager to christen my new jumping skis. There was still snow on the Hochalm above Garmisch, so we spent a whole day leaping down a homemade ramp and rushing back up again. Admittedly, I could still only ski in a straight line, but for ski jumping nothing more is required. I smiled pityingly at the others as they practiced their turns, feeling immeasurably superior, until suddenly I planted my tips and had to be carried down again. The doctor made silly faces as they brought me into the same Munich clinic that I had only left just a few weeks previously. I comforted him with the thought that the leg he had healed had stood up to the strain, and this time it was a knee. It turned out to be the meniscus. By the time they let me go, spring was over.

Anderl Heckmair (standing) with companions at the Elmauer Tor in the Wilder Kaiser Mountains in the 1930s

My studies were finished. On the strength of my final report I got a job in the Munich municipal gardens. They had no idea what they were taking on. On Sundays I would do a difficult climb and often help carry down an accident victim. On Monday and Tuesday I would be tired, on

The leap from the Friedrichsturm in the Wilder Kaiser

Leo Rittler, 1929

Wednesday I would have to go to the funeral, which they could not very well refuse, and on Friday and Saturday I would be saving my energy for Sunday's climb. So it went on week after week, month after month, throughout the summer. It's little wonder that my superiors looked on me with disfavor. To me, my achievements in the mountains were of far more importance than my job. I had already evolved a philosophy of climbing for my own pleasure rather than to impress others, so before concentrating on first ascents, I determined that I wanted to climb all the classics within reach.

The summer of 1929 was filled with wonderful mountain experiences. With various companions I climbed all the hardest faces in the Kaisergebirge, the Wetterstein, and the Karwendel one after another. Nowadays, these climbs no longer count as anything very special, but at that time they had been done less than a dozen times. Few people were interested, and those climbers tended to be either praised to high heaven or condemned. Either way, we did not care; we had battles of our own to attend to. For example, the southeast face of the Fleischbank, climbed a few years earlier by Wiessner and Rossi, had still had very few ascents. Leo Rittler and Peter Aschenbrenner had climbed it the weekend before our turn came, but during the following week a party came rushing down with the tale that all the pitons had been removed. So what? Those who had made the first ascent didn't have any pegs either. We decided to go anyway. My companion was Wiggerl Gramminger. We climbed the face, found enough pitons, and took out as many of them as we could.

The following weekend saw us on the Laliderer Wall in the Karwendel Mountains. As a boy I had walked along the foot of this gloomy north face in the course of a solitary expedition. This time I went up to the Karwendelhaus, got a place in the attic dormitory, and then, because the shutters were closed to the light, overslept in the morning. Furious, and therefore all the quicker, I clambered up the Birkkarspitze and along the west ridge to the Kaltwasserkarspitze, then down to a very steep gully that turned into a chimney, then uphill again to the Hallerangerhaus—I cannot remember the whole route exactly. On one narrow ledge, however, I came round a corner to find myself suddenly face-to-face with an outsize chamois buck. I do not know which of us was more startled. When the buck began to back away, I thought it was preparing to charge, but suddenly it turned around and dashed away with a clatter of stones. I reached the Falkenhütte by evening. Never again has any face impressed me so much as that incredible wall, not even, strange as it may sound, the north face of the Grandes Jorasses and the Eigerwand. The awed impression of youth remains the most profound.

Now, however, we stood at the foot of the wall. We were well equipped, as we had a description of the route from Dr. Wilo Welzenbach, who explained all the hidden dangers and pitfalls. Of the two of us, Wiggerl Gramminger was the more experienced mountaineer, and leading is what brings the most pleasure, but he unselfishly let me go ahead. Nevertheless, I felt as though I was the one being led as he directed me upward meter by meter. By early afternoon we had climbed the face. On the way down the Spindler gully, a storm broke and we had to climb back up in order to avoid being hit by stonefall.

Now began a twelve-hour march along the Rossloch toward Scharnitz, then over past the Karwendelhaus to the Falkenhütte, which we reached in the gray light of dawn. After a little reviver we carried on down to the Eng, where we had left our bicycles, and pedaled back to Munich. Passing through Grünwald it occurred to us that it would be fun to play around for a while on the training crag, since we were going to miss work that day anyway. On the crag we ran into friends who greeted us excitedly with the words, "The mountain rescue (to which we belonged) is sending out a search party for you." Somebody had the idea of telephoning from the nearest pub to say that they had found us on the training crag. Instead of praise we got a good telling off.

We had made the mistake that beginners often make, whatever their age, because they fail to realize that others worry about them. But that was not the only charge that we brought upon our guilty heads. The same weekend another party had set out to climb the southeast face of the Fleischbank and found very few pegs, some of which, moreover, had been hammered flat. Forced to retreat, they blamed their failure on us. Our fellow climbers treated us like outlaws. I did not care too much about that, however. My view was and is that if someone has confidence enough to tackle a particular climb, there should be no expectation that others will have prepared the way first. Wiggerl did not agree. He felt we should make up for what we had done while at the same time demonstrating that we ourselves could climb the route without the *in situ* pitons. So back we went and replaced the more necessary pegs. Honor was satisfied, at least in our own minds. Now I had earned the respect of the extreme climbers.

What I could never understand was why climbers are so often judged according to the difficulty of the climbs they undertake, when there were so many other beautiful things to experience in the mountains. In this respect I owed a lot to my work, which gave me an eye and a taste for botany and geology. But even the roughest lads among us were sensitive to all the beauties of nature. I am convinced that it has always been so with mountaineers and always will be.

Mungo Herzog,
Anderl Heckmair,
and Hans Brehm
after the Civetta
trip in 1929

2. Mountain Vagabonds

The next winter, I was determined to learn to ski properly. I had had enough of ski jumping and was now keen on touring, since the whole business of climbing up, breaking trail, and running down through the deep snow—even if only in a straight line—was devilish good fun.

One day, however, it happened that there was a cross-country race, and some of my friends, knowing my powers of endurance, insisted that I take part. At least, I thought, it will be safer than jumping. A further incentive was that the start and finish were in Bayrischzell, where my brother had settled and was working as a goldsmith and photographer. He lent me his cross-country skis and, shortly before the start, took me into a field for a quick lesson in how to use them. With a warning not to tire myself out at the start he tied on my number bib. The starter announced "Three, two, one . . . Go!" and I was off. Mindful of my brother's warning, I walked rather than ran, and was naturally overtaken by all and sundry. I thought to myself, "Just you wait. When I cut loose I'll get the lot of you." It was the 18-kilometer race for the Munich championship, and when after 10 kilometers I decided that the time had come to put on a spurt, I found I was too tired and just plowed on doggedly. I was deeply ashamed to finish last.

The Bavarian cross-country championships were held soon afterward, also at Bayrischzell. I wanted to redeem myself in my own eyes and therefore set out from the beginning to race until I dropped. Putting the plan into practice, I did not drop at all and even overtook some big name racers. Coming into the finish I passed a skier who had started ten places in front of me. He was a good sort, since he stared at me in an astonished way, shook my hand, and congratulated me. Much later I learned that this was Wiggerl Vörg, who was to play an important part in my life. This time I was satisfied with my performance and did not care what place I had obtained. But when the finishers list appeared, Vörg, whom I had overtaken, was credited with a time superior to mine by several minutes. Wiggerl could not swallow this and immediately lodged a protest, only to be shot down in flames and summarily disqualified. A judge never makes a mistake! Well, if it was like that they could stuff their races. I preferred ski touring anyway. But I never forgot Vörg's fanatical sense of justice and sportsmanship.

I wanted nothing more to do with racing. My technique had improved, but I was well aware of just how little I knew how to do. Others evidently hadn't noticed, as I was invited to join a relay race. They thought I was the ideal man for the first leg from the Rotwand to the Spitzingsee. I had strong doubts about this, but I could not let my friends down, so I duly plodded up to the Rotwandhaus and the starting line.

It was cold, with wind-driven snow, and a lot of strong racers were waiting for the sign to start. I knew this descent . . . and now I had to race down it. I could feel the apprehension in my guts. This kind of emotion can affect your insides, and shortly before my number was due to come up I felt a powerful call of nature. The "place" was perched above a trench. No sooner had I sat down than there was an explosion, presumably caused by gas under the frozen crust. I was blown right off the seat and covered with stinking muck. At least I was only plastered from behind—another person who had just opened the door to go into the next compartment got it in his face. Once the initial fright was over there was a great roar of laughter that put me into a towering rage. I stripped off my underwear, wiped myself down with them, hurled them away, and dressed again as best I could. As soon as I reappeared, my number was called. I

was happy to get away from the malicious guffaws and grinning, and also to get ahead of my own stench, so much so that on the climb up to the col I overtook two men whom I never would have caught on any other day. On the descent I hurled myself downhill with such fury that the slopes seemed flat and I lost all sense of speed. The inevitable happened. Shortly before the end of the leg, at the place where the next racers were waiting to take over the batons, an almost invisible stone stuck out of the snow. I crashed into it. On arrival at the hospital, I was given a good bath, for which I felt distinctly grateful to my broken coccyx. My craving for ski racing was entirely satisfied.

"I really wanted nothing more to do with racing. It was true that I had improved my technique slightly, but I was well aware of just how little I could still do."

It was understandable that my employers at the city gardens regarded my mountaineering ambitions without enthusiasm, and I was not surprised to be given notice while still in the hospital. Widespread unemployment was beginning. But, by law, so long as I remained in the hospital, I could not be dismissed. I continued to receive my wages, as well as a sickness benefit and more money from an insurance policy. By the time I was let out I had saved 1000 marks. I had never been so

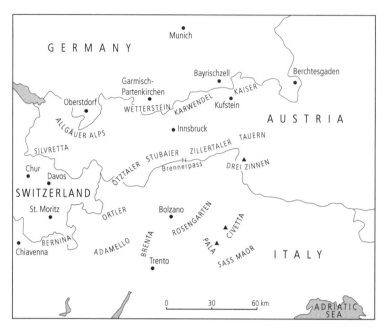

rich and decided to stay up in the mountains as long as the money would last. Friends were soon found to join me. Hans Brehm did not need to be asked twice, and Hans Ertl promised to follow with another companion. We fancied a trip to the Dolomites. At the Bavarian branch of the Deutscher Alpenverein (German Alpine Club) we heard a famous climber, Walter Stösser, talk about the fourth ascent of the northwest face of the Civetta. In the course of his lecture he mentioned that "the number of ascents may be limited, as the hand traverse that starts the climb is crumbling away, and when it goes there will be no way to get onto the face." We believed this quite literally—presumably he did too—and suddenly we felt drawn to the Civetta.

Lacking another option, we would go there on our bicycles. To solve the problem of luggage transportation we built ourselves "the gig," a little trailer that we loaded with our substantial rucksacks and towed behind a bike. Everything went well as far as the Brenner, but from there to Bolzano the roads were torn up for construction. This is where the trailer gave up on us, so we ended up carrying not only the rucksacks but the trailer as well. Days of pushing over the Karer and Pordoi Passes did not worry us too much. There was hardly any motor traffic. After a few days we reached Alleghe, where for the first time we were able to take a refreshing bath in the lake before starting the climb up to the Coldai hut. The rucksacks were strapped to the gig, but we did not get far with it and soon we had to shoulder both the sacks and the damned gig again. To cap everything, we were caught by a storm on a col below the hut. But we quickly pitched the tent and crawled inside, feeling safe and secure. It was still early in the year, and the face was full of ice and snow. This did not stop us from heading up it first thing the next morning. The initial hand traverse was indeed earthy and loose, but only about half as bad as we had imagined from the description. It seemed you shouldn't believe everything you heard from these great alpinists.

The wall was tricky, but we made rapid progress until we came to another traverse. It was 10:00 A.M. by the time I got across it. Hans Brehm lobbed off after a few moves and swung at least 10 meters until he was hanging below me. Haul and tug as I might, I could not shift him, and finally had to let him down a couple of meters to a place where he could at least stand. There was no recourse but to rappel down to him. So we sat there with our heads hanging and thought of giving up. "Let's just try it again." I fixed a rope across the traverse, and finally we had it in the bag. At 2:00 P.M.

Roast chicken dinner in the Dolomites, 1929. Hans Brehm, Anderl Heckmair, Hans Ertl

we stood on the same stance that I had reached four hours earlier—and this on the biggest and hardest face we had ever tried to climb. We did not even have a bivouac bag with us. The only solution was to climb fast. We managed to keep up our speed clear to the summit, which we reached at 8:00 P.M. It was still light enough for the descent, if only we could have found it. Thick clouds had built up from the side of the ridge. There was nothing else to do but sit down behind a rock and wait for better weather. However, we were in a lively mood after our efforts on the face. Neither the wet nor the cold bothered us in the least. During the night, the cloud thinned and it started to rain. By dawn it was pouring down, but we could at least see and managed to find the way into the corrie. Here we met a track and began to argue whether we should go left or right. I got my way, though I was by no means sure. For hours we followed it to and fro from one corrie into another. Thick fog closed down again as the path vanished into a grassy pasture. "Now you're in the shit," grumbled Hans mutinously. Suddenly we heard something. We were standing 20 meters from the Coldai hut.

We celebrated our success with a plate of pasta asciutta and a jug of wine, and then continued on down to our tent where Hans Ertl and Mungo Herzog, brother of the famous Otto, who was known among climbers as a "Rambo," were waiting.

Every climber lives according to a personal style. When I am not actively doing something, I tend to be lazy. Here, I could not be induced to stir from our splendid campsite for eight days. Hans Ertl, who was a first-rate chef, spoiled us lavishly and kept our spirits up until we recovered some drive. Our next route was the east face of the Sass Maor. First climbed by Solleder and Kummer in 1926, it was still awaiting its second ascent. We had started to think of ourselves as the masters of the mountains, but our knees buckled at the sight of this 1100-meter yellow wall. All our expectations and fears were duly fulfilled. Remember that, knowing nothing about étriers and other artificial aids, we had to free-climb everything. We were already using double-rope techniques, however. We hit on the idea of using two ropes for a simple reason. In those days the only ropes readily available were 12- and 13-mm hemp lines. As they had to be 40 meters long for the climbs we were doing, they

"When I am not actively doing something, I tend to be lazy. Here, I could not be induced to stir from our splendid campsite for eight days."

were simply too heavy. When we observed the leader of another party fall and the rope snap (probably it was an old one), we decided to start using two thinner, lighter ropes, and to carry one each. It never crossed our minds that we were contributing to the development of new climbing techniques. We only thought that if one rope broke in the event of a fall, the other would hold. Plus we quickly realized that overhangs were much easier to climb if one of the ropes was clipped to a piton with a carabiner, and then held in tension while the leader leaned back, placed

Anderl Heckmair during the second ascent of the east face of the Sass Maor, 1929

another piton, clipped the slack rope into it, and then took tension on this second rope while the first one was left slack. We climbed quite respectable overhangs using this method.

Incidentally, I wrote my very first article about the ascent of the Sass Maor. I sent it to an Alpine journal, which printed it. When a fee eventually came I was amazed at first, then indignant, "So little money for such a big climb. They ought to be ashamed!"

As a "dessert" after the Sass Maor we plumped for the Schleierkante, climbing it the following day. It was to remain my favorite route in the future. After this I indulged my craving for laziness, spurning any further routes, and set off for home. In spite of the state of the roads but without the gig, I managed the stretch from Bolzano to Bayrischzell in a day. I wanted to bring a present for my brother, so I carried Italian cheese, sausage, bread, fruit, and chocolate in the rucksack. At 11:00 P.M. that night, 3 kilometers before Bayrischzell, I was suddenly overcome by such ravenous hunger that I sat down on a woodpile and scarfed every bit of it. I couldn't stop myself. A few minutes later, with empty hands and troubled conscience, I reached the house where my brother lived. He was not there. There were few pubs in the village, so it did not take long to find him. He was in the process of celebrating his victory in a chess tournament. I joined in the festivities, and neither of us knows how we got home that night.

Playing chess with brother Hans (right), 1947

The summer of 1930 was not yet over, when, to give my brother a treat, I took him up the west face of the Totenkirchl. Fate played a part, and the trip turned out to have a decisive effect on my mountaineering future, as I met Gustl Kröner from Traunstein on the route. He had done some difficult ice climbs in the western Alps that summer. I could not get enough of his tales of these climbs. He told me about the Grandes Jorasses and the north faces of the Eiger and the Matterhorn, all of which he had at least seen. If we teamed up, he said, we could attempt one of these faces. I thought he was crazy, as I had never climbed on ice. "That's not a problem," he said. "Anyone who can rock climb like you can certainly climb on ice." Moreover, he said, we did not have to go for one of the big faces right away; we could just take a look and then do something else. That made sense to me, but the question was which one to take a look at. The Mont Blanc range offered the most possibilities, and I liked the name of the Grandes Jorasses best. By the time we parted company it had been decided that we would travel to the Mont Blanc area together the following year, 1931.

But all that was still a long way off. First, I had to survive the winter. I was registered as unemployed, but it was hardly possible to survive on the benefit payments, let alone get out to the mountains. It was no different for other members of the Hochempor Club. Therefore, we decided to do without the pitifully inadequate welfare money and parked ourselves at our ski hut at Spitzing. Those who still had jobs brought us so much food on the weekends that we could always get through the following week. It was here that I struck up a particularly close friendship with Bartl Hütt, with whom I had already done some climbs in the Kaisergebirge. Now that fate had thrown us together again, we noticed that we complemented one another to a remarkable extent. Bartl was as strong as a bear and rather the silent type. He was an infinitely better skier than I and took the trouble to teach me the basic skills I needed for cross-country skiing, and this was exactly what I wanted as I was through with any kind of racing. We stayed up at the hut until spring, at

Bartl Hütt

which point he proposed a plan for us to go to the central Alps. My objection that I had not really done enough cross-country skiing was dismissed out of hand. As for financial considerations, he said, "If we wait for money, we'll never go." That seemed clear enough, and preparations were made.

We set off on March 1, 1931. Each of us carried two rucksacks, one on our back and one in front, stuffed full of food we had cadged. We had 30 marks between us. Thus equipped, we left Garmisch station with the intention of reaching the Ötztal. We chose not to follow the road over the Fernpass, but humped our four rucksacks up the track from Lermoos to the Wolfratshausen hut, having conceived the crazy idea of skiing down to the Fernpass from Grubigstein. Moreover, we intended flitting from hut to hut, since the rules of the Alpenverein guaranteed us an emergency overnight stay in a hut for a fee of just 40 pfennigs, the utmost we could afford. And somehow we did succeed in getting down to the Fernpass, though I went flying over a little cliff in the process. I held on to the precious rucksacks, but broke a ski pole. Once we reached the road we built a sled with the skis, loaded the rucksacks on to it, and sledded off down the pass.

Bartl had been a vagabond once before, and knew how to get a night's lodging at a monastery. With piously raised eyes he asked the brother porter at the little fortified cloister below the Fernpass for alms and a spot to curl up for the night. Both were granted to us after a prayer for the poor. We spent the night in the straw of the pigsty with one of the devout brethren. The next day we tramped on into the Ötztal. A heavy truck gave us a lift as far as Zwieselstein, at which point the driver noticed with horror that he had lost one of our ski poles. I could not bring myself to protest and kept silent as, with many apologies, he bought me another pair. For weeks we wandered through the Ötztal range, making ourselves useful in huts, sometimes guiding tourists, and constantly under the impression that each tour would be the last and that we would soon be booted home. Yet miraculously it went on and on, and for now we had more money in our pockets than when we set out. Gaining in confidence, we crossed over the Gepatschtal to the Silvretta. Above Compatsch we reached the Heidelberger hut without realizing we had passed through Swiss territory. Again we moved on from hut to hut, making our situation known on arrival and asking for odd jobs. We chopped wood, fetched mail and provisions, folded blankets and swept dormitories. No task was beneath our dignity. Most of the hut custodians were reluctant to see us move on, but we did not want to get bogged down.

There were many highs and lows, not only on the mountains we crossed, but also with tourists, hut wardens, and guides. Even now I wonder how our inadequate equipment survived weeks and months of tough, unrelenting use. Yet never once did we get stuck because of it. With the steel edges of the skis, however, we waged unremitting war, until finally we nailed them right through the skis and hammered the points over. We climbed every single summit within reach. When new snow fell we nearly always broke the trail. Tourists and even guides behind us were so grateful they would buy us a meal and a drink in the hut afterward. We also humped rucksacks from hut to hut for tourists. We had long abandoned our original idea of carrying two sacks of our own, so we generally had capacity for a tourist's sack on our chests. Bartl frequently went so far as to carry three, but I preferred to make two trips. Whenever we reached a new hut we had generally been talked about in advance by tourists and therefore were expected. At the Wiesbadener hut the warden greeted us with the words, "Ah, there you are at last. Go into the kitchen and have a bite, and then ski down to Galtür, spend the night there at my expense, and tomorrow bring up everything on this list."

"We had started to think of ourselves as the masters of the mountains, but our knees buckled at the sight of the 1100-meter yellow wall on the Sass Maor."

We were a little surprised at this presumption, but it was Easter, and when we saw the hordes staying in the hut we understood well enough. Moreover, it turned out to be an advantage. When we got back to the hut with the mail for the guests, they had a gigantic Easter dinner waiting for us.

We had been traveling now for six weeks. On reaching the Tübinger hut we sat down and raided the piggybank. It came to precisely two Austrian shillings. What should we do? Head for home or slip over the border into Switzerland? We couldn't get home on two shillings anyway, so Switzerland it was.

Down in Klosters it was already spring. We had an idea to look for work at construction sites. Everywhere they said they would have been glad to take us on, but it was against the regulations. Next we tried a plant nursery. Of course I had no references with me, so the manager was mistrustful at first. However, I reeled off the names of all the plants in the cold frames, and he began to believe my claim to know something about laying out gardens. Now he became brightly enthusiastic, found quarters for us, and said he would soon sort everything else out. In the meantime, we were to go around to his house and get a meal from his wife. With stomachs rumbling from having gone hungry for a week, we did not need to be told twice. It was nearly suppertime.

Anderl Heckmair (standing) and Bartl Hütt at the Lötschen Hut

The good lady placed an enormous bowl of noodles and sauce on the table and told us to dig in; the others would be along presently. That was a mistake. Our hunger was so great it was out of control. Bartl normally ate enough for two anyway, and now he ate for four while I ate for two of the absentee dinner guests. In a few moments we had gobbled the bowl clean. When our new boss came in and found nothing left his eyes bulged and his wife was horrified that we had devoured the lot in such a short time. However, the Swiss cannot be accused of inhospitality. The others had to make do with coffee and we kept up with them manfully.

After we had worked for a week the local *gendarme* appeared and demanded that we leave the country. Our patron gave us some money and told us to disappear up to a hut while he arranged work permits. Nothing could have suited us better. We went to the Parsenn hut, spending our time enjoying the marvelous ski runs, the fame of which we never suspected, until the boss came to fetch us down. He had indeed succeeded in obtaining permits, but after a few days the policeman came around and withdrew them because we had previously worked illegally. In darkness and fog we set out, albeit provided with food and generous pocket money. The boss had tears in his eyes at losing us. We were supposed to leave the country at once, but instead we wandered over by way of the Vereina hut to the Engadine and then went up into the Bernina range.

At the Boval hut we ran into two famous climbers from Vienna, Dobiasch and Vaitl, who were guiding some tourists up Piz Palü the next day. We had intended to have a rest day, but the fine weather and ready-made tracks were too tempting. We set out late in the morning and caught up with the other party on the summit. Far from being applauded for our speed, however, we were reprimanded for taking advantage of their tracks. I would have thought such great men would be above all that. The next morning we got up at three o'clock and broke the trail all the way up to the Piz Bernina. This time it was Dobiasch and Vaitl who followed. They came over to compliment our tracks afterward. Vaitl stared at my hooded anorak, an article of clothing completely unknown in those days. "Where did you get that?" he asked. I explained that I had found it at the foot of the Civetta. "Then it's mine," he said. "I brought it back from Lapland and left it lying at the foot of the Civetta." Such coincidences happen. A friendship was struck up, and we had no more need to worry about food supplies or hut fees.

It was now the end of May. We had thoroughly explored the area around the Coaz hut (in particular, I remember a sunset as I skied down from the Fuorcla della Sella on fresh snow as one of the most beautiful moments of my life). And so our thoughts began to turn to making our way home.

Our skis and anything else we did not need we dispatched by rail from St. Moritz. We ourselves set out on foot, annoyed at having failed to forward the rope as well, as we now considered it to be an unnecessary piece of ballast. In this we were mistaken. Just before reaching Zuoz, we spent the night in a haystack. In the gray light of dawn we were dragged out by our feet by a farmer whose use of language in his Romansch dialect was truly awful to hear. It seemed to me that we should be the ones cursing since he had woken us so rudely. But he showed no sign of ever stopping, and suddenly I said to Bartl, "Get rid of him!"

That was all Bartl needed. The next moment the farmer took an involuntary headfirst dive into the hay, then he picked himself up and ran

off toward the village. As our rest had been disturbed anyway, we decided to get going. We innocently ambled along, suspecting nothing, when our path through the village was suddenly barred by two men, one of whom was our farmer and the other a policeman, although in civilian clothes. It was the most critical moment of the entire trip. One false word and there would have been a brawl.

Bartl had already adopted an attitude of eager anticipation. The policeman said soothingly, "Don't do anything crazy. We just want to know who you are and whether you're on the wanted list." That sounded reasonable, and we went with them meekly. They led us to a house, up a steep staircase, ushered us politely into a room, slammed the door shut behind us, and locked it. It wasn't very nice to lure us into a

After the escape. Bartl Hütt stands before the village tower of Zuoz, 1931

trap like that. Looking out the window we saw that our prison was a turret room, and below the window was a smooth wall 10 or 12 meters high descending into a garden. What were we carrying that rope for? In a few minutes we were standing in the garden. You should never imprison mountain climbers in towers.

Circumventing the border crossing, a forced march through steep forest brought us to Ehrwald, from where we had just enough money for the train fare to Pasing, a suburb of Munich. A kindly official at the ticket counter made up the extra out of his own pocket so that we could continue through to the main Munich station. No such Good Samaritan in ticket collector's guise appeared to help us with the tram out to Giesing, where we lived, so we marched along through the city, blisters and all.

The blisters soon healed, the bad moments of the adventure were quickly forgotten. What remained was an experience that the thickest wallet in the world could not have purchased. And already the next adventure beckoned.

Anderl Heckmair
(right) with Gustl
Kröner, training in
the Wilder Kaiser
Mountains, 1930

3. Attempts on the Grandes Jorasses

To make ends meet, Bartl had to report back to the labor exchange. I, however, had an outstanding arrangement with Gustl Kröner to visit the Grandes Jorasses. It was time for us to go. Gustl had been making initial preparations, and just four weeks after my return from Switzerland we saddled up our bicycles and pedaled off for Chamonix. We were not alone this time. Leo Rittler and Hans Brehm had their sights firmly set on the north face of the Matterhorn. We traveled together as far as Lucerne, where our roads diverged, and our parting was a crude and uproarious affair. It would have been more emotional had I known that I would never see them again.

We made a detour en route to take in the south face of the Drusenfluh, a climb steeped in hideous myth. Walter Stösser made a direct ascent of the face and reported finding no fewer than five bodies during his climb. An aura of disaster weighed heavily upon the face. The first ascender had survived, the second-ascent party fell to their deaths, the third made it, the fourth perished . . . and so on, right up to Stösser on his—the ninth—ascent. The face devoured all the even-numbered parties. It was there in black and white for all to read in *Bergsteiger,* which we acquired just before we set off. It meant that the next party—the tenth—could expect disaster.

We wanted to test the theory, so we turned left at Feldkirch and at 3:00 P.M. the next day we stood at the foot of this notorious mountain face.

It did not look especially fearsome. For a moment we even doubted whether we stood below the actual face that enjoyed such a horrific reputation. We were not disappointed. After just a few pitches we came across tatty pieces of frayed rope hanging in a chimney; in a few meters more we met the first of the bodies. They did not look too gruesome, since they were largely covered with soil and debris. According to the route description, we now had to arch up to the left for 150 meters to find the next corpses. The description was correct—the bodies made exceptionally good route markers. By six in the evening we were on the summit. It was a pleasant climb, not too easy but not too hard either.

The next day we went down to Schruns to report our findings. We were directed to the local priest, from the priest to the mayor, and from the mayor to another esteemed official, but no one showed any interest in the body count, and our offer to help with salvage operations was received without enthusiasm. Suit yourselves, we thought. We had only wished to dispel the "curse," which had not inconvenienced us in the least, and with a light heart we continued our carefree journey through glorious Switzerland to Chamonix.

We arrived at our destination much faster than we expected. We set up our headquarters at the Leschaux hut below the Grandes Jorasses, ferrying our loads up from Chamonix via Montenvers. Each trip took five or six hours, since financial considerations made using the mountain railway out of the question. Our undertaking was financed partly by the Bavarian section of the German Alpenverein in the strictest confidentiality, and partly privately. In particular, Gustl Kröner, who though not exactly rich was not poor either, sank his entire savings into our campaign. I had nothing to offer apart from my comradeship and ambition. As long as the latter did not become too excessive, Gustl was in agreement.

There was a double-burner gas stove in the hut. We soon learned how to cope with it; so well, in fact, that it would not work unless we wanted it to. Whenever we saw a party coming up the glacier to the hut—we could spot them a good two hours in advance—we would switch it to "not working." After letting the new arrivals fuss with it for a while, we would do our rescuing angel act, thus

The north face of the Charmoz above the Mer de Glace. Anderl Heckmair and Gustl Kröner made the first ascent in 1931. Montenvers is in the foreground.

earning their gratitude. In bad weather we would have hot tea waiting for them, so our relations with all the hut visitors were immediately of the best.

It was mid-July when we made our first cautious approach to the face. It disappointed us from every angle, and from directly below it looked as though we could be up it in a couple of hours without any special effort. My powers of judgment were not dulled by any experience whatsoever with ice. Gustl merely grinned. We made considerable ceremony of donning our crampons, since it was the first time I had ever had the pointy iron things on my feet. The 'schrunds were soon crossed, and after a couple of pitches of steep ice, Gustl let me assume the lead so that I could get the feel of it. I felt at home immediately.

"It's splendid," I shouted down. "You don't have to mess around looking for holds." The steepness did not bother me in the slightest. The fickleness of ice was something I only learned about much later in highly disagreeable circumstances. Gustl, however, was careful, hammering in pitons at stances and as running belays, and therefore wasting far too much time in my estimation. On his leads he cut his way upward step by step. When my turn came, although a complete beginner on ice, I did without steps and just walked straight up on my ten-point crampons. After that Gustl would not let me lead anymore. This was undoubtedly a piece of luck, as we had put only half of the ice field behind us when a storm blew in from the west and forced us to beat a hasty retreat. As we rappeled down, I really noticed for the first time how steep the ice field was. We were hardly across the bergschrund when the storm broke. Soon stones and avalanches were hissing down the gully we had intended to climb. That such a little storm could achieve such an effect! Was it possible that the gully was not the safest way up? With this revelation we walked back to the hut and celebrated the fact that we were still alive.

The weather was decidedly bad all that summer of 1931. There were never more than two or three nice days before another bad period set in. It was nearly a week before we could get back onto the face. Having learned to avoid the gully we climbed diagonally toward a buttress on the right. Even here we came under fire. A stone the size of my fist strafed

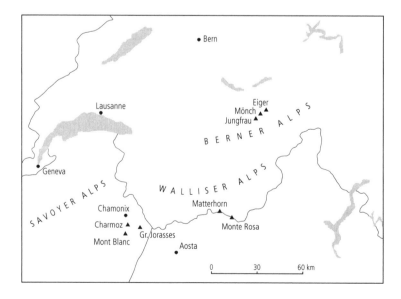

me, knocked the ax out of my hand, and sliced half through the rope. By some miracle I was unhurt, but we had had a shock and beat another hasty retreat.

Three more times we went up on the face; we even attempted the line of the Walker Spur, which later became so famous. But the time was simply not ripe for the north face of the Grandes Jorasses. Today I realize that what we thought of as bad luck was in fact a colossal stroke of good fortune, since ambition and technical rock-climbing ability are sometimes not enough. The necessary equipment and experience for such a great climb did not yet exist. Far greater mountaineers than us had fared no better—Welzenbach and Merkl had been repulsed some years earlier.

After a while we decided it was dumb to concentrate always on the same face, and then turn back without having achieved anything, so we moved on to other projects. On our return from the East Face of the Grépon we bumped into Welzenbach and Merkl at the Leschaux hut. They told us about their attempt on the north face of the Charmoz. A storm had forced them to traverse out to the right from the top of the big ice slope. Naïvely, and not very tactfully, we announced that we would go up and finish their line. Apparently this idea did not appeal to them, as a couple of days later they set out from Montenvers to finish the climb. Again a storm surprised them on the upper half of the face, and they remained nailed to the spot for three days. The newspapers were already anticipating a high-mountain drama and reported us missing too, while we sat in the warm hut frying one pancake after another. When the flour finally ran out we went down to Chamonix and learned of our disappearance.

"On arriving in Nice we dashed into the waves with loud shouts of delight."

However, we were seriously worried about Welzenbach and Merkl, and went back up with the intention of starting up the north face of the Charmoz the next day. First of all, however, we wanted to find out at Montenvers where they had last been seen. At four o'clock in the morning, to our amazement, the window of their room stood open. As we stood there wondering what it might mean, a shape materialized. It was Welzenbach. Through continuing bad weather, they had traversed across to the east side of the face, passed over the summit, and finally got back to Montenvers at midnight, five days after starting out. As if they had not had enough fresh air in the course of three bivouacs, they slept with the window

wide open. Hearing our muttered conversation, they invited us to their room, where at four in the morning we drank a bottle of wine to celebrate their return.

Meanwhile, the day had broken, and as we had all our equipment with us it seemed wise to make the most of the day, so we walked up to the Requin hut to do the Dent du Requin. Another storm caught us in an icy chimney just below the summit. This time we had really had enough. *Requin* means shark, we remembered, and decided to head for where those beasts swim around—it would certainly be warmer. Down to Chamonix we plodded, then jumped on our bikes and pedaled off toward Marseilles. On the way we saw a signpost that said 250 kilometers to Nice. Marseilles was beyond that. We emerged from the mountains 20 kilometers before reaching the town. On arriving in Nice we dashed into the waves with loud shouts of delight.

Next we cycled leisurely along the whole Riviera to Marseilles. The Tour de France was on, and despite our rucksacks we were often taken for strayed racers and treated to the appropriate celebrations. We were perfectly happy to go along.

In the old port at Marseilles we ran across some Germans who arranged work for us on the docks. Keen to refresh our travel funds we accepted gladly. We were expected to carry 100-kilo sacks. Gustl, who was even less robust than I, refused this hard labor at once. However, I had been watching an aged, emaciated Arab trot down the gangplank with one sack after another without batting an eyelid. Ambition seized me, and I joined the line. The first sack almost crushed me, then I seemed to get the hang of it, but after a couple of hours I was suddenly finished. My knees buckled. In the meantime, Gustl had been rolling barrels and watching me with sadistic pleasure, but now he hurried over and helped me back to my feet. All my "colleagues" were extremely friendly and sympathetic.

I was ashamed of my collapse, but the hard cash we were paid was an effective and comforting remedy. We immediately invested in a mighty lunch. As for accommodation, someone recommended that we try the poorhouse, where one paid nothing and got a bowl of warm bread soup. You had to be inside by 6:00 P.M. and were released again at 6:00 A.M. We were not keen on the idea as we wanted to see something of the sinful city, where there were many opportunities to go astray in the old port area. But not without money. We were ready

"I had been watching an aged, emaciated Arab trot down the gangplank with one sack after another without batting an eyelid. Ambition seized me, and I joined the line." In the port of Marseilles, 1931.

for adventure, but as the "lady" generally demanded that we "pay 'er" in advance, and we could not pay, we always got tossed out. Nevertheless, we had good fun until one in the morning. Since there was nothing doing that night, we got on our bikes again and headed for Chamonix. We arrived there after two and a half days and went straight to the Leschaux hut.

The north face of the Grands Charmoz looked so inviting as we passed under it that we said, "Let's do it now!" Good sense prevailed, however, and we decided to have a decent night's sleep, a rest, and a meal, and then put our plan into practice. Around lunchtime the next day we were satisfied that we could feel no trace of fatigue, so we set off intending to bivouac at the foot of the face. We were there by 3:00 P.M. It seemed much too early to bivouac. We were sure to find something higher up, we reckoned.

So up we went. The first part of the face, a kind of pedestal some 600 meters high, presented no difficulties. It was indeed loose, icy, and streaming with water, but at the speed we were going we had no time to think about such things. By six o'clock we had reached the main ice slope. We thought that was about enough for today, so we started setting up a bivouac between the rock and the ice. That's when the whole sheet of firm snow covering the ice slope suddenly slid off and went thundering down over the pedestal. We were lucky we were not still on the pedestal. And we were lucky that it happened to one side of where we were standing. After this our little bivouac site seemed less attractive; who knew what else might be on its way down? It seemed prudent to go up at least as far as the upper edge of the ice slope.

Never again have I experienced such curious conditions. The surface of the ice was hard, but as soon as we cut a step meltwater came pouring out of it like a spring. I felt like Moses smiting the rock, only I had no one to provide water for. The surplus water merely trickled into our boots. Okay, so we won't cut steps then! We had no twelve-point crampons, we had not even heard of them; in fact they had yet to be invented. Stamping all my ten points hard into the slope, I ran out a whole pitch as fast as possible, then cut a stance, hammered in an ice peg, and let the water spray over my feet. Using risky methods like this it is no wonder that we made rapid progress and soon reached the upper edge of the ice field.

Unfortunately, the ice here was so steep and rotten there could be no

Gustl Kröner "training" at the Leschaux hut, 1931

Anderl Heckmair ice climbing on the Grandes Jorasses. Drawings by Gustl Kröner, 1931.

thought of a bivouac. Which way had Melzenbach and Merkl made their exit? We would have been glad to find any way off, but only succeeded in reaching the eastern ice gully leading to the summit. It began to grow dark; down at Montenvers the lights twinkled brightly. We had just enough light to see that a bivouac here was impossible. The start of the gully looked almost vertical. However, over on the rock bordering the ice there was a crack parallel with the slope that was just the right width for jamming in the hands and the right distance from the ice so that we could continue to claw up on crampons. It went excellently, only I could not find a single place to take a stance. Gustl did not relish this piece of gymnastics, but he just had to climb.

At last I reached a dogleg; there was snow in the bed of the gully and I could stand in it. It was high time, as the crack in the rock wall had petered out and it was now almost totally dark. The exit was now almost close enough to touch, though garnished with a monstrous cornice. I did not trust the weird edifice at all and directed Gustl to take cover in a place where he was even able to take a couple of turns of the rope around a rock spike and belay. It was a good thing, as I had hardly begun to dig a channel diagonally through the cornice when the entire wave of snow broke over my head and carried me down with it. Gustl hung on to the rope with a will of iron and I found myself gasping on the end of the rope. But not for long. Clambering up again, I encountered no further problems now that the cornice had broken away. After another short stretch of individual rock climbing we reached the summit together just as the full moon rose. Beyond ourselves with happiness, we fell on one another's necks and yodeled our traditional climbers' greeting.

The word "wet" does not adequately describe the state we were in, but there was nothing we could do to change that. The ever-cautious Gustl had brought a sleeping bag with him. Though it was only designed for one, we managed to squeeze into it. He also had a handful of rice. What more could we want? We had moonlight, we were wet, we had the most wonderful view imaginable, and although we were cold there was no wind and in due course morning came again.

These things, combined with the sense of danger overcome and inner satisfaction at one's own performance,

Gustl Kröner on the summit ridge of the Charmoz after the first ascent of the north face with Anderl Heckmair, 1931

are what a mountaineer experiences. Any external recognition would have felt quite alien. Down at Montenvers in the morning we celebrated with a glass of beer as we sat and gazed up at the north face we had climbed. Every phase of the adventure came back to us now, together with the danger we had been exposed to. We had challenged fate to such an extent that we almost felt ashamed to be alive. Now, however, we were able to grant ourselves a few days of well-earned rest at the hut. Gustl looked after our physical well-being while I reveled in an orgy of botany and geology, filling the hut with flowers and crystals. We had no difficulty finding customers for the latter in Chamonix, which provided the means to carry plenty of goodies back up to the hut with us.

Meanwhile, we were acquiring an ever-growing respect for the north face of the Jorasses. With our inadequate equipment it was clear that we could not survive bad conditions, and there seemed no likelihood of getting a whole week's fine weather.

Another spectacular storm chased us back home from the traverse of the Aiguille du Dru. This expedition took nineteen hours. We stumbled back up the Leschaux Glacier with only the dazzling lightning to show

The north face of the Grandes Jorasses. Drawing by Gustl Kröner. The lines show the routes that Heckmair and Kröner thought possible.
1) lower bergschrund;
2) upper bergschrund;
3) high point of the 1931 attempt. The black triangle marks the presumed point at which Hans Brehm and Leo Ritter fell to their deaths. The circle denotes the high point reached by a party in 1928.

us the way. We were close to exhaustion when we arrived back at the hut. For lack of anything better we put potatoes on the stove to boil, lay down for a rest until they were ready, and promptly fell into a deep sleep. By the time one of us woke up the hut was full of blue smoke and an odd smell. It was still dark. Then we discovered that it was not still dark, but dark again. We had slept for a whole day, and the potatoes in the saucepan looked like shriveled lumps of coal.

Presumption caused us to seriously underestimate the time we needed to do the Dru. A couple of days earlier on the Rochefort Ridge good conditions had made everything seem so easy that we jumped to a conclusion that if the guidebook said it would take two hours, we could do in twenty minutes. We therefore figured on six hours for the Dru, which in fact required nineteen. It was a real blow to our morale, and our formerly overweening pride shrank to nothing. Hence our hesitation concerning the Jorasses.

However, we were far from idle. Moving over to Courmayeur, we walked up to the Gamba hut with a view to climbing the Peuterey Ridge, only to be dogged by bad weather yet again. By the time we got back to the valley it was fine, so we went up again to the Torino hut—all this was on foot, naturally, as there was no cable car in those days—then down the Mer de Glace, reaching the Leschaux hut in a snowstorm.

The hut was shut on the outside, as usual, but inside reigned the disorder of a hurried departure. It hit me like a slap in the face: "Leo Rittler and Hans Brehm are here!" We had heard at the Torino hut that the north face of the Matterhorn had been climbed, not by Leo and Hans, who had left Munich with us and cycled to Zermatt, but by the Schmid brothers. We did not begrudge their success; on the contrary, it gave us great pleasure, as Franz and Toni Schmid belonged to our own close circle of friends. But how would Leo and Hans feel about it? A thought formed in my mind: Perhaps they had come and gone on to Chamonix to join in our struggles on the Grandes Jorasses. The suspicion that they had been there became a certainty when I reached into the pocket of a jacket hanging on the wall and found Hans Brehm's passport.

Inscription on the tombstone of Hans Brehm and Leo Ritter at the graveyard in Chamonix

Outside the storm raged with unimaginable power, and our friends were up on the face. Of course it was also possible that they were down in Chamonix stocking up on provisions, but I did not believe that. I knew

Leo and Hans too well. In their disappointment over the north face of the Matterhorn they had almost certainly gone straight up to the Grandes Jorasses. There was a slim chance that they would turn back; it was still early afternoon. We brewed some tea, just in case. The clouds seemed to be thinning a little—there, almost at the foot of the face, something was moving! I rushed out and shouted. Nothing. I had imagined the movement. It was just a rock, not so far away, with the cloud shifting over it. We drank the tea ourselves. As night fell, hope began to fade. The weather was still bad the next morning. "Why don't we check down in Chamonix? Maybe we'll run into them down there," Gustl suggested.

In Chamonix we met a lot of climbers, but no Leo and Hans. With hanging heads we went back to the hut, not looking at the people we passed on the way past Montenvers. What did they know of our struggles and worries? Toward evening, as we neared the hut, the weather cleared slightly, and hope revived for a moment. But again there was nothing. It was now certain that they were on the face. Not being so close to them as I, Gustl was able to be a little more optimistic, although he understood and shared my disquiet.

The next morning dawned fine at last. Immediately we trekked up to the bergschrund with the intention of setting off up the face and climbing until we found out what fate had befallen our comrades. We did not need to go to such lengths. At the lower 'schrund I saw a hand sticking out of the snow. We found our friends stiff in the new snow, still roped together. The sun was now touching the summit of the mountain and the face was coming to life. It was no time to hang around; we were standing exactly in the fall line below the central gully. We dragged the bodies of our friends out of the danger zone, buried them again in the snow, marked the spot, and hurried back to the hut to report what had happened. On the way we ran into climbing friends

"We dragged the bodies of our friends out of the danger zone, buried them again in the snow, marked the spot, and hurried back to the hut to report what had happened."

who took over the task, and before long the rescue team arrived. Reduced to the role of mere onlooker, for the first time I was overcome with grief. Many important personalities attended the funeral in Chamonix. Where they had come from and why they came I did not understand. All of a sudden our presence was no longer required, and we followed the tail of the procession. Our homemade wreath of pine and erica was the last to be laid upon the graves.

We had had enough of Mont Blanc and the Grandes Jorasses for one year, but before setting off for home we looked at the face once more and swore a solemn oath to return.

"No one wanted
to come to blows
with Bartl!"

4. Spring Ski Tours

The journey home took several days, whereupon it was again necessary to concern ourselves with the problems of everyday existence. This presented no great difficulty for Gustl, as his father had a flourishing painting and decorating business in Traunstein. For me it was a real problem. Timidly I reported to the Munich labor exchange, partly hoping to find work, partly fearing I would find it. And, indeed, an amiable young woman informed me, "Someone has been looking for qualified gardeners to work on a project in the Rhineland." Travel expenses would be paid to Opan. A tremor of panic ran through my limbs, not at the prospect of the work, but at the thought of having to move. There was no obligation to take any job offered, but a refusal would mean that I could draw no unemployment benefit.

When times are hard it is best to keep out of the way of people you know, especially if the problems are of your own making. I found it downright disagreeable when a delivery van stopped beside me and a childhood playmate jumped out and greeted me affectionately with "How are you? What are you doing these days?" and so on. When I told him that all I had in the world was a rumbling stomach he suggested I become his partner. He made his living buying fruit and vegetables in the city markets and selling them in the country. He urgently needed someone to help. I accepted with enthusiasm. The van, however, was temperamental. It was a Model T Ford and looked more like a hearse than a fruit and vegetable van. To get it to start we had to get up at 3:00 A.M. to light a small fire under the engine and then crank it by hand for half an hour.

The goods were bought at the wholesale market and sold to country shops with a 100-percent markup. We needed this profit margin because the old vehicle not only consumed an enormous amount of gasoline, but also gulped three liters of oil per 100 kilometers. In addition, as we had no spare, we would have to stop and patch a tire three of four times per trip. Wheel off, tire off hub, inner tube out, clean puncture, slap on prepared patch, put it all together again, give 600 stokes with the hand pump, and then drive on until the same thing happened with another tire. In time we became so well practiced at it that it hardly bothered us anymore. The one drawback was that we could never be punctual and this antagonized several customers. We muddled through like this all winter, until one day near Pasing as I was driving home alone there was a horrible noise and the peevish old truck refused to move another millimeter. It steamed like a locomotive, while at the same time brown icicles hung from the radiator—it was always leaky, and we used to plug the holes with chicory coffee powder.

I peered under the hood, knowing already what had happened. The crankshaft had broken. A policeman strolled up and remarked that the van seemed to be on its last legs. "It's given up," I replied. "What should I do?" After intense deliberation the policeman advised me to remove the license plates, since I would have to unregister the vehicle and everything must be dealt with in the proper order. The van could be left where it was and would be towed away in due course. My friend and partner was sad to see it go, but there was nothing else to do. We therefore divided our takings, and I went off to see Bartl to ask him if he would like to do another spring ski tour.

This time we decided to venture a little farther afield to the Bernese Oberland and, if we could make it, go on to the Valais. Having had a happy experience with bicycling, we forwarded our equipment and skis to Gletsch, hopped on our bikes and pedaled off down the Rhône valley. The start of our trip was not very auspicious. It was three in the morning on April 1, 1932, when I went around to collect Bartl, and a snowstorm was in full swing. At Pasing we had to go into the station waiting room to warm up and dry off. This did not bother us too much, however. The snow stopped, it grew light, and we continued our journey in good spirits, reaching Kaufbeuren on the first day.

Like the temperamental April weather, our mood changed from lighthearted optimism to self-absorbed pessimism. Was this adventure going to happen at all? This time we had only 50 marks between us. Nevertheless, we were at least on our way, and in due course we reached our first objective. On inquiring about our luggage at Brig we learned that there was indeed a station at Gletsch, but no trains, as the timetable had been suspended for the winter. A kindly railway clerk telephoned half of Switzerland before learning where our things had gone. They would take at least two days to arrive. Seeing what a pair of poor devils we were the clerk offered us his hospitality, feeding and sheltering us until everything arrived. In the course of our conversation, he wondered what had impelled us to set out on such an adventurous journey. When we explained that rather than fritter away the time waiting for work and living on charity we preferred to accept hardship, privation, and hunger if by doing so we could fill our lives with experiences. He understood. The mountains were our ideal, we told him. Up there we felt no social distinctions, and what we needed would always turn up. Out of his honest heart he wished us good luck and loaded us up with as much food as we could carry. Traveling this way we met people and certainly got to know them better than those who travel with a bulging wallet.

We pushed our heavily laden bicycles up to Fiesch, where we stayed in the youth hostel. Two days of ascent took us up to the Concordia hut, which we pronounced our headquarters. No summit in the vicinity was safe from our attentions. Every time we thought we were running out of money for wood—every stick of wood we burned had to be paid for—

or running low on provisions a party of tourists would arrive who had more than enough. It was astonishing to observe how many tried to get away without paying the hut and wood dues. We watched them like hawks, and no one wanted to come to blows with Bartl! During one such dispute when it got quite tense, we were silently observed by a couple of Swiss. As we triumphantly put the carefully reckoned dues in the safe, they came forward, introduced themselves as officials of the Swiss Alpine Club section to which the hut belonged, and presented us with a free pass to all their huts.

The whole of April had passed by the time we decided to go down to Fiesch again. An army group occupied the hut and salami sausages hung from the coathooks in the vestibule. Unable to resist the temptation, we stuffed one into the rucksack and headed out onto the wide expanse of the Aletsch Glacier. Mist and a diffuse light prevailed, and we were unable to find the way through the maze of crevasses to the Märjelensee. The decision whether to bivouac or to return to the hut where we had filched the sausage was a difficult one to make, but common sense prevailed. After all, we thought, even if the soldiers noticed the missing sausage they can't very well put us up against a wall for it. In fact, all that they had noticed was that we had gone; they even seemed glad that we were back before dark, as the weather had taken a turn for the worse. We hung the sausage back in its place, and, spiritually relieved, took our place in their circle. Before long we were telling them about the tours we had done and our intention to travel on to the Valais. We were taken for veritable prodigies, and the next morning there was

The Concordia
huts, above the
Grosser Aletsch
Glacier, 1930s

no need to pinch sausages; they loaded us up with as much of their rations as we could carry.

We had now been up in the mountains for more than three weeks. In the youth hostel where we had left the bikes an atmosphere of panic reigned. They had reported us missing to Bern. It was difficult to grasp that we mattered enough for anyone to worry about us. Finally, we were bid farewell with the admonition to give news of ourselves now and again when we wanted to be away for long.

Down the hill to Brig we went, along to Visp, and then up into the St. Niklaus valley to Zermatt. On the last stretch there was no road, only a path. We not only had to push the bikes, but often had to carry them too. As a prelude to our stay in Zermatt we were treated to three days of unrelenting rain. We set up house in a hay barn. Our provisions were better suited to staying in a hut than in the valley; our staple was polenta, supplemented with fat, salt,

"We not only had to push the bikes, but often had to carry them too."

and sugar. We wanted to preserve the small remaining quantity of sausage for special occasions. With his special brand of gallows humor, Bartl chanted fervently, "Our father, who art in heaven, send us this day some money so we can get enough daily bread to make the table bend, then let us get on up the mountain!"

However, our heavenly father did not take pity on us, and so we walked up to the Monte Rosa hut with hungry stomachs, where we filled ourselves with the polenta. This gave us enough fuel to tackle Monte Rosa, which, being in good shape, we easily managed in a single day. On the upper slopes there was powder, then a short zone of breakable crust, and then on the moraines such perfect firn that at every turn the snow sprayed up over outcropped rocks. The joy in our faces found an echo on those of a group who had been following our descent from the hut. It must be admitted that at first we were not so overjoyed to see them, as it is always more pleasant to have a hut to yourself. Our gloomy mood was rapidly dissolved by their friendly reception, however. The guides Friedrich Schneider and Toni Matt had tea ready for us and were horrified when we wanted to make do with our polenta alone.

The next day the group attempted to find a way up the heavily crevassed Zwillingsgletscher to the summit of Castor, while we went up the Grenzgletscher and climbed the Lyskamm. The double-corniced ridge gave us a lot of trouble, as it has many another party. More than once the cornice collapsed under one of us, forcing the other to jump down the other side of the ridge. We wasted no time discussing the maneuver, as we had practiced the technique on the Grünhorn in the Bernese Oberland. We summited at about midday and arrived back at the hut in the late afternoon.

Soon afterward Matt and Schneider arrived back with their party, having failed to find a way through the labyrinth of crevasses on the Zwillingsgletscher. "How far did you get?" they asked.

"To the summit."

"You can't be serious?" They thought it was empty bragging and left us sitting there with our polenta.

The next day we exchanged objectives. We did not try to get through where the other group had failed, but where it looked possible to us. We struck lucky and reached the summit. By following our trail the others did not have too much difficulty reaching the summit themselves, and that evening they were profuse in their apologies for their mistrust and disbelief. Good relations were restored. As the conversation came around to the Civetta, the Grandes Jorasses, and the Charmoz, their respect knew no bounds. It was natural, therefore, that they, the best skiers in the world in those days—this was before a distinction was made between skiers and mountaineers—should invite

On the Lyskamm

us to accompany them up Castor. The weather turned bad, but it was huge fun. The conditions forced us to set such a pace that Toni Matt could only just keep up. The others had to wait on the col for our return. We all skied down together, with Bartl and I out in front without ropes, since we did not really like using them, and the others carefully roped up following behind. This went on until Schneider barked, "I don't care what you may have done, you're going to rope up. I can't tolerate this recklessness any longer!" Bartl replied, "But there's enough of you to haul us out if we fall into anything!" Nevertheless, we obeyed his demand. After a few more tours together we parted the best of friends. They left us all their surplus provisions and settled our bill for hut fees and wood taxes, so that in a roundabout way our heavenly father seemed to have helped us after all. We stayed at the hut until the last crumb was consumed.

An attempt to climb the wintry Matterhorn did not succeed; in fact we failed to reach even the Hörnli hut, and with the realization that in certain conditions the mountain will always get the better of the mountaineer, we set off on our journey home.

With Arwed Möhn
in the port of
Barcelona, 1932

5. North African Impressions

artl got himself fixed up with another job. In my case, I did not even inquire, as something quite different had cropped up through the intervention of Gustl Kröner. Somehow the idea of an expedition to the Atlas Mountains had arisen in the Bavarian section of the German Alpine Club, and Gustl had been invited along as a junior member. He immediately made it a condition that I could come along too. Some were in favor, others decidedly against the proposal. While awaiting the decision, I went up to our club hut at Spitzing. Even there, however, I needed something to live on, and when I finally ran out of everything I decided to go over the Rotwand to Bayrischzell and bunk at my brother's for a while. It was not a decision I particularly liked though, so I was glad to accept the invitation of a fellow Bavarian club member I met at the Kleine Tiefentalalm.

"Anderl!" he called. "Come on in and have a cup of tea." I stayed with him for two months.

In the meantime, our Africa expedition had been abandoned because of financial difficulties. We made up our minds to go anyway on our bikes. We were offered some support, but only on the condition that we form a team of at least four. The hut companion who had invited me to have tea at the Kleine Tiefentalalm was Arwed Möhn, famous for having traversed the Alps from Vienna to Chamonix on skis, and he suggested his brother Felix as fourth man. We accepted his suggestion.

Traditional Bavarian fare before the trip. Arwed Möhn, Gustl Kröner, Anderl Heckmair

Before we departed something happened that was to have a decisive effect on the course of my life. Here I must go back to the year 1930. Leo Rittler had set out to climb the west face of the middle summit of the Predigtstuhl with Karl Brendl. In the course of the ascent, Brendl, who was rated as one of the best climbers of his day and had made the first ascent of the south ridge of the Aiguille Noire de Peuterey, took a leader fall and was killed. In an attempt to hold the fall, Leo burned his hands on the rope. Immediately afterward he had an engagement to guide an American who was especially keen on difficult routes. With his badly burned hands Leo did not trust himself to lead the south face of the Scharnitz in the Wettersteingebirge, so he asked me to join them. Thus, indirectly, I obtained my first guiding job. After Leo Rittler was killed

Last-minute preparations.

on the Grandes Jorasses, the American, whose name was Edwards, re-mained faithful to me and engaged me as his guide on trips to the Gesäuse and the Dolomites.

Two years later we were back in the Kaisergebirge again. With us was Hans Steger, a friend of mine from Bolzano and one of the best moun-taineers in the Alps. We guided our American client up the southeast face of the Fleischbank, and were mighty proud to have taken just two and a half hours for the route despite climbing as a rope of three. The American did not share our pride; he was annoyed. "For the money I'm paying you," he said, "I expect to spend at least ten hours on the face. We'll go back and repeat the climb tomorrow."

Such an attitude was not only alien to us, but absolutely incompre-hensible. However, the next day we obediently went back up to do the face again, wondering what to do to fill in the time. We practiced climb-ing up and down the cracks, did all the traverses two or three times, and soaked up the sun on the belays. In the end we found it all such fun that we decided that Mr. Edwards's approach was the way to de-rive the maximum pleasure from a day in the mountains.

The next day Mr. Edwards insisted on climbing the Schleierkante. I was restless and impatient, as I had arranged to depart for Africa with my friends in the middle of July and time was ticking by. When we got back from the Schleierkante, Mr. Edwards put his car and chauffeur at my disposal and I was driven out to Bayrischzell, where I had just one hour to get my kit packed up, say goodbye, and head back to Munich where the others had been waiting the whole day with freshly greased bicycles. It was four in the afternoon when we set off in the direction of

Africa, stopping, however, in a beer garden for a tankard as we knew it would be the last little luxury for a long time to come.

We cycled through Switzerland, then down the Rhône valley past Nîmes, Monpellier, Sète, and over the border at Port Bou into Spain. In this age of motorized transport such a journey is no problem at all, but on bicycles and with road conditions as they were back then it may be regarded as something of an achievement. We surprised ourselves by reaching Barcelona in a week. Here we discovered that a group rail ticket would be far cheaper than the time-consuming journey by bicycle, and also that we would have to go via Madrid as Felix's visa was not in order. We encountered no particular difficulty getting the visa organized at the consulate in Madrid; problems first arose when we tried to get a night's rest on a bench on the lawn in front of the ornate post office building. Some kind of minor revolution was in full swing, and a number of fugitives sprinted past with the police in hot pursuit. As they were unable to catch up with the fugitives, they arrested us instead. It was clear to them that our ice axes were highly suspicious instruments of death. We were clapped into a cell, where to our profound satisfaction we discovered quite passable bunks. However, we had hardly made ourselves comfortable than we were hauled out and led away for interrogation. There was an interpreter to do the translating, but they had only the foggiest notion of mountaineering. Nevertheless, the situation became a little friendlier.

Once they found a climber who could speak German, the tone grew positively hearty. They offered us coffee and cigarettes, and we had to explain exactly what the ice axes were for, and how to use ropes and pitons. Our nailed climbing boots were particularly admired; they had never seen anything like them. Finally they decided to let us go. However, as we had no quarters for the night and sleeping out in the fresh air seemed too dangerous to them, they allowed us to stay in the cell. The next morning we were escorted to the station. This turned out to be an unexpected

Roadside break in Southern France

"There were fancy buses for Europeans, but they cost too much for us and we preferred to travel on the bus the locals used." On the way to Marrakech.

advantage, as the station was crowded and in tumult. The trains were so crammed that without our escort we never would have got on.

From Algeciras the ferry took us across, past the Rock of Gibraltar to Ceuta. The first swim on the African coast was something of a swindle. Despite the midsummer heat, a cold wind was blowing; the rocks were not exactly beautiful and were covered in spiky sea urchins on which we promptly stepped. Next a couple of jellyfish stung us on the hands. It stung worse than nettles. Thus served we retreated to dry land where our dilemma continued. A pack of street urchins attached themselves to us, screaming with joy whenever our nailed boots slid on the up-and-down streets, polished by the bare feet of generations of Arabs, and we crashed to the ground. In the end we took off our boots and went barefoot too.

A short trip by rail brought us to Tetuán, from where we had to cross the Rif Mountains to Larache by bus. There were fancy buses for Europeans, but they cost too much for us, and we preferred to travel on the bus the locals used. It was supposed to leave the market square at eight o'clock in the morning. Like good Germans, we were punctual, but the bus was not. We were assured that it would be coming presently, so we did the same as the Arabs and resignedly sat down in the dust to wait. The bus arrived at about noon and was boarded in a general uproar. We found a place for ourselves and our baggage on the roof, where there was fresh air, a nice traveling wind, and a splendid view. We sat there feeling pleased about it all until, as dusk drew over the mountains, shots rang out. The driver drove full speed down the steep dirt road causing us to almost fall off the roof.

Postcard of
Marrakesh sent by
Anderl Heckmair
to his brother
Hans: "Marrakech
is lively and
boisterous, but a
little warm. 43-
45° in the shade.
Happy as the
proverbial
pigs . . . "

The following evening we reached the Atlantic coast, where we were
treated to a marvelous sunset. The journey went on past Rabat and
Casablanca to Marrakech. Here we were as close to our first goal, the
High Atlas, as Munich is to the Schliersee. We could see nothing of the
mountains, just the city. Marrakech is a big city built on an oasis, with a
European and an Arab quarter. In between lies a wonderful park full of
palm trees where we settled down to make ourselves at home. Once
again unexpected difficulties arose. It was not so long since Marrakech
had been, as they say, "peaceably subdued." Our objective, the High
Atlas, lay beyond the demarcation line. To obtain authorization to cross
this line we had to leave a deposit, which we did not have. Instead we
had letters of recommendation from the German Alpine Club and the
Swiss Alpine Club. These had to be verified, and telegrams were sent
back and forth. All of this took several days, which Gustl and I wanted
to put to good use.

Our explorations into the Arab medina became increasingly adventurous, and we soon discovered that life really began at sunset. The
market grew lively, and storytellers and snake charmers found their
audiences. In between were stalls offering every kind of delicacy. As we
nibbled some of these we noticed two deeply veiled Arab women gazing at us with lightning in their eyes. The lightning struck and taking
them by the arm, we indicated that we would like to go home with them.
It seemed as though they understood and were not averse to the idea.
So that everything should go with a swing we purchased a bottle of wine
and followed them full of gleeful anticipation. The districts through
which we made our way became progressively gloomier and shadier.
Finally one of the women knocked on a gate which was forthwith opened.

A romantic-looking inner courtyard appeared, lit by several dim paraffin lamps. A lot of Arabs lay sprawled in all directions sleeping or dozing on mats. They took not the slightest notice of us.

At the back of the courtyard a completely unromantic iron staircase led up to a row of cubicles on the first floor. Our two beauties led us into one of these cubicles where we settled back expectantly on leather hassocks. We could not say much and were thus all the readier to make a grab. To lift the atmosphere we drank a toast and passed the bottle over to our new conquests. Gustl was suddenly inspired to seize the moment and find out just what we had let ourselves in for and whipped the veil off one of them. We saw a flattened nose; projecting, over-rouged lips; and a face no longer young. Horrified, we sprang to our feet, whereupon the two women began to scream as though they had been stabbed. Grabbing our bottle of wine, we bolted along the passage and stormed down the iron staircase as our nailed boots struck a shower of sparks. My foot landed on the belly of a sleeping man, but by now there was such an uproar in the house that no one knew what was happening. The gate opened as though by miracle and we tumbled headfirst into the street. Still rolling in the dirt, I called out, "Gustl, are you all right?"

On the streets of Marrakech

"Nothing missing. Still with you."

At that moment a Foreign Legion patrol came down the alley, and an astonished voice called out, "Germans, are you? Well you're in luck." The Arabs recoiled at the sight of the legionaries, the gate thundered shut, and we got to our feet. "What are you doing here?" asked our rescuers. "We're German too, serving in the Legion. Come with us and we'll get you out of here. This is a very dangerous district."

We had been lucky. After the usual questioning as to where we came from, where we were headed, and what for, they sat us down in a café with instructions to wait for them. It was no ordinary café, but more of a cabaret where exotic beauties danced breast and belly dances. Compared with the adventure we had just been through we found it a little dull, and we were glad when our newfound friends appeared again. When they returned, they were in civilian clothes. They paid our tab and said, "Come on, now we'll show you Marrakech." We were tense with anticipation.

They led us straight to a brothel where the "ladies" sat around unveiled wearing what looked like nightdresses and made eyes at us. One by one our companions disappeared with the woman of his choice. Gustl also picked one out. Finally only I sat there with pounding heart, feeling exactly what Karl Valentin so classically formulated as, "I would have gladly, but did not trust myself to dare."

Under the pitying glances of the legionaries—"nothing to be done with him then"—we left the "free" house and were led through tortuous alleys to a quarter where Arabs who had come in from the desert left their wives and children under lock and key while they went on to do business in Casablanca. The district was closely guarded and was off limits to legionaries, but as tourists, once we had given proof of our identity, we were allowed in without obstruction. We remained for three days and nights. Money did not come into it, but my innocence was a thing of the past. When we emerged and went back to our friends, who had been told by the legionaries where we were, they greeted us like prodigal sons. In the meantime, permission had been granted for us to continue our journey.

On a peak in the High Atlas: "We had a fascinating view southward into the desert. The desire to one day penetrate those unending wastes began to germinate in my mind."

The mountains of the High Atlas were interesting, but not imposing. We sought out the most interesting ways up rocky ridges and precipitous faces, and climbed the highest peak, the 4100-meter Toubkal, from which we had a fascinating view southward into the desert. A desire to one day penetrate into those unending wastes began to germinate in my mind, though I did not dream that the desire would be fulfilled one day. We climbed numerous summits, but what do such "first ascents" mean? It was fun, but after four weeks we had had enough.

The journey home was no less adventurous. In Barcelona we picked up our bikes, happy not to be at the mercy of schedules and timetables any longer. We traveled along the Riviera to Marseilles, this time without stopping, then on past Genoa, along the plains of the Po and back over the Brenner to home. There were still a few lire left in our pockets, which we quickly changed into schillings so that we could spend a week in the Kaiser, a perfect way to wind up our mountaineering and other experiences.

Anderl Heckmair
as a ski instructor
in Switzerland

6. A Man Has to Live Somehow

On arriving home I found myself faced with my usual problem of how to make ends meet. I had already given up my apartment in Munich, so I moved up to my brother's place at Bayrischzell. However, I could not sponge off him forever.

"Why not give a lecture on your experiences!" he suggested. I was far from excited about the idea, but necessity prevailed and I cobbled together a lecture called "Difficult Climbs on Rock and Ice," which I gave for the first time in Bayrischzell, reading from the manuscript. The response was highly enthusiastic. Most of all I was impressed by the appreciation of a millionaire who lived in Bayrischzell. He shook my hand and said, "I have seen the whole world, but I envy you your experiences." A millionaire said that to me! I received ten marks for the lecture, which was a considerable sum to me at the time. Several climbing clubs in Munich also showed an interest in my lecture, and soon I earned from 20 to 40 marks a time.

I used the money to buy food and retreated to our club hut at Spitzing, where I remained the whole winter. A lecture a month gave me enough to live on. During this time I put together another lecture on our Morocco trip. Its "premiere" in Bayrischzell was no less successful than before. Among the audience were visitors taking the cure at the spa; one of them belonged to the Alpine Club, which invited me to give a lecture to the Hamburg branch.

Thus it was that I traveled to what seemed to me the remotest north. An elegant, chauffeur-driven car met me at the station and drove me to a distinguished-looking villa on the Alster, where I was entrusted to the care of the grown-up daughter and the son of the house. I almost forgot my lecture.

I still do not know how, all alone and clad in an off-the-rack suit, I inquired my way to the lecture hall in time. It was an enormous building. Before the imposing portal stood a uniformed commissionaire who refused to let me enter until somebody from the Alpine Club arrived to fetch me. When I saw inside I was more than a little alarmed. It held an

---

Bayrischzell

Interessanter Lichtbildervortrag.

er Schneller als gedacht, löste der hiesige Skiklub sein Versprechen ein, durch Herrn Andr. Heckmair Lichtbilder vorzuführen über dessen heurige Atlasbesteigung. Im Saal der Postwirtschaft vor dichtgedrängtem Zuhörerkreis wechselten auf der Leinwand die vielen schönen Bilder, welche das vierblättrige Bergsteigerkleeblatt Arweb und Feder, München und Kröner und Heckmair als Ausbeute von Nordwestafrika mit heimgebracht hatten. Die Bilder, welche die Reise der vier Herren, ihre Erlebnisse zu Fuß, zu Rad, im Auto, in der Bahn, auf dem Schiff, auf den Bergen veranschaulichten, waren begleitet von erläuternden Worten des Herrn A. Heckmair, welche aus noch frischem Erinnern an Erlebnisse nur so hervorsprudelten und mit natürlichem Humor gewürzt und so manches selbst abenteuerliche Ereignis schildernd einen großen Eindruck hinterließen. Da war nichts Gemachtes, Gesuchtes, Gekünsteltes, sondern eben Selbsterlebtes und so wie es erlebt war, wieder Erzähltes. Bilder und Worte schlugen alle Teilnehmer in ihren Bann, der sich wiederholt in überraschtem Staunen und anerkennendem Beifall auswirkte. Das Viele, was geboten wurde, kann nicht im Einzelnen berichtet werden: so was muß man selbst gesehen und gehört haben. Berechtigt war der in begeisterten Worten ausgesprochene Dank des Vorsitzenden des Skiklubs, Fritz Pellkofer, in welchen alle Anwesenden mit dreifachem kräftigen Ski-Heil einstimmten.

Heckmair, the "mountain guide" in the film *La Croix des Cimes*, 1935

audience of 2000, was packed to the eaves, and positively radiated carefully fostered atmosphere. And that was where I was supposed to speak! Somebody sat me down at a table and calmed me down with a glass of wine. I surrendered my box of slides, arranged my script on the lectern, and steeled myself for whatever might transpire.

At last the moment came. After a few introductory remarks from one of the officials I stepped up to the microphone, opened my script—and went rigid. The pictures were of Africa, but the text was "Difficult Climbs on Rock and Ice." I was rendered speechless. Throughout the hall there was a breathless silence. There was no mouse hole into which I could disappear. I had to do something. Suddenly seized by anger, I thumped my fist down on the accursed manuscript. Magnified by the microphone, the noise thundered through the hall. I simply said, "I'm terribly sorry, but I brought the slides for one lecture and the script for another. As you only half understand my dialect anyway, you may as well at least look at the pictures." There was a great roar of laughter throughout the hall, but nothing could shake me anymore. This is how I came to give the first improvised lecture of my life, without notes or script. It was a tremendous success, and I never used a script again.

A thought had been preoccupying me for some time. Leo Rittler had applied to become a mountain guide. As we had about the same Alpine experience, why shouldn't I take his place at the examination? I once again sought Dr. Wilo Welzenbach's advice, and he promised to see what could be done. Welzenbach had great influence; in June 1933 I was invited to attend the training course and examination for guides at Innsbruck.

The course lasted six weeks. Four of these were spent cooped up in a room in the university studying theory, followed by two weeks of practice up at a hut, and then the examination. Thanks to my training at the school of gardening and all the practical experience I already had on rock and ice, I did not have too hard a time of it. I got an A grade, which did not make me feel any particular pride.

The Grandes Jorasses were far from being forgotten. On the contrary, Gustl was pushing for a new attempt, but it was precisely on his account that I felt inhibited. He had gotten engaged, his father had a business employing ten men, which would eventually be his, and Gustl himself had artistic talent to bestow. He had studied at the Munich Art School, and *Die Mappe*, the leading review of applied art, had published a special issue dedicated to his work. He took his sketch pad with him wherever he went so that he could capture any image that appealed to him. Thus, on the north face of the Grands Charmoz he had committed scenes to paper in places where it was impossible to take photographs. My view was that with so many advantages piling up on his side he shouldn't

Ski instructor in
Davos, c. 1935

accept risks of the sort that we were envisioning. We almost quarreled over it. He would not give credence to my arguments, and instead joined forces with a no less fanatical climber from Pforzheim, Walter Stösser. He was killed by stonefall while trying to make a second ascent of the north face of the Matterhorn. I was deeply upset by the death of my friend.

I received the news while in the Dolomites, where I had also just done a climb that was dangerously prone to stonefall. Steel helmets from the First World War were all over the place, and I took one home to test its effectiveness as a means of protection against falling rocks. I wanted to find out exactly how it felt to receive a violent blow, so I donned the helmet and challenged my brother to belt me over the head with an iron bar. The helmet stood up to the force of the blow very well, but my neck hurt so badly for a week that I had to go to the doctor.

As guiding jobs were too infrequent for me to live off, I worked as a tourist guide for a travel agency that had previously hired me as a ski instructor in winter. The first trip went through the Bavarian Oberland. I was surprised to realize how much more I knew than was in the program I was given. Mountaineering, it seems, can be educational. The next trip was to the Dolomites, followed by one to Venice and three to the western Alps. On one occasion my coach party was unlucky with me, or I with it. A group of Swabian schoolteachers had hired the entire coach. I was looked at askance from the outset, and while we were still in the town someone decided to test me by asking about some monument. "I'm sorry," I replied, "I am a mountain guide and have only been assigned to this trip because it goes through mountain country." After that I got some peace until the first mountains appeared. Immediately someone piped up, "What mountains are those?" They were the Myths, but as I did not know that then I just said "foothills." Only a schoolmaster could have delivered the kind of dressing down I received.

Finally we came to Zermatt. To my malicious pleasure it rained continuously for two days. We were due to stay for three, but during our second night it cleared up suddenly. At three o'clock in the morning, clad in his nightgown and holding a candle in his hand like Wee Willie Winkie, one of the teachers patrolled through the corridors of the hotel intoning loudly for the benefit of all who cared to listen (and those who did not care to as well): "The Matterhorn is clear! The Matterhorn is clear!"

In no time several of the tourists were rattling my door with the urgent request that I should reserve the first train up to the Gornergrat for the group. This I succeeded in doing, and once up there I was surprised by the radiance of the day. Everything was thickly sugared with new snow, the sky an improbable blue. I stood on a rock and pointed out the mountains around, when they were first climbed, and recounted a few of the victories and dramas that had occurred on them. My audience grew and began to include bystanders who applauded enthusiastically. Not so a puny little runt of my own litter who followed my discourse with map and guidebook. "You called that mountain by the wrong name!" he yapped. Probably he was looking in the wrong direction. "And you've missed this mountain entirely." That was because it did not seem very important to me. Suddenly I was overcome with rage. Leaping down from my rock, I offered him a little bit of the "Iron Hand of Götz von Berlichingen" and told him what I thought of him in no uncertain terms. For this he brought a court action against me. It was rejected in Germany and waved away as trivial in Switzerland.

The Hörnli hut and the Matterhorn at the beginning of the 1930s

I had had enough of being a tourist guide. When I arrived home, however, the next group was already waiting; teachers from the same association who wanted to make the same trip. The agency implored me to take the job. What else could I do? This time the atmosphere was exactly the opposite. Everything went off in perfect harmony. It taught me that the mass of mankind simply follows along behind a minority whether for better or worse, and that a collective judgment is the most perverted thing in the world. It was a useful lesson to learn at a time when nationalism was beginning to run wild.

With this second group I again spent three days in Zermatt, this time to my great satisfaction in beautiful weather. As I was able to take a day off, I wanted to climb the Matterhorn, but having neither suitable clothing nor equipment I did not take my project particularly seriously. Nevertheless, I did a quick nailing job on my walking shoes—Vibram soles did not exist yet—and bought a pair of stockings and a pullover.

Thus equipped, I stole out of the hotel at four o'clock in the morning with a packed lunch under my arm. I stuffed the essentials from the lunch into my pockets and threw the rest into the raging torrent of the Visp for fish food. By 7:30 A.M. I had reached the Hörnli, where I was recognized by an Austrian guide who greeted me with, "You're going up the mountain, aren't you?"

"Well, no, only as far as seems easy and safe."

"At least take my ice ax with you."

So I did, and hurried on, overtaking the first party near the Solvay hut. I had no intention of racing or breaking any records, but I slipped into a fast pace and there was no one to hold me back. Up near the shoulder, I had to wait for a party descending one of the fixed ropes. After five minutes I grew impatient and looked for another way.

Above the steep section I traversed back along the line between rock and ice to rejoin the normal route. A guide was sitting there, belaying his tourist. At the sight of me he started as though confronted with a mountain ghost or a lunatic. He could scarcely be blamed, as despite the cold weather I was clad in flannel slacks and a pullover, not to mention walking shoes, and to keep my hands warm I had stuck them in my pockets and was carrying the ice ax under one arm. Finally he got his breath back and stuttered a question, "Where did you spring from?" Tickled by the comic aspect of the situation, I could not forbear answering, "Out of the mountains."

At that he got angry and began to curse, "My God, that's tempting fate." I had to admit that he was right, but before he could curse again I drew his attention to a fault in his technique. In his astonishment he was neglecting to keep an eye on his rope and his client, who was climbing down, blissfully unaware of our exchange. The rope was running out free.

"What would you do if your client fell now?" I asked.

He hastily grabbed at the coils and I went on my way at once, having neither the time nor inclination for further explanations. After overtaking a couple more parties I reached the top, alone. The air was so still that the match flame did not flicker as I lit a cigarette. I was often to visit this summit, but I never experienced such stillness there again.

The unforgettable
Memy

I started down as soon as the last party I had overtaken arrived. I did not want to speak to anyone, as no one would have understood me anyway. It was embarrassing to overtake all the same parties again on the way down, so I deliberately wandered out onto the east face. The same guide with whom I had had the dispute called out to me, "The route is much farther left, out on the ridge." I thanked him and thereafter stuck to the route like a good boy.

By five o'clock I was back in the hotel for tea. No one believed that I had been to the top. It did not matter. I had had my fun and, to be honest, my inner satisfaction, which was worth more to me than any recognition from others. The only one who didn't doubt me was the Austrian guide. When I returned his ax, he said, "I knew right away you were going up. No matter how you disguised yourself, you couldn't fool me."

He indeed had eyes in his head. I proved to be less clear-sighted that summer of 1933 when, on my way up from Ellmau to the Gaudeamus hut, I ran into Hans Steger guiding two eye-catchingly delicious young ladies. Why on earth would anyone want to take anyone like that up into the mountains? I thought to myself, and slipped into the bushes along the side of the path. Up at the hut, however, we met again. For the next few days bad weather set in, so we whiled away the cabin fever in our usual way, which was neither quiet nor always appreciated by the squeamish. The two ladies sat in the corner and obviously enjoyed the cabaret. When we sat down to our simple—but at Mother Maria's, always abundant—meals, invariably there was wine on the table. The ice melted and out of gratitude for the many flasks of wine we invited the women to join in our games. When the weather cleared up we did a couple of climbs together and they acquitted themselves not too badly at all.

Not long after, the one to whom I had been paying particular attention invited me to spend the winter in St. Moritz as a ski instructor to her club. This was a dream come true. A friendly relationship developed, which led to my "girlfriend's" husband, who was a film producer, bringing a crew to the Kaiser to make a film with our collaboration. Its title was *La Croix des Cimes* (The Cross of the Summits). When the time came for voice-over recording we all went to Paris. There I sampled a completely different side of life. I will never forget Memy, the woman who made it possible.

Throughout my life when I came to a crossroads I always chose the path that led back to the mountains, even when a woman stood in the other road. Had I chosen otherwise, the course of my life would have been different. Perhaps I would have become a playboy, perhaps the adoptive son of a charming, influential French family. Perhaps. . . .

But that's not what happened.

1935 in Paris –
Anderl Heckmair
the film star

7. Ready for the Scrap Heap?

was tired of being a tourist guide. I also had some money. I could go back to the mountains. A friend in Munich, Martl Maier, was one of the best climbers, and I knew he was keen on the Grandes Jorasses. I told him about my ideas and he was enthusiastic. We agreed on the essentials and went our separate ways for a while.

In the meantime, I had a guiding job in the Dolomites. Before heading out, I went back to Munich to settle additional details with Martl, but he was nowhere to be found. I was told that he had gone traveling. Where and with whom, no one knew. Deeply disappointed, I slouched off through the streets of Munich. Turning a corner I bumped into another climbing friend, Ludwig Steinauer.

"Weren't you interested in the Grandes Jorasses, too?" I asked.

"With you, I'd go any time. When are we off?"

"First, I have to go to the Dolomites, but I'll be at the Leschaux hut on the third of August. I'll need my ax, crampons, and miscellaneous other items."

"Agreed. I'll bring all the gear with me."

I headed off to the Dolomites in a happy mood, completed my guiding assignment, and reached Courmayeur on August 1. The next day I wanted to walk up to the Torino hut and down the Mer de Glace to the Leschaux hut, but did not feel comfortable about crossing the glacier alone. The idea of engaging a guide never entered my head. As I wandered around Courmayeur, I noticed a tent on the outskirts of town; maybe it was climbers who also wanted to go over to Chamonix. They turned out not to be climbers but some young Danes who did wish to visit Chamonix.

"Then you're in luck. I'm a mountain guide and I'll take you over Mont Blanc," I announced.

They had planned to do the modest walk over the Little St. Bernard Pass. At 6:00 A.M. they stood ready to receive their marching orders, and by noon we had reached the Torino hut. After a brief rest we were able to continue; they had done well despite their heavy packs. I didn't worry too much about the fact that they were wearing shorts and thoroughly unsuitable footwear. Before setting foot on the glacier I roped them up and gave them the necessary instructions. We had not gone 500 meters before the one in front fell into a crevasse. We quickly had him out, looking rather pale. "Don't worry about it," I reassured them. "That kind of thing happens on glaciers all the time. That's why you're tied on." Secretly, I was relieved to be tied on too. Despite several more little excursions into crevasses, I escorted them safely on toward the Requin hut.

Another group came toward us, with a lone figure walking about 100 meters away from them. As they drew nearer I recognized Martl. We hugged each other with howls of joy.

"Why didn't you leave word for me in Munich?" I asked.

"But I did leave you a letter!"

"Well, I never got it, so I arranged to meet Steinauer at the Leschaux hut. He'll be there today or tomorrow with my gear. There's nothing we can do about it. We'll just have to climb as a rope of three."

Martl was not over-enthusiastic about the idea, but I tied him on close in front of me and let the Danes go ahead without paying much attention to them while we chatted. Presently we became aware that we had wandered into a frightful maze of crevasses. We had no choice but to rappel into a wide crevasse and clamber up the other side, which was more or less climbable. The poor Danes, who were unaccustomed to such maneuvers, were completely undone by the time we reached the Requin hut. From here on, there was a path to Montenvers, so we left them there to spend the night and hurried on toward the Leschaux hut, where Steinauer was indeed waiting.

The greeting between him and Martl was a little frosty, but he too had to accept the situation as it was. First off, we had

The Leschaux hut and the heavily crevassed Leschaux Glacier

to spend a couple of days preparing for the climb. The Leschaux hut was being renovated, so we moved to a convenient shelter stone some 100 meters above. Then competition appeared on the scene in the form of two other Munich climbers, Peters and Harringer, who pitched a tent 100 meters below the hut on a slab of rock. Each party kept a close eye on the other. I made an attempt to establish diplomatic relations by undiplomatically suggesting to Peters that they should wait and see how we did. Peters replied that he had his own ideas as to what he should do, and I withdrew in a huff. In any case, the weather was so bad that even with the best will in the world it was impossible to try anything at all. One day it got so unpleasant that the construction workers invited us to leave our cave and join them in the hut. We accepted gladly, and the workmen indicated that we should also fetch our friends from the tent. I scrambled down and called out, "Don't be stubborn. The workmen are letting us use the hut. Come on up, all your gear is floating away."

Rudolf Peters (left) and Martl Maier, who made the first ascent of the north face of the Grandes Jorasses in 1935

Harringer responded, but not Peters, who remained sulking in the tent. For this breach of good manners we begged the pardon of the kindly French workers. They believed that we must have had an almighty quarrel.

The storm raged around the hut as it only can in the mountains. We were happy to have a dry corner and could not understand Peters's attitude. Suddenly flames flared below the hut as Peters's tent caught fire. His gas stove had exploded. We ran down and helped him to stamp out the blaze.

"Now you'll come up and join us, surely?"

"Why on earth? I can sleep in the bushes. I still have a sleeping bag, and I'm not bothered about the wet."

I doubted his sanity, but he steadfastly held out and remained in excellent humor even though the bad weather continued for several days.

I had other duties to attend to, and as it would take a good week or ten days for conditions on the face to get back to normal, I suggested to my friends that they should take a look at it without me. They were not happy, but they conceded that my arguments were logical.

Once I had departed, Steinauer and Maier grabbed the first available opportunity to attack the face, so that Peters and Harringer should not get in before them. They bivouacked on the top of the first buttress to the right of the central gully. During the night Martl got hungry and tucked into the provisions; his actions caused a terrible bout of swearing from Ludwig in the morning. They quarreled; there could be no question of going on and they came back down. Steinauer left, but Martl remained in the hope of joining forces with Peters and Harringer. Peters had no intention of climbing as a threesome, so he left Martl where he was and set off up the face with Harringer. Conditions were still bad, and on the third day they turned back. As they were preparing their bivouac, Harringer, who was unbelayed, slipped and fell wordlessly to his death, taking with him the rucksack containing the bivouac equipment.

Peters spent a terrible night, and the next day continued to rappel down with the remaining length of rope. As time went on he became snow-blind. In this state he reached the big ice slope, where he was observed by climbers at the Leschaux hut, among them Martl Maier, who hurried to his rescue. Only now was Peters willing to join forces with

Maier and took him on his now-
vacant pillion back to Munich. In
the summer of 1935 they made the
first ascent of the north face of the
Grandes Jorasses together.

I was dogged by bad luck that
year. I had no grudge over Maier
and Peters teaming up together; all
that mattered was finding a new
climbing partner and getting in
ahead of the competition. The
companion was soon found in the
person of Hans Lucke from

Kufstein, a climber with whom I had done many climbs in the Kaisergebirge and whose unshakeable good humor made him always ready for
any adventure. We had plenty of time to prepare and organize our fi-
nances. I earned my money in Switzerland working as a ski instructor
for the travel agency where I had played at being a tourist guide. Every
mark, every franc I earned I saved, as we could not expect to receive
any kind of grant. I had connections with several wealthy people but
was unwilling to saddle them with feelings of moral responsibility in
the event that anything went wrong.

Hans Lucke,
Eugen Minarek,
and Anderl
Heckmair

It was mid-June, still quite early in the season, when we left for
Courmayeur, this time by train. On the way up to the Torino hut we ran
into snow below the level of the Pavillon de Mon Fréty. It was so slushy
that we decided to bivouac there. In the morning, however, there was
breakable crust over the slush, which was even worse, so we waited for
another day. To cap it all, the weather turned bad.

"You know what?" I said. "We're three or four weeks too early. Let's
catch a train to Portofino. I know some people who have a little house
there. We can stay there until conditions improve." Hans was all for it,
so we headed off to Genoa and Portofino, where our skis, ice axes, and
nailed boots excited considerable attention.

We were welcomed with open arms. Our hosts believed they could
talk us out of our foolhardy project, but we were happy to let them spoil
us and passed three marvelous weeks swimming, walking, and even
climbing, as we found some excellent rocks in hidden bays where we
could train in complete privacy.

We had now fixed the day of our return to the Mont Blanc range, and
out of sheer high spirits we dashed down to our training crags the afternoon before we were due to leave. That's when it happened. I jumped
off and broke my foot. It was a bitter blow. Instead of Courmayeur it
was back to Munich after ten days with my leg in a pot. I had written to

a friend in Munich to tell him of my misfortune. He met me at the station with a wry smile on his face and a newspaper under his arm bearing the headline "Grandes Jorasses North Face Conquered by Peters and Maier." They had done it! My friend tried to comfort me.

"Don't let it get you down," he said. "Your bad luck may have been a blessing in disguise. In any case, you'll be thirty soon. It's time to join the ranks of the has-beens. Find yourself a steady job and give up all this frantic competition." His blunt words were well-meant, but they hit me hard.

I was forced to spend the next few weeks in a hospital until my foot was all right again. I was not very talkative, but lay all day in tortured self-examination, staring at the ceiling. Was I a failure? Was my place really with the has-beens? Well, if so, there was nothing I could do about it. I would just go on being a mountain guide, living in the mountains and doing the climbs I enjoyed, and leave off harassing myself with ambitious projects. As time wore on, however, I became bright and cheerful again and not only my broken leg healed but my spiritual wounds too, of which the doctor knew nothing.

Hardly had I been discharged from the hospital than I was engaged by a lady schoolteacher to do some guiding in the Dolomites. On our way up to the Lavaredo hut we encountered a couple of friends from Nuremberg, beaming with joy at having done the fifteenth ascent of the north face of the Cima Grande. Originally climbed by Comici, in those days it was considered to be the hardest route around. Instantly I felt twinges of the very ambition I had so solemnly renounced while in the hospital. Secretly, I sized up my schoolteacher, wondering whether I could talk her into trying the face. But no, it would have been insane. I put away the thought and steeled my will to be a staunch, honest guide who would never encourage a client to attempt anything beyond his or her ability.

The hut was not too busy, and I noticed a lanky, pleasant looking young man wolfing down a triple-sized evening meal with evident relish. Drifting in his direction, I opened with the question, "Did it taste good?"

He glanced at me in surprise and simply nodded. I tried another tack. "Did you get hungry doing a hard route?"

At last he deigned to answer, "My friends have left. I had another day's holiday left and was just using up the last of my lire." As soon as he spoke I detected his Nuremberg accent. He had been with my friends and was put out at missing out on the north face.

"We could do it together," I exclaimed. He accepted with delight, and my teacher readily agreed to a day or two's rest.

Anderl Heckmair on the north face of the Cima Grande, August 3, 1935

I was brimming with enthusiasm and could hardly wait for the next day. But the next morning rain drummed the roof of our attic dormitory. Paradoxical as it may sound, mountain climbers generally like their comforts and are often even lazy, qualities to which I am by no means immune. If bad weather thwarted my plans to climb, I could usually sleep through the whole day with pleasure and a clear conscience. On this occasion, however, I was so vexed that I could not sleep another wink. Toward seven o'clock the rain eased, and an hour later nothing worse than cold, damp clouds drifted around the mountains.

My companion, who went by the name of Theo Erpenbeck—we finally got around to introducing ourselves—had already packed his sack to go down to the valley, remarking, "You can't do a climb like that in this kind of weather, and anyway it's much too late."

I begged him to walk up to the foot of the face and do the first two or three pitches with me, after which I would feel satisfied and we could rappel off. Thus it was that at 9:30 A.M. we stood at the start of a climb that had never been done without a bivouac. As we tied on to the rope above the first easy rocks I reassured him that I would just do two or three pitches, then I began. There was no need to place any pitons; there were far too many already for my taste. I wasted no time trying to take any of them out, but simply did not bother to clip in to all of them. In any case, I did not have enough carabiners. After three pitches I had no thoughts of turning back. Theo had no say in the matter; no sooner had he reached the stance than I whipped off the belay and climbed on.

Only once, after climbing at least fifteen meters without seeing any pitons, did I feel that something might be amiss. At this point I noticed a row of pegs running up a slightly overhanging corner about five meters to one side. Without any protection, the traverse across to the corner was far from easy, but if I hammered any in my companion also would be obliged to deviate from the proper line. As I reached the stance and shouted to him to come on, I heard a reproachful voice ask, "Have you given up clipping in at all now?"

Shortly before the gully in the upper part of the face there was a roof about half a meter across. I had heard that others had used a sling for aid here. As I had no slings, I leaned out backward in desperation and found a fantastic hold, big enough to get both hands on while I leaned back in tension from the rope. On the command "slack" my legs swung clear of the rock. It was lucky that I had been a good gymnast in my youth. A quick pull up, a mantelshelf, and I was up. In the gully above I would have taken off the rope, but, as poor Theo's arms had no feeling left in them, that would not have been the right thing at all. The real difficulties were over now, and there was no more talk of turning back. By three o'clock in the afternoon we were sitting on the summit. Theo pulled a flask of red wine tea out of his sack, which he had only intended to carry as far as the foot of the face. I have hardly ever tasted anything so delicious.

By now we were firing on all four cylinders, and like mad dogs we tore back down to the hut, where we were greeted with the question, "Where did you turn back?" Once again I was stared at with patent suspicion when I replied, "We climbed the whole face, and we can't help it if we're back already." My peace of mind was restored; I now knew that I had no need to fear the scrap heap alongside other has-beens, and patiently I led my schoolmistress up all the routes she wished to do. Theo left for home the next day, and I next saw him several decades later, after he had recovered from a serious illness. He wanted nothing more to do with climbs of such severity. I, on the other hand, still could not get enough of them.

One face above all remained unconquered and now that I had my self-confidence back I concentrated all my thoughts and my will on the north face of the Eiger.

Anderl Heckmair
studies the north
face of the Eiger
through
binoculars,
summer 1937

8. The Eigerwand— Prehistory

M any years went by before the time was ripe, but in 1935 the first attempts were made to climb the Eigerwand. I followed the events with interest, knowing from my experiences on the Grandes Jorasses that such a face does not yield to the first attack. It was one thing for it to happen on the north face of the Matterhorn, a very different matter on the Jorasses, and quite impossible on the Eiger.

Max Sedlmayer and Karl Mehringer were the first to try this murderous wall. Max's brother Heini was a good friend of mine, though he was more of a skier than a climber. Both climbers came from Munich, but I had heard nothing about either. However, they certainly made an all-out attempt on the Eigerwand. Their breach of the first rock step after the initial pedestal demands great respect even today. They reached the third ice field, although not until the fourth day. Then the weather broke and both men lost their lives. It was the first round in the struggle for the Eigerwand.

The excitement among the so-called experts was enormous. Some praised to high heaven the daring and spirit of sacrifice displayed by the protagonists, while others bitterly condemned the foolhardiness and fanaticism of those who attempted, and died on, the face. In Switzerland feelings ran so high that a law was passed forbidding any attempts on the face, but this was later repealed following protests by leading Swiss mountaineers who rightly asked where the limit lay. For some people, they pointed out, a simple Alpine walk might be a risky affair, while for others even the Eigerwand might be just another climb, albeit a difficult one. As future events were to show, they spoke the truth, and the ban was lifted. The prohibition probably would not have bothered us too much, as the first ascent would have been worth more than a couple of weeks in prison. But a lot was to happen before that.

Throughout the winter of 1935–36 I worked as a ski instructor at Arosa, Davos, and St. Moritz, and when summer came I did more climbing in a professional rather than private capacity. An operation on my meniscus put me out of action for a considerable while, but eventually it healed and I soon got fit again.

During the summer of 1936 there was a lot of activity on the Eigerwand. Independently of one another, three parties arrived at the foot of the face, bent on the same objective. These were the Munich climbers Herbst and Teufel; Andreas Hinterstoisser from Bad Reichenhall and Toni Kurz from Berchtesgaden; and two Innsbruckers Edi Rainer and

Karl Mehringer and Max Sedlmayr, the first victims of the North Face, August 1935, Alpiglen

Willy Angerer. Temporarily at least, there was absolutely no thought of joining forces. On the contrary, they avoided one another as much as possible. It was too early in the season for a serious assault on the wall, so Herbst and Teufel, who were unwilling to sit around doing nothing, did a training climb that became the first ascent of the north face of the Schneehorn in the Jungfrau group. As they were descending through the ice bulges of the Jungfrau Glacier, Teufel slipped and pulled his companion after him. Teufel was killed immediately, while Herbst was seriously injured and had to be brought down. The rescue was made by Swiss guides. Although the latter received some compensation, it was not in proportion to the effort, hardship, and danger involved, and it was understandable enough that they had nothing good to say about the so-called Eiger candidates. What if something should happen to them up on the Eigerwand? And precisely as the guides feared, something did happen.

The victims of 1936: Edi Rainer and Willy Angerer (top), Anderl Hinterstoisser (bottom)

No doubt influenced by the recent accident, the two other parties decided to join forces. At 2:00 A.M. on July 18 they set out on their fateful attempt.

The leader was Andreas Hinterstoisser. After they had surmounted the pedestal, he turned from the overhanging zone on the right, climbing the pitch below the Rote Fluh now known as the "Difficult Crack." After a relatively easy stretch he then made a tension traverse down and across to the first ice field, a pitch that would achieve notoriety and become known as the "Hinterstoisser Traverse." Yet it was this very pitch that proved their undoing when sudden bad weather later obliged them to retreat. In icy conditions it proved impossible to reverse the traverse, and they were forced to make the fateful decision to seek safety by a series of free rappels to the pedestal. During the retreat Hinterstoisser fell, Rainer and Angerer were killed by stonefall, and only Toni Kurz remained. His shrill shouts for help were heard in the valley. Three guides immediately volunteered to mount a rescue operation, despite the official

declaration that "guides shall not be required to intervene when an accident occurs on the Eigerwand."

The Jungfraujoch railway made a special train available to take the rescuers up to a garbage disposal chute (the Gallery Window) leading from the tunnel to the face. From here they only had to traverse a few hundred meters across the pedestal until they were able to make verbal contact with Toni Kurz, but they found it impossible to reach the spot where he was hanging. Kurz explained that Hinterstoisser had fallen off and that the other two were hanging dead on the rope below him. The guides advised him to cut the rope linking him to the bodies, to unravel the remaining rope (it was a hawser-laid hemp rope), and tie the strands together, then weight the line with a stone and lower it down to them. All this took hours

to accomplish, and in the meantime it grew dark. The guides were forced to retreat to the gallery, leaving Kurz suspended over the cliffs like a condemned man. By dawn the guides were back again. To their surprise, Toni Kurz still sounded reasonably fresh as he answered their questions. The unlaid rope was lowered, and to it they attached two new ropes, pitons and food, all of which Kurz hauled up.

At last Kurz came sliding down the new ropes. He reached the level of the guides, but was still hanging too far out from the overhanging wall. At this point something unforeseen occurred. The knot joining the ropes would not go through the carabiner with which Kurz was rappeling. He mumbled something incomprehensible. The guides tried to give him advice, but he had reached the end of his strength. Suddenly he tipped over and hung dead on the rope. Not until a week later was it possible to cut down the body with a knife attached to the end of a pole, and, as there had been no

Toni Kurz hangs
dead on the rope

way of tying him on, he vanished over the cliffs of the pedestal not to be seen again until some time later when his body was discovered in a deep bergschrund at the foot of the face. Deeply as I regretted the fate of these four climbers, it was clear to me that they had been mistaken about the nature of the face. To undertake climbs of this order in the western Alps one needs western alpine experience, and they had none. Climbers cannot rely on luck alone, especially not on the Eigerwand.

By now I was so obsessed with climbing the face that nothing would induce me to abandon the project. Nevertheless, I was fully aware that it was not just a question of catching a train, wandering up the climb, and coming home with the laurels. One might have a lucky break, but I had no intention of relying on that. It should be possible to gain a certain advantage by studying the face for a period of some weeks and perhaps climbing a certain distance up it with the intention of turning back.

Toni Kurz

Such were my considerations, and when Theo Lesch and I set off again on our bicycles to lay siege to the face in 1937, I stuck to them. Secrecy was now more essential than ever, less on account of rivals than of public opinion. We did not wish to be regarded as fanatical lunatics so fueled by ambition as to be willing to risk our own lives. Things had reached such pitch that it was considered bad form among mountaineers to speak of the face at all.

So it came about that in the spring of 1937 I did a number of difficult climbs in the Kaiserbirge with Hias Rebitsch with the unspoken aim of training for the Eigerwand. I had dark suspicions that Hias nurtured the same plans, but neither of us said a word about it to the other. Perhaps things would have turned out differently if we had not adhered so rigidly to the mountaineers' unspoken code. However, the underlying reason for our reticence was probably that neither of us needed the other

Anderl Heckmair with Theo Lesch at the Interlaken swimming pool, July 1937

to realize his objective. Each of us had another companion, and in July I pedaled away toward Switzerland with Theo Lesch.

Intent that no one should see us in Grindelwald, we hired a beach cabin from the lifeguard at Interlaken, who was a friend of mine. It was there we learned of the ban on attempting the north face of the Eiger. Taking every precaution not to reveal ourselves as "Eigerwand candidates" we cycled to Grindelwald without rucksacks and walked up to Alpiglen, where the

alpenhorn player offered us a hideout and kept our secret. When anyone approached he would warn us with a blast on the horn. Bit by bit we assembled our equipment up there and reconnoitered the foot of the face. When the weather was unfavorable we went down to Interlaken and mingled harmlessly with the bathers.

In spite of our precautions we were run to ground by two journalists who had disguised themselves as walkers and engaged us in conversation. Our suspicions were first aroused when they began to take snapshots of us. And indeed, two days later our photographs appeared in the newspapers with the caption "Two anonymous Eigerwand candidates who were unwilling to give their names." We had at least avoided making that mistake. In effect, it would have been a matter of complete indifference to us, but as we were no longer unknown in climbing circles it would have caused a certain amount of sensation.

Unfortunately, other parties sought to achieve the exact opposite. Courting publicity, they informed everyone about their designs on the North Face, whether they wanted to know or not. In the full glare of publicity and in the company of those whom they had invited to observe, they climbed around the foot of the face, let people stand them drinks in Grindelwald, and generally tasted the fruits of victory in advance wherever they could find them. To our embarrassment they were also from Munich. The Grindelwald guides were rightly annoyed. It is comforting to report that the publicity hounds duly got the thumping they deserved and were expelled from Switzerland for their misdeeds. We became more circumspect than ever and no longer trusted anyone.

The day came when we collected ourselves for a serious attempt. The plan was to start at 2:00 A.M., but when we awoke the sun was shining into the tent. We had overslept! "What the hell, it's bound to stay fine for more than one day," we remarked, refusing to worry, and lazily lay down again. Perhaps this was fate raising a warning finger, as around midday a black wall of cloud gathered about the mountain and a terrible storm broke. That was all we had been lacking. We had been there for six weeks and our funds were dwindling alarmingly. During the past few days we had even cut back to one meal a day to save money. We could not starve ourselves much longer, and even if we did we would be in no physical condition to withstand the massive effort that would be required. We therefore made the difficult but correct decision to cancel the siege for the time being and return without fail the following year.

Once the decision was made there was no point in waiting any longer. We packed up our gear, ran down to Grindelwald, swung our legs over our bikes, and rode home. That day was another fateful date in the history of the Eiger. Our giving up was only a minor incident. The same day Hias Rebitsch and Wiggerl Vörg appeared on the scene, but we did not meet. Also on the day of our departure a pair of climbers from Salzburg started up the North Face and were caught by the storm. They succeeded in traversing off to the Mittellegi Ridge, but Gollackner died of exhaustion and Primas was rescued in a state of collapse.

Rebitsch and Vörg collected Gollackner's body. Right from the outset, their party stood under an unlucky star. No sooner had they recovered from the effort of the rescue than they made an attempt on the face, but had not climbed 300 meters before they found one of the victims from the year before. It was Hinterstoisser. They gave up their attempt and carried down the body.

Thus they lost several fine days. The weather became unreliable, but they made another reconnaissance as far as the traverse to the first ice field, which they christened the "Hinterstoisser Traverse." Here, they fixed a rope taken up especially for the purpose. Satisfied with this achievement, they turned back. Their careful preparations and wary approach to the mountain showed that this time there were experienced men at work who were up to the task they had taken on. Three weeks now elapsed before they ferried their comprehensive equipment loads in two stages up to a niche beyond the Hinterstoisser Traverse, where they spent the night. The serious work would begin the next day.

The body of Edi Rainer lies broken on the rocks at the foot of the Eigerwand, July 1936.

On the Mittellegi Ridge, where Hias Rebitsch and Wiggerl Vörg found an exhausted Franz Primas and the body of Bertl Gollackner

Even they had underestimated the scale of the face. Instead of the five pitches they had anticipated, the second ice field gave them twenty, and instead of one hour, it took them five to climb it. In the process of hacking steps in the glass-hard ice, Vörg broke his ax and from then on had to work with his ice hammer, which is always a poor substitute.

The rock step dividing the second ice field from the third was running with water. In vain they looked for a way around, but finally Rebitsch went ahead and worked his way up through the spray of a waterfall. On the way he found an old piton with a rappel sling left by their predecessors.

In the course of the struggle they failed to notice the dirty gray clouds forming around the face. They were shocked by the realization that they too might be condemned to retreat. They had not yet reached the headwall.

It was another 100 meters over steep ice interspersed with rocks before they reached the point where Sedlmayer and Mehringer had last been seen. They expected to find Mehringer's corpse, but the only trace was two pitons hammered into the wall. From here on it was up to them to find the way. After an attempt to continue in a direct line to the summit they realized that rapid progress was now impossible, so they rappeled back down and attempted to traverse leftward toward a conspicuous ramp. Here they were surprised by such a stream of water that they again hurriedly retreated. They settled down for the night on the ledge below the two pitons and waited with chattering teeth for morning to come. The hope of better weather proved illusory, but they waited on for a while. Then a gap in the mist revealed a bank

of black cloud rolling in from the west. They began their retreat at once.

All through the day they rappeled downward on the hard-frozen rope in their soaking clothes. Menaced by stonefall and avalanches, it was 5:00 P.M. when they reached their first bivouac site at the end of the Hinterstoisser Traverse. There was still plenty of daylight and they easily could have crossed the traverse and descended somewhat farther. It was not a trap, as the fixed rope guaranteed an easy return to the rocks below the Rote Fluh. But perhaps the weather might improve after all?

Hias Rebitsch at the Hinterstoisser Traverse bivouac

They spent the night thinking and talking about the tragedy that had played out the previous year a few meters below where they lay. If only the others had left a rope across the traverse too. . . .

Wiggerl Vörg

The next morning the weather was more miserable than ever. There was no more to discuss; they had to get off the face. The rain was torrential, and the rappels ran down a line of temporary waterfalls. The two climbers had to slit their breeches at the bottom to let out the water that poured inside their anoraks. It took them the whole day to reach the foot of the face.

Their joy at winning their way back to life outweighed the disappointment of failure. When all was said and done, they were the first to spend more than 100 hours on the Eigerwand and live to tell the tale; moreover, they had demonstrated that with the necessary prudence and foresight the face could be climbed.

Anderl Heckmair
in a wide bridge
on the Torre del
Diavolo in the
Cadini Group,
Dolomites, mid-
1930s

9. Hitler and Leni

learned about the travails on the Eigerwand much later. Back at home, I felt far from downcast or defeated. If Hias had succeeded I would have been genuinely pleased for his sake. The dream of the Eigerwand would have been over, the dream that had already become a nightmare. I had enough other experiences to keep me abundantly happy.

One morning in Bayrischzell I got a telegram from my friend Hans Steger in Bolzano. For many years he had been the best and also the best-known rock climber in the Südtirol, and he was now a qualified guide. The telegram said that Leni Riefenstahl wanted to climb with him, but he had an engagement with the king of Belgium.

"You take her. Rendezvous Wolkenstein today."

Everyone knew about Leni Riefenstahl from Arnold Fanck's mountain and ski films, and she had produced and starred in a fine mountain film of her own, *Das Blaue Licht* (The Blue Light). It was also well known that she belonged to Hitler's most intimate circle. Party leaders often had film stars among their friends and followers, but in her case the rumor was that she was one of Hitler's closest friends, if not more. That she was a celebrity did not trouble me, but the connection with Hitler gave me pause. Up until then I had had no contacts with government or party big shots. No matter. It did not occur to me to turn down such an offer. I traveled to Wolkenstein and asked at the hotel for Miss Riefenstahl. Immediately I was treated with exquisite courtesy. The bowing and scraping and dashing back and forth occasioned by names and money is quite remarkable.

Leni Riefenstahl had gone out for the day with a climber I knew well, Xaver Kraisy from Kaufbeuren who, however, was not a professional guide. After a few hours she appeared looking radiant and more beautiful in reality than I had imagined her. Her feminine charisma and un-trammeled naturalness dissolved my inner reservations. Whatever her relationship with Hitler might be she was obviously a fabulous woman, and her years spent in the company of Arnold Fanck's casts of outstanding climbers and skiers had taught her not to play the star or the temperamental diva among mountaineers, myself included. What she was worth as a climber, I would soon find out.

When we discussed the routes we might do I suggested the west ridge of the first Sella Tower as a warm-up and familiarization climb. I knew full well that there was a Grade 5 pitch on it. If she had trouble there, she could find another guide and I would go home. I was arrogant in those days and interested in nothing but the difficult stuff.

To my huge surprise, and to my pleasure also, she had no difficulty on the crucial pitch. Indeed, she positively danced up it. Knowing little

"To my old friend Anderl Heckmair. Yours, Leni." Card sent by Leni Riefenstahl, December 1940

about women, I would never have believed it of such a delicate-looking creature. When she explained that before going into films she had been a ballet dancer I began to understand why her movements were so graceful and sure. Thereupon we undertook a series of harder and harder climbs, including the Schleierkante, which we knocked off in two and a half hours as a party of three. I was in high spirits after this success and for our next climb I suggested the Guglia di Brenta—not the ordinary route but the Preuss Route.

As we walked up from Madonna di Campiglio to the Brentei hut we talked about her film, *Das Blaue Licht,* which she had shot in the district. Hitler was so impressed by it that he commissioned her to make the films of the National Socialist Party Meeting and the Olympic Games.

My brother had filled me in on these details before I set out from home, drumming into my head that on no account should I let on that I knew next to nothing about her and had never seen one of her films. That was bad advice. At every bend in the path she asked if I could remember the scene she had shot there, until like a fool I confessed that I had never even heard of the film. She was offended and went into a sulk. Just wait till tomorrow, I thought to myself, and I'll cut you down to size so that you forget your film. In fact she was to be cut down much smaller than I intended, and that was my fault again because after the experience on the Schleierkante I overestimated her ability. I fixed our time of departure at a leisurely 10:00 A.M. We strolled gently up to the Tosa hut, had an agreeable midday rest, and reached the foot of the route by two o'clock in the afternoon. I was planning on three hours up and one down, so there was plenty of time even though we were a party of three. I was feeling my oats, and right at the start of the route decided there was no point in following the ledges across the Bergerwand when a corner led straight up toward the Preusswand. Unfortunately, this corner turned out to be much harder than it looked. Halfway up Leni suggested, "It would be easier out there on the left."

I was of the opposite opinion, but wisdom gave in to inexperience, something that should never happen in the mountains. The somewhat easier rock led around to a good stance on the east face, but there everything came to an end. So back to the corner. I took some tension on the rope, then climbed the whole corner to the top and gave the word to follow. That was easier said than done. Leni peered around the edge, took one look at the smooth wall and overhangs in the corner, and refused to move another step. In this she was fully within her rights. I called down that I would rappel back so that we could return to the hut. At this she grew angry and insisted on continuing up, but not at this particular place. In reality we had no choice; there was not enough time to go any farther. At this point, however, she made the mistake of informing me that she had engaged me as her guide and that I must do as she said. In a sense she was right, but not in these circumstances. There was nothing else to do but go down so that she could find another guide who would do what she wanted.

I kept the belay rope over my shoulder while I hammered in a ring piton for the rappel. Suddenly, without any warning, there came a violent tug and Leni pendulumed across into the corner. I winched in the rope with all my strength and before long she was standing in front of me, her eyes red with weeping. Xaver followed, grinning with embarrassment. Only now were we at the foot of the Preuss route proper. Climbers normally allow four hours for this, and it was 5:00 P.M. already.

"The sensible thing would be to turn back."

"No, I want to go up."

Okay by me. We went up. Without further ado, I addressed myself

Leni Riefenstahl with Xaver Kraisy in the Dolomites, summer 1937

to the climbing. Even today the route cannot be described as easy, and it kept us busy until 8:00 P.M., which was dusk. A bivouac was now inevitable. The thought did not bother me, but out of the west a black wall of cloud was bearing down on us, flickering with blue lightning. It was essential to get off the summit and into a little niche between two blocks on the north face.

"Right, this is where we bivouac. Now it remains to be seen how we survive the storm."

"You don't expect me to spend the entire night here?" moaned Leni. "I must not catch cold, I'm not well. . . ."

The rest of her words were drowned in a terrifying crash of thunder. Hail poured over us, while the lightning flashed and glimmered incessantly in the black wall of cloud.

"This is unpleasant. Let's get down farther."

Going on implied rappeling, hammering in pegs by the harsh glare of lightning. Xaver had to descend unbelayed on the two 40-meter ropes in the pitch darkness. Leni could only be belayed on a 25-meter length of thin cord. The shower of hail had turned into a cloudburst. We rappeled all night, arriving exactly where we had left the sacks at the bottom of the climb. This was due to either pure chance or sixth sense, as most of the time I had no idea where we were.

It was far too dark to follow the route back to the Tosa hut, but in the gully running down to the corrie below a faint light shimmered off the ice. Nothing much could happen to us now as long as we kept moving, so we cut our way with the peg hammer, step by step, down the gully. The weather had relented a little, but clouds came up from the valley, enveloping us in a Stygian gloom of fog and darkness. Luckily, we had just got off the ice. Although we had no lights, we could at least move forward in a sitting position. For me there was nothing new in that. Leni and Xaver were not pleased about it, but wanted even less to bivouac. We missed the little track leading through the corrie and found ourselves in a wilderness of blocks the size of tables and even houses. After I had tumbled over one of these I found I had exhausted my readiness for self-sacrifice, so I stretched out and announced, "I am going to sleep until it gets light." In a moment I was snoring. Xaver had to spend the rest of the night comforting and rubbing Leni to keep her warm. They woke me as soon as day broke; despite the wetness and cold I felt fresh and recovered. By climbing back up again we soon found the little track, up which the hut warden and his wife were already coming to look for us in a state of great concern.

Three days of rest at the hut. Then a banquet at the Hotel Greif in Bolzano given by Leni's friends. There were heated discussions over the table concerning modern mountaineering techniques. The subject of the

Eiger was aired. One of the older men, clearly convinced by his own rhetoric, looked deep into my eyes and said "Heckmair will climb the north face of the Eiger."

I was taken aback, having believed that no one knew of my intentions. However, his confidence did me good, as, remembering my ill-luck and defeat on the Grandes Jorasses, I was not at all sure of it myself.

It was now September, and Leni had to attend the Party meeting at Nuremberg as Hitler's guest of honor. As she wanted to "convert" me, she insisted on my coming too. Afterward I was to accompany her to Berlin, where everything I needed would be placed at my disposal at the national stadium so that I could train as much as I wished. For an offer like that it was even worth attending a Party meeting; what harm could it do to go along to view the spectacle?

At Nuremberg we were lodged at the Gauleiter's house. Everything was pompous and reeked of refinement—with the exception of the Gauleiter himself. So this was the face of National Socialism! Hitler was residing at the Deutscher Hof Hotel. Naturally, the whole place was sealed off, but Leni had a pass that opened all doors. We went to the hotel for afternoon tea. Leni positioned herself so that the Führer would see us when he came in. It worked perfectly. He went straight to her with outstretched arms and complimented her appearance. We were invited to sit at his table in a neighboring room. Thus I came to be sitting beside Leni in immediate proximity to Hitler and could study his face at leisure. I make no claim to being a connoisseur of men, but I could see absolutely nothing extraordinary about him.

Leni told Hitler about her experiences in the mountains, but he seemed neither impressed nor enthusiastic. Instead, his brow darkened and he growled, "How can you risk your life so lightly when I have entrusted you with so great a mission?" She answered that for this very reason she had engaged a guide to guarantee her safety. Now, for the first time, he looked at me and the conversation turned to me. Far from being stupid, the questions he put to me were direct and to the point, although it was clear that he had not the slightest idea about mountaineering. What interested him was the "why" of it all—what one would feel and experience on a severe climb as compared to a simple walk in the mountains. With no intention of embarrassing me, he bored his way relentlessly into every aspect of the subject. In all this, my own person interested him not one bit. It was the facts that absorbed him; apparently he had never before spoken with a mountaineer.

Thus the meal went by. Outside darkness had fallen and a torchlight parade began to march past. The Führer's adjutant—I do not know if it was Bormann—came up behind him and murmured that it was time to go out on the balcony. As we got to our feet, Hitler asked another question that called for a lengthy answer; no one dared to interrupt us, and so it was that I accompanied him out onto the balcony, still talking, there to find myself in my gray suit amid all the uniformed Party dignitaries.

Below us the crowd shouted its unceasing cry of "Heil!" The torchlight procession came to a halt. Hitler saluted it with a stiffly outstretched

arm, something rigid in his gaze as though staring into the distance. For the first time in my life I raised my hand in the Hitler salute. My situation as a completely apolitical and disbelieving anonymous climber standing beside the fanatically acclaimed leader struck me as so grotesque that I felt like laughing out loud. The parade lasted two hours, and throughout this time I stood at Hitler's side on the balcony. As the umpteenth thousand marcher paraded past us yelling I thought of the loneliness of the mountains and of the hordes of humanity below. I came to no conclusion; I simply found the whole thing remarkable, disturbing, and inexplicable.

The following day I stood beside Leni Reifenstahl on the honor platform watching the parades and marching Party members, wondering how people could be herded

Working as a guide in the Walsertal, 1937-38

around like that and why they let it happen. You could not help admiring the organization, yet I felt a little horror in my soul. I understood that something was in motion that was going to sweep everything away with it, but where to I could not tell.

In Berlin I needed a period for reflection to digest the experience. Leni was set on dragging me to the mass gathering on the occasion of Mussolini's visit, but I had had enough and preferred to go running in the woods. Each time I ran farther until I was doing 40 or 50 kilometers every second or third day. Deliberately I suited my training to my projects for the following year. This time I intended to climb the Eigerwand.

All this preserved me from the temptations of city life and prevented me from becoming embroiled in politics. I was unwilling to be entrapped by the suggestive urge that I felt could not be rationally explained. It

As a ski
instructor for the
Strength Through
Joy initiative,
winter 1937-38

was too alien to me and I was too matter-of-fact for it. Above all, I had
my own goals.

Not until the mountain winter had set in did I return to Bayrischzell.
A couple of weeks later I took a job as a ski teacher in the Strength
Through Joy (*Kraft durch Freude*) organization. Introducing these simple,
mostly working-class people to the beauties of the wintry mountains
was far more satisfying than instructing the would-be socialites of the
St. Moritz travel agencies.

Anderl Heckmair
on the north face
of the Eiger

10. The North Face of the Eiger

began to tie up the loose ends for the summer. My first act was to write to Hias Rebitsch in Innsbruck and say that we should stop being stupid and competing with each other and what about teaming up instead? He replied by return that in principle he was in favor of the idea, but that he had been invited by the well-known expedition leader Paul Bauer to go to Nanga Parbat, an 8000-meter mountain in the Karakorum. In his place he recommended his companion of the previous year, Wiggerl Vörg, "a man with whom you could happily steal horses."

Wiggerl Vörg. Wasn't that the nice guy I had once overtaken in a cross-country ski race who had protested on my behalf when I had been placed behind him? I had no idea that he was a climber into the bargain. If Hias recommended him, he must be good. I wrote to him at once.

Again the answer came by return of post. He had been invited to join an expedition to the Hindu Kush, but he was not at all sure whether anything would come of it, and he would be glad to join me. So it came about, and we agreed to meet in the Kaiser on a particular date to begin training.

For a whole week I sat at the Gaudeamus hut waiting for sight or sound of Vörg. Perhaps he was on his way. What should I do? First of all a few climbs, even if I had to do them solo.

I wandered up the south ridge of the Karlspitz—steep chossy scrambling with a lot of flowers and the odd overhang between—taking pleasure in it all. As I strolled back down to the hut in the evening light I saw two climbers looking at me expectantly. Both were on the short side, one thin, the other plump. Yet there was something in the bearing of the heavier one by which I could recognize the extreme climber. That would be Wiggerl Vörg. And so it proved to be. The introductions were short and hearty; the thin man was his brother. After a few minutes it was as though we had been friends for years. From time to time, however, we looked long and penetratingly into one another's eyes, and each of us had his own thoughts.

We had heard too much about one another to have any doubts, yet it is a little strange to be face-to-face with a person with whom you are intending to be bound in a life or death situation. The same evening a couple of friends from Munich arrived to stay for a few days. Our plans remained a closely guarded secret. Only the hut warden, Mother Maria, so called by everyone because she really was a mother to all mountaineers, knew or suspected what we had in mind, and organized the menu accordingly.

We stayed at the Gaudeamus hut for two weeks, doing all manner of climbs. Quite against our will it worked out that although Wiggerl and I were sometimes on the same face at the same time we were never on the same rope until, on the last day, we did the hardest climb of the holiday, the east face of the Karlspitz. Never had I had a climbing partner so much the opposite from myself yet with whom I could climb in such perfect harmony. He was outstandingly kindly and good-natured, which I cannot claim for myself. This was a factor destined to play a major role in the ascent of the Eigerwand; without it events might have been different.

We decided on July 10, 1938, as our date of departure for Switzerland. The week beforehand was spent in Munich assembling our kit, which had been worked out down to the last detail. By contrast to all earlier attempts, including our own, equipment was selected in light of the concept that the north face of the Eiger was an ice climb rather than a rock climb. Nowadays this discovery

Training in the Wilder Kaiser: Anderl Heckmair and Wiggerl Vörg, early summer 1938

seems ridiculously obvious, but up to then all our predecessors had come to grief on account of their primitive and unsuitable equipment. Not only did pitons, crampons, and rope need to be of appropriate design, but so did our clothing and bivouac gear so that we could stand up to bad weather and several bivouacs without coming to harm. This process of selection postulated not only experience but also the eradication of deeply rooted traditions and attitudes.

The question of packing arose. To avoid being recognized as Eiger candidates, we packed everything into suitcases. Only the ice axes caused a headache; try as we might we could not get them in. In the end we had to carry them under our arms, thus rendering all our camouflage pointless.

"From our earlier attempts we already knew a place where we could camp safe from the eyes of the inquisitive tourists and still more inquisitive journalists. Wiggerl pitched the tent while I went off to gather wood."

According to plan, we left on July 10. We deliberately selected this date because I knew from the previous year that in June and early July melting on the face causes such waterfalls and consequent stonefall and avalanches that an ascent during that season is beyond consideration. We wanted to keep the nerve-racking period of siege as short as possible. For this reason we purposely started training late. Our strategy received tragic confirmation when two Italians, Bartolo Sandri and Mario Menti, tried the face during the critical period in June and lost their lives in the attempt.

It was not easy to stick to our chosen date. Even while we were up at the Gaudeamus hut we received the news that four Viennese climbers had set up camp below the face, among them Fritz Kasparek and Heini Harrer, whom we knew by reputation. However, we managed to remain calm and stick to our plans. If by doing so we lost the first ascent, it would simply mean that Fate had decided otherwise. I held to this notion with a stubbornness that surprised even me, and still does in retrospect.

Upon reaching Switzerland we stocked up with special food for the face and also certain medicaments that were easier to obtain there than at home. Among these was a roll of Thermogene. This product had been earnestly recommended to me by a concerned lady friend. It consisted of pink cotton that people suffering from rheumatism placed over the afflicted part, whereupon the skin burned like fire. What burns cannot freeze, I reasoned to myself, and in view of the well-meant advice bought a jumbo-sized pack.

The weather was rainy, so we lazed away a couple more days in Zürich, enjoying the pleasures of the big city. We didn't reach Grindelwald until July 12. The visibility was good, and a single glance was enough to sum up the condition of the face. It was still damnably white. This was comforting, as it meant that our rivals could not have snatched the prize from us. We now had the advantage, in that (a) we were fresh from training; (b) we probably knew the face better; and (c) we were surely better equipped. The combination of these factors gave us a feeling of great security, which soon drove us up to the foot of the climb.

From our earlier attempts we already knew a place where we could camp safe from the eyes of inquisitive tourists and still more inquisitive journalists. Wiggerl pitched the tent, while I went off to gather wood. I disregarded the smaller sticks that lay around in abundance and instead dragged over thick branches and trunks, which I then attacked violently with an ice ax, with the result that after about five minutes the shaft broke. I pulled a face and Wiggerl grinned meaningfully. There could be no question of attacking the wall the next morning; first we should have to go back down to Grindelwald for another ax. However, the delay was not without a favorable side. We would be acclimatizing to the altitude and could make a few minor adjustments to our supplies. The weather also was not quite what we wanted.

The next day turned out decidedly rainy again. We passed the time in a peculiar way, improving the campsite in spite of the weather. To keep our clothes dry we took them off and ran around naked as Indians. It was not long before we began to feel the cold, so to warm ourselves we set to work like wild men. First we dug a ditch around the tent to keep the surface drainage away from it. Soon the ditch grew so deep that we needed a bridge. Wiggerl dragged over some enormous slabs of rock which I then made a professional job of laying. Next the trampled area in front of the tent began to trouble our aesthetic sensibilities, so we paved this too and in between the slabs I planted grass and Alpine flowers—what was the use of being a gardener otherwise?—so that we finally had a beautiful terrace.

On Sunday, July 17, the weather began to improve, but the Eiger was still wrapped in thick cloud; in any case, it is a more hopeful sign when the conditions do not improve too suddenly. On Monday we went down to Grindelwald, having thought of a few more provisions to take on the face. In front of the tourist office stood a man from Vienna intently studying the weather forecast. He told us that our arrival in Grindelwald had been in the news, and that Kasparek and Harrer were going to attack the mountain that very day.

Now there was no holding us. We went straight back to our camp and made our plans: a good night's sleep and a good meal, then pack our sacks and set out by midday.

Ice and rock pitons, carabiners, crampons, ice axe, and stove—just some of the equipment for the north face ascent

The plan was carried out to the letter. We got up at ten o'clock and I started cooking while Wiggerl carefully laid out all the gear we required for the climb: thirty ice pitons, twenty rock pitons, fifteen carabiners, two ice axes (one long and one short), an ice hammer, a piton hammer, crampons, a liter of fuel, a package of Meta-fuel for priming, bandages, climbing shoes, two pairs of socks each, a change of underwear, two pullovers, a spare shirt, two anoraks, over-trousers, sou'westers with chin straps, face masks, two pairs of mittens, not forgetting the bivouac sack and the roll of Thermogene, which weighed nothing but was unbelievably bulky. On top of this Wiggerl slung his Contax camera, at which I protested. In the first place I thought it weighed too much, and in the second I did not want to waste time taking photographs. Wiggerl, however, was of the opinion that any photographs we took could afterward prove to be an important record. I gave in on the condition that the camera would be the first thing to be jettisoned if the going got tough and we had to lighten our loads. Knowing that I was in deadly earnest, Wiggerl agreed. Not until much later did I realize that he was right.

Food was another whole problem, and one that gave us many headaches. Again and again we argued the question through, bringing all our experience to bear on the matter, and at last we thought we had a solution. The basis was hot drinks—chocolate, tea, coffee, Ovomaltine, sweetened and unsweetened condensed milk—together with three kilos of lump sugar, glucose (especially Dextro-Energen), crackers, bread, bacon, and sardines in olive oil. Wiggerl was against these last but I insisted on them, much to my subsequent regret. On top of all this we took a cured shin of pork which we later had to leave behind on the mountain on account of its weight and indigestibility, a deed that haunts me even now.

As we sorted everything out we kept glancing up at the north wall. Meanwhile the morning slipped by. We forced ourselves to gulp down all we could, and by 12:30 in the afternoon we were ready to go.

A shiver passed through my limbs as I lifted my rucksack. It weighed at least 20 kilos, and Wiggerl's was just as heavy. It seemed impossible to climb with them, yet there was nothing we could leave behind. Somehow I could not bear the thought of parting with the shin of pork. We plodded up the steep ground below the snow slope at the foot of the face. Even at this early stage we had to stop a couple of times to catch our breath. My morale was close to zero; I could not see how we could climb with our overloaded rucksacks. Wiggerl comforted me, "After the first bivouac they'll be a lot lighter because we'll put on all the spare clothes for the night and leave them on after that. Anyway, you'll get used to the weight." Cold comfort indeed.

Right from the start the snow slope was steep and compacted down hard by the avalanches that had swept across it. We were glad to have this excuse to strap on our crampons, which seemed to lighten the load.

As we climbed, Wiggerl told me about a chimney with a jammed block in it at the end of the first snowband. It seemed that this might offer a good way onto the face. Instead of a chimney with a fallen block, however, we found a steep, snow-choked groove. Clearly, there was significantly more snow than at the same time the previous year. That was a good thing, as with our crampons we could gain height quickly. By making a rising traverse across to the right we reached the first buttress after 300 meters. From there, we were on rock, which tended to form ledges and terraces.

At this point we found a splintered ice ax handle, then a tattered rucksack a few meters higher, and above that some other bits and pieces. We did not search any farther, as we knew there were two bodies still on the face. Only one of the Italians had been brought down, and Karl Mehringer had never been found either. We had no desire to disturb the peace of the dead in case they disturbed ours. However, we resolved to return and do a body search after we had climbed the face. Unfortunately, we did not keep this resolution.

Meanwhile, we had reached the split pillar. The climbing was more difficult and we began to feel the encumbrance of the sacks. We tried hauling them after us over one of the overhangs. It proved a complicated maneuver and wasted a lot of time.

Above the pillar we came upon a cave, and what should we find there but two full rucksacks with a note attached to them saying: "Please leave where found. Belong to Kasparek and Harrer." Well, well! So they had already been up and cached their gear. The certainty that they had gone down again had a kind of liberating effect on us.

"All right then, we'll just carry on for a few pitches and the others can see if they can catch up!"

The next few pitches were not pleasant. Water was pouring from the second ice field, and there was nowhere suitable for a bivouac. We therefore decided to retreat to the cave and spend the night there. There were

drips in the cave too, but Wiggerl declared, "They'll stop when it gets properly cold."

It got cold soon enough, but the dripping failed to stop. I lay right at the back where it was worst, with a rock lodged in the small of my back just to help matters. Wiggerl lay unbelayed at the edge, so that I did not dare make the smallest movement for fear of pushing him off. Our first night on the face turned out to be neither exciting nor romantic. The perpetual dripping on my face and down my neck became positively unpleasant. At about four o'clock in the morning we crawled out and made coffee. Our enthusiasm had waned considerably, and the weather, or rather the outlook, was not very encouraging. The horizon was an angry red with black, fish-shaped clouds outlined against it.

"Take a look at the altimeter."

"It's gone up 60 meters!"

This meant that the pressure had dropped about three points. Our morale dropped correspondingly. Wiggerl chose his words carefully:

"Of course, I don't want to go down, but. . . ."

I agreed at once that the idea was not to my taste either. However, if we wanted to play it safe we must have settled weather. An old proverb says "Fish clouds in the sky bring rain by and by." Quoting these ominous words to one another, we decided to leave the sacks in the cave and descend.

The sacks were packed away and we were about to start when suddenly a form hove into view on a snow slope to the left of the pillar, closely followed by another. Not particularly pleased with this development, I called down, "Hi-yo!" and received the same reply. It was Kasparek and Harrer. As we had never met, we introduced ourselves somewhat formally and with some embarrassment.

"Sleep well?"

"Not too well," we admitted, and then asked in our turn, "Are you going on in spite of the weather?"

"Yes, we're going on. It has to be done sometime. We've been camping

"My morale was close to zero; I could not see how we could climb with our overloaded rucksacks."

in tents and barns for five weeks now, and we're down to a franc and a half. We think the weather's going to hold out, so we're going for it."

"Our altimeter's rising and the weather doesn't look too hopeful," I warned them. But Kasparek repeated obstinately, "We're going on."

Wiggerl looked at me.

"What do you think?"

At this moment yet another party appeared on the scene. They were two Viennese, Freissl and Brankovsky. "Are you all together?" I asked.

"No, it's each party for itself."

The six of us laughed a little forcedly at the coincidence. In fact it was not so extraordinary, since obviously all the parties lurking around were bound to meet on the first fine day. I would not have been surprised if several more parties had appeared, since we knew that there were some Italian climbers in the vicinity who represented serious competition. The name of Cassin had even been mentioned, and of all possible rivals he was the one I feared most. The arrival of the second party was, however, enough to confirm our decision to retreat. No matter how good they are, six men cannot help getting in each other's way. On a face such as this, the objective dangers would be heightened to a point where an accident would be inevitable. That was my opinion at the time. Nowadays, when the conditions are good, parties climb one behind another. Have the conditions or the climbers improved?

However that might be, we had resolved to turn back and remained true to our decision; things would have to take their own course. Nevertheless, we assured the others that if anything went wrong they could count on our help.

Heinrich Harrer, photographed by Wiggerl Vörg as the two parties meet for the first time

Secretly we believed in our own weather forecast and reckoned that the others would soon be back too. As we descended, however, the weather got better and better and our faces grew longer and longer. By 10 A.M. we were sitting in grass below the face, knowing that far above us "the competition" were at work. Wiggerl, normally so placid, was utterly discouraged and in despair. When I spoke to him he was too lost in his thoughts to hear. However, I was fortified by the thought that we had acted correctly throughout.

Since we were already down, we decided to continue on to Alpiglen at once so as to follow the progress of the other parties through the fixed telescope. Before long we were standing among a crowd of inquisitive tourists who had

Fritz Kasparek
works his way
laboriously up the
first snow field.

nothing very intelligent to say. A woman announced importantly, "I saw them on the way up yesterday afternoon,"

This in fact referred to us, who stood in their midst, but no one had noticed us climbing down. A man who had elected himself spokesman explained to his eager listeners, "Those are doomed men. Do you see that tree growing in the ice field? That's where they are now. Today they'll get to the ledge, tomorrow they'll reach that one, and then it'll be all over for them because they'll be out of food and they won't be able to climb down."

Seldom had I been forced to listen to so much earnestly intended drivel. I began to wonder whether it was we who were sane or they. Meanwhile, we had pressed forward to the telescope, where we found to our astonishment that the first party was making extraordinarily slow progress. The second party was not visible at all. This perplexed us, but after a few more hours of observation we came to the conclusion that for some reason or other they must have turned back. The idea affected us like an electric shock. If that was the case, we could go back up; four on the face was not too many.

Immediately we placed a telephone call to Grindelwald for a weather report. The meteorological chart showed a flat anticyclone over the Baltic, a flat depression over the British Isles. It seemed as though everything was flat except the face. If we weren't scared of that, surely there was no need to be scared of the flat depression. Now we felt no more doubt. We were going up again.

I could have turned cartwheels of joy. We ate a good lunch at the Gasthaus at Alpiglen, where the kindly landlady knew us and kept our secret. The accompanying tankard of beer restored our mental equilibrium. Another look through the telescope showed Kasparek working his way up from the first to the second ice field, hacking away furiously with his ax. Probably he lacked twelve-point crampons and was having to cut his way step by step up the almost vertical ice gully, a tedious and time-consuming task. It suited us all right, as it meant that they would not build up too great a lead.

Wiggerl was in favor of heading straight to the bivouac without further ado, but I still had horrible memories of the night before and also thought that an immediate assault would be premature. We agreed to delay departure on the condition that we set off at midnight. I agreed to the plan sanctimoniously and undertook the responsibility for waking up at the right time, thinking to myself: "You can stuff your midnight. Two o'clock is early enough." Once before I had set off for a big climb at midnight and well remembered how we had sat freezing and shivering at its foot until daylight came. I wanted to avoid a repetition on this occasion.

During the afternoon we crawled into our sleeping bags and lay down under a shady tree by our campsite. Seldom had I felt so well in myself; not a trace of nervousness. We were in a mood of supreme confidence. At six o'clock we had an ample meal. There was pineapple for dessert. Originally we had intended this for victory celebrations, but we philosophized: "Success is not so certain after all. The pineapple will taste just as good now, while we are alive, and if something happened to us somebody else would eat it." An hour later we lay down again in the tent and fell asleep immediately; it was incredible that we could sleep so deeply and peacefully. I woke up in the middle of the night. It was exactly two o'clock.

Enough of this inactivity. Out!

The night was cool and clear. As we looked up at the pale gloom of the face a light suddenly flared up from the rocks below the second ice field and went out. We learned later that the other party had lit their spirit stove at this moment.

Three-quarters of an hour later we left the camp, finding our way with the help of a candle lantern. It was a good thing that we knew the way so well, as the darkness was intense. We did not go astray by so much as a meter and reached the snow slope in the gray light of dawn. By the time we set foot on the rocks it was daylight, so we stuffed the candle lantern into a cleft with the intention of returning for it after the climb, though that never happened. At 4:30 A.M. we were already at our previous night's bivouac site. We recovered our kit, roped up, shared out the pitons and carabiners, and pulled on our climbing shoes.

"No more messing about. Let's go."

The crack leading up to the Hinterstoisser Traverse was choked with ice, and I found it so difficult to lead that I had to take off the sack. This pitch is now popularly known as "the difficult crack," and more than one party has met its match here. The ability to cope with extreme technical

Anderl Heckmair
on the
Hinterstoisser
Traverse

difficulty is only one of the preconditions for a successful ascent of the face. We were fully aware of this, and our intensive training and long period of mental conditioning now stood us in good stead.

The sack-hauling once again proved extraordinarily time-consuming and exhausting. As I started to take in the sack, it immediately got caught up. I heaved enough to thin the rope with the strain, but still it would not budge. Finally Wiggerl had to climb up and butt it free with his head, so that at last I could haul away. We resolved to avoid sack-hauling as much as possible, and as we had now reached easier ground we began to climb at top speed.

The Hinterstoisser Traverse, over which a waterfall usually pours and which had proved to be the undoing of the 1936 party, was dry but plastered in ice. The fixed rope with which Rebitsch and Vörg had kept open their line of retreat was still there. That was good, as it saved us valuable time. Damaged as it was by avalanche and stonefall it was risky to use, but by protecting myself with our own rope the worst I had to fear was a nice big swing.

In 1957, a German and an Italian party met at dawn at the beginning of the traverse. For reasons no one can explain it took them a whole day. Their ascent ended in particularly tragic circumstances. In my judgment it was doomed to failure from the start; the north face of the Eiger is not the place to learn how to do tension traverses.

At 8:00 A.M., climbing on our twelve-point crampons, we reached the first ice field. As we stepped onto the slope we found ourselves in the fall line of a hail of ice chips and stones dislodged by the others, who were cutting steps above us. The steps which they had cut the previous day were of no use; meltwater had flowed over them in the afternoon and frozen solid during the night, so that no trace remained even of the biggest. This did not worry us, however, as with twelve-point crampons no steps are needed, except that a stance must be cut out and protected with an ice piton at the end of each run-out, since climbing at high speed on the front points only is very hard on the calf muscles. It was the first time that I had used twelve-pointers, which in 1938 were still absolutely new. Everyone has them now, even for stomping around on flat glaciers, although their only real advantage is in climbing steep ice.

I was surprised at the way the two front points bit in and the security they gave even on ultra-steep ice. After no more than a few minutes the first ice field lay below us. The route to the second ice field lies either up the notorious "ice hose" or else up a black 40-meter wall of rock. We opted for the rock. Off came the crampons, the sacks were tied to the rope, and in the end the wall turned out to be not nearly so bad as it looked. Nevertheless, there were a couple of overhangs, and hauling the sacks caused yet more drudgery.

In the Difficult Crack

The second ice field consisted of bare water-ice. Very carefully but steadily Wiggerl balanced upward, while I panted behind with the big rucksack. We had allocated the weight so that the leader could climb with a lighter sack, the second managing as best he could with the heavier one.

At eleven o'clock we reached Kasparek and Harrer's line of steps at the upper edge of the second ice field. Our troubles were over. We could have romped along with our hands in our pockets.

"Hey, Wiggerl, look, we're catching them already!"

The ice fields had not looked particularly big from below, but in reality they were huge; the second was a good twenty rope-lengths across. The pair in front of us had performed a Herculean labor, cutting their way step by step. Indeed, "steps" was not the word—they were real bathtubs. Now we could stroll along together. Quite soon we were within shouting range and yodeled happily to one another. By 11:30 A.M. we had caught up with them.

The use of twelve-point crampons. Drawing by Gustl Kröner 1931.

Now I saw why they had moved so slowly and needed such big steps. They had made the same mistake as all the parties that had been lost on the face, and that we ourselves had made on our first attempts. They were equipped for rock rather than ice. In fact they did not have so much as an ax, and Harrer did not even have crampons. Kasparek had had to cut all the steps with an ice hammer, working the whole time bent double. I pointed out to them that at this rate they stood little chance of getting up, and advised immediate retreat. However, climbers are obstinate souls, and Kasparek particularly so. He simply replied, "We'll do it all right, even if we do take a little longer."

It was a ticklish situation. We were faced with the grave decision whether to overtake them and press on, leaving them to their fate. I was close to doing this, but not Vörg, who was far better-natured. It was he who found the redeeming words.

"Then let's form one party and rope up together."

I did not want to start an argument and therefore agreed, albeit against my will. However, during the ascent our forced association turned to comradeship and afterward to lifelong friendship. That was by no means an inevitable development, for mountaineers are only human

Fritz Kasparek moves across from the third ice field to the "Ramp."

and endowed with their share of human frailties. Among us, however, there were no petty jealousies about who was the best climber. On the north face each had his job to do and did it, and could rely absolutely on the others to do theirs.

Joining together also brought some undeniable advantages. With the weight distributed among four, I could lead with only a very light sack. The bivouacs were not so lonely, and above all the other two knew the way down the other side of the mountain. But for this it would have gone badly for us.

Before long we were standing under the rock buttress below the third ice field. The way up was supposed to be a difficult chimney, but the ice made it invisible. It was an example of how changeable conditions are on the face. Well, we were equipped accordingly.

By the time all four of us sat beside the third ice field it was 2:00 P.M. Wiggerl pointed at the rock, "Look, there are the pitons placed by poor Sedlmayer and Mehringer."

Silently our thoughts turned to the two friends. We hacked out big stances and heated some Ovomaltine, which did us all good. We wanted to eat as much as possible to lighten the sacks, so we chewed away at some bacon, but no one really cared for it. Our stomachs simply refused to absorb solid food. The shin of pork began to annoy me, but I was reluctant to abandon it in case my appetite returned with a vengeance.

About this time the previously cloudless sky began to haze over, but we did not worry unduly. The route, by which I mean the route that we had worked out in advance, was so firmly fixed in our minds that there was no peering around wondering where to go next. The weak points of the wall and where to attack them had been worked out in advance. We were all in agreement about the line.

So the four of us crossed the rib of snow on the third ice field onto untrodden ground. To get across to the so-called "Ramp" we first had to down-climb a short stretch of steep ice where the differences in the lengths of our ice axes became significant. The longer ax came into its own on the downhill step-cutting.

The Ramp is a gully that cuts diagonally up the face. One side of it

128

proved relatively easy to climb—almost too easy, I thought. I became anxious lest it should continue like this to the top. Before long, however, I was fully reassured on this point.

For about 150 meters the route went comparatively easily up snow-covered, icy slabs which then culminated in a belt of cliffs. The only way out of this was a vertical chimney that ended in a rib. One side of the chimney was yellow, overhanging and loose, in a word, unclimbable. The other wall was smoother but more amenable, except that a waterfall tumbled over it so merrily that anyone attempting to climb it would be soaked through in a minute. None of us wanted to bivouac in wet clothes.

It was seven o'clock when the four of us stood together in the hollow below the belt of cliffs. We decided to celebrate. The hollow did not seem a good place, as its floor was covered with avalanche debris that had built up into a steep, icy surface, over which the water sprayed and flowed. We therefore climbed back down to the ramp and set about preparing for our bivouac. Suddenly the clouds parted and we found ourselves gazing down into depths so tremendous that although we were accustomed to such sights we shuddered slightly. For the first time we understood how exposed our position was, and with a couple of powerful

Heinrich Harrer (left) and Fritz Kasparek at the bivouac on the Ramp

Anderl Heckmair (left) and Wiggerl Vörg at the bivouac on the Ramp

Heinrich Harrer brews tea at the bivouac on the Ramp

blows hammered another belay piton into the rock.

We pulled on every stitch of clothing we had with us. With loving care I took out my Thermogene and packed it around my knees and toes, informing the others that it would keep me nice and warm. Next we got into our long underwear, over which came climbing breeches and overtrousers, two sets of pullovers and anoraks, and anything else available. Wiggerl, the voluptuary, even had a pair of fur booties. I had to wear my big boots, as my climbing shoes were still wet through from the Hinterstoisser Traverse. Ropes, rucksacks, and everything else was laid on the ice as an under layer to sit on, and the sleeping bags spread out and ready. Had I been a fakir I would have sat on my crampons with the points upward, which might have added further warmth.

Coffee was what we most craved, and Wiggerl busied himself producing mighty quantities. We were thirsty but not hungry. I could still not get rid of any of the damned shin of pork. One must eat something, however, so I opened a tin of sardines. No one else wanted any, so I ate the lot. They were to cause me trouble during the night.

In the meantime it had grown dark. The lights of Grindelwald glittered up at us and we felt fine on our airy perch. Before long we got into our sleeping bags and everyone settled down to get as much sleep as

he could. By the light of my torch I took a last glance at the altimeter. It showed 3400 meters, which was extremely satisfactory for the first day. As I was trying to put the altimeter away, something slid down the slab and vanished silently into the abyss.

"Damn it, what was that?"

It had to be the altimeter, which was nowhere to be found. Cautiously I inquired how much such a gadget might cost to replace.

"Oh, about 150 marks," replied Wiggerl dryly.

I could not get to sleep for anger. Only the parts covered in Thermogene remained marvelously warm. I thought with gratitude of the fair lady who had given me this good advice; it was as though the padded places were being caressed.

The time would not go by. When I thought it surely must be almost dawn it turned out to be only eleven o'clock. It is a form of natural compensation; as the hours fly past like minutes when you are climbing by day, the minutes have to turn back into hours at night when you are bivouacking.

Just as I was starting to get really bored I was seized with a violent stomachache. I said nothing about it so as not to worry the others. But the fevers and chills and dizziness were so powerful that I began to fear that there was something seriously wrong with me. Presently Wiggerl noticed, and everyone sprang into action. Heini Harrer was of the opinion that hot tea would be the best thing, and immediately got his cooker going. A few minutes later I found myself sipping peppermint tea, a drink I had never been able to stand, yet never had a brew tasted better or done me so much good. The sardines promptly settled down in my stomach and we all nodded off for a while.

Cooking started again at 4:00 A.M., but not until seven o'clock were we ready to go. As we packed up the altimeter was found. You should avoid getting angry; it seldom helps and is often pointless.

Our first movements were a little stiff, but the sight of the wall that I now had to climb made me feel warm. The waterfall over the smooth left-hand wall was no longer there, but in its place was an icy crust. As the chimney was free of ice higher up, I started up it without crampons, prudently placing a couple of pitons, one of which was really firm. To avoid the ice I used holds on the loose, overhanging side, and managed to surmount the overhang, if not very elegantly. Just half a meter more and I could get in another peg. My right hand reached a hold above me but it broke off even before I could put much strain on it and a lump the size of a coffee pot landed on my head. I found myself hanging from the good piton under the overhang.

That was the first fall. Well, these things happen, I thought to myself. Strapping on my crampons I tackled the left-hand wall. I had never done anything like it before. It was ice climbing in the purest sense, but it went.

Well above the level where the hold had broken off, I returned to the chimney, and after a few more meters found myself standing in an ice-filled groove where I cut a stance and belayed the others. While doing this I glanced up to see where we could go next, but the possibilities did not seem clear. The only remotely feasible line appeared to be an ice-choked corner capped with an ice overhang.

Summit icefield

Exit cracks
Second bivouac

Spider

First bivouac

Ramp
Third
icefield

Second
icefield

Hinterstoisser
transverse

Difficult
crack

Gallery
window
Shattered
pillar

First pillar

It was the task of the last man to take out all the pitons, not so as to complicate the task of subsequent parties but to economize our stock in view of the unknown above, where we might need all we could muster. As leader on this difficult ground I no longer wore a sack at all. The others were thus all the more heavily laden and arrived so out of breath that they needed a few minutes to recover.

Every meter gained in the direction of the ice overhang made me more uncertain how to get over it. Finally the difficulties came to a head at the end of the corner, right under the roof. In front of me a curtain of beautiful icicles hung from its edge, but at this moment I was little disposed to appreciating the beauties of nature. In fact I was in despair to know what to do to get any farther. The first thing was to place a secure piton under the roof. Now I could take tension and knock down the icicles with the ax, naturally after warning the others to take cover, as these icicles weighed a good 50 kilos and went whizzing down most impressively.

Leaning out as far as I could against the rope tension, I was finally able to reach the stump of one of the icicles. In those days we did not have the now common étriers, or we would have used them. As I swung my weight on to the icicle it snapped off and I shot down as far as the last piton, which luckily held. It was clearly impossible to get up here, but there was no alternative. Were we to be defeated by this ridiculous overhang? This was the Eiger, and we had to expect some difficulties.

I prospected to the left and then to the right, but it was no good. By this time I was really in a temper and resolved to go for it all out. Above the ice piton that had just held so well, an icicle as thick as my arm had grown down until it joined on to the ice again, thus forming a handle-like structure through which I threaded a sling. Once again I took tension on the rope and leaned out. With a supreme effort I managed to hammer in my biggest ice piton just at the edge of the overhang. When it was only half in I could tell by the ringing noise that it was sound. That was enough—quick, a carabiner—"Take in tight!" I got the upper part of my body over the edge. Now the battle was as good as won. With my left hand I swung the pick of the hammer into the ice, with my right the ice ax. A quick pull-up, and I cramponed my feet up onto the slope.

"Slack!"

I took a few hasty steps. Five meters higher I could finally cut a good stance and plant two ice pitons for protection. Then it was the turn of my companions to climb up with their heavy rucksacks—we had long ago given up sack-hauling. It had been the hardest part of the climb so far. I was satisfied, but not inclined to wish for any further heightening of the satisfaction.

The Heckmair Route on the north face of the Eiger

The slope to which we had won our way was bare and steep. The ice was so hard that I had to cut some steps even for the crampon wearers. We were getting close to its upper end when suddenly a fearful uproar broke out. Thinking it was a stonefall we all ducked, only to find that the racket came from an aircraft flying close to the face. Seen from below, the slope on which we stood looks tiny, but it was almost ten pitches long and took more than two hours to climb. Next we followed a band to the rocky step that bars access to the long gangway leading across to the "White Spider." The Spider is the ice field in the upper third of the face from which ice gullies and ledges reach out on all sides into the surrounding rocks.

The previous year, as Wiggerl and I had carefully studied every possible line up the face through the telescope, this step had looked distinctly doubtful to us, and the others had independently come to the same conclusion. Now that we stood in front of it, it did not look bad at all. Though vertical and about fifty meters high it was finely articulated and therefore probably well-endowed with holds, so I did not think of taking off my sack and crampons but simply tied the ice ax to the sack.

However, starting up the step was not as easy as it looked. The holds were small and the rock overhanging. Placing the front points of my crampons on tiny holds I forced my way upward. It was a completely new technique to us; none of us had ever climbed on such iced-up rock before. What would we have done without our twelve-pointers? Nevertheless, it was hard on the arms, which were going numb with the effort. I was not far from falling off when suddenly the airplane came blasting by again shamelessly close. A thunderstorm approaching out of the west was shaking it, and I had visions of it crashing into the cliffs at any moment and the whole of it raining about my ears. I was genuinely relieved when it disappeared into the clouds.

Three o'clock in the afternoon; where had the hours gone? We felt no trace of hunger or tiredness. On the contrary, when we heard the first rolls of thunder our wills hardened with the resolve to fight a way through. There could be no more thought of retreat. In the interests of speed we divided into pairs again. I wanted at all costs to reach the Spider and get a view of the way forward before the arrival of the cold that always goes with a storm. To get onto the Spider we had to cross a few meters of bare ice. I found I was out of ice pitons.

"Wiggerl!" I called, "Bring the ice pegs."

"Yeah, er, Heini's got them!"

As last man, it was Heini Harrer's task to take out all the pitons, and as we had used them all he now had all of them. It seemed best to wait for the others to catch up, but several stones went whistling past as we stood there. If one of them hit one of us, that would be the end. Suddenly we found our stance very inhospitable.

"Come on, never mind the pitons. We'll belay with the shafts of the ice axes." And as this technique seemed to me of doubtful effectiveness, I added, "Only we must not fall off!"

In fact the ice had softened and steps were not absolutely essential. Nevertheless, 150 meters had to be climbed in this way. After each run-out we cut a stance, which was to prove the salvation of the others.

We did not take long to reach the foot of the rock bastion before the summit. Initially there was nowhere to stand, but it was possible to chop a couple of stances out of the ice. I also found a crack in the rock that would accept my very last ice piton, which was a particularly thin one. It is extremely rare to be able to place an ice piton in rock, but if it can be done it constitutes an especially safe anchor. With heavy blows I drove it deep into the crack, little guessing how vitally important it was to prove to us. A glance up at the face comfortably revealed a whole system of cracks and grooves, one of which must surely provide a way forward. Now the storm could come, although to half stand, half hang where we were was not the most agreeable prospect. Thirty meters below, a pulpit of rock cropped out of the ice, offering a level, tablelike top.

"What do you say, Wiggerl? It would be pretty good to sit down there."

Having joined forces, the climbers make their way along brittle ledges. The photograph was taken from an airplane. From left to right are Harrer, Kasparek, Vörg, and Heckmair.

"I'm all for it, only the rope won't reach."

"It doesn't matter. Go on, I'll belay you."

As soon as the rope had run out, I unclipped from the piton and climbed carefully down without any security. We settled down on the rock as though it were a throne and looked around critically at the weather.

"Doesn't look too good."

Meanwhile, our friends were just traversing onto the Spider. The light was gradually growing more and more dismal, and before long it began to sleet. Lightning and thunder followed, but we had endured enough storms in the mountains not to be dismayed. Only the increasingly frequent whistling and hooting of invisible stonefalls in the mist got on our nerves.

Climbing in our tracks, the two Austrians had now reached the middle of the Spider. The sleet had changed to hail, and we had pulled the tent-sack over our heads for shelter. We raised it to see how the others were getting on. Suddenly Wiggerl gestured toward the ice groove directly above us:

"There's an avalanche coming!"

Out of the gully came hissing a stream of ice granules that broke over our heads and poured into the depths. I jumped up and stabbed the pick of my ax into the ice so as to resist the pressure. Wiggerl was unable to emulate me because there was no room to do so, and sat exposed on the edge of the rock. We had no belay whatever. I held on to the pick with one hand and grabbed Wiggerl by the scruff of the neck with the other, convinced that our comrades had been swept away by the mainstream of the avalanche that had broken over them, and that we were about to follow them at any moment. In the meantime I just tried to hang on as long as possible. In my imagination I already saw us tumbling over the edge.

However, things had not reached that point. I was astonished at how long I was able to withstand the tremendous force. The bare hand that held on to the ax had turned white with cold, and I took the risk of letting go for a moment to draw on a mitten. The sleet and hail particles had banked up in a wall as high as my hips, over which the avalanche split into two and rushed past on either side. Luckily, the steepness of the ice slope had caused the enormous mass of powder to slide by quickly. Slowly the air cleared and the pressure eased. We hardly believed that we had come through it, but so it seemed. What had happened to the others? The cloud thinned out, and . . .

"Wiggerl! They're still there!"

It seemed impossible, almost a miracle. We were overcome with joy.

Anderl Heckmair clips a running belay on the traverse across to the Spider.

Only when you again see friends you believed to be dead do you realize how deep the feeling of comradeship can be.

"I'm hurt!" called Kasparek. "Throw me a rope."

First we had to get back up to our piton, and that turned out to be
not so easy. The stream of hailstones was still rushing down. When we
reached the rock wall above the Spider we found ourselves separated
from the peg by a runnel down which the hailstones were pouring like
a torrent. I was all for risking a jump, but Wiggerl would not hear of it.
It was a good ten minutes before we could get across to our piton. It
and the carabiner had grown icicles several centimeters long. The phenomenon was curious, but we had no time for scientific reflection. However, it did occur to us to wonder how we would have fared if we had
remained standing there.

The belay was clipped in, the ropes tied together, and the end thrown
down to our friends. To reach where it landed on the ice some 60 meters
below us, Kasparek had to climb up about another 10 meters. Finally
he was tied on. The knowledge that we were all linked together again
was like an assurance of salvation, and from that moment we remained
roped in one party all the way to the summit and down to Scheidegg.

The others soon reached our stance.

"Where are you hurt?"

"Ugh, my hand looks awful."

All the skin had been torn off the back of Kasparek's hand, and at
the time it looked much worse than it really was. In order to be sure I
gave it a hard squeeze, reasoning that if a bone was broken he would
feel it, whereas if the injury was superficial he would only start swearing. To my relief it was the latter that occurred. Quickly I got out the
first aid kit and bound the gaping wound. By this time it was 6:00 P.M.

"Shall we bivouac here?"

Following the storm the weather improved, but still did not look
promising. We had just had a taste of what snowslides can be like when
concentrated in a funnel. If the weather turned really nasty it would be
fatal to try to climb the ice gully up which the rest of the route lay. After
a short council of war we decided to continue despite the Alpine rule of
thumb that one should settle down to bivouac two hours before dark.
Our reasoning was that it was still relatively warm and the ice soft, so
this was the most favorable time to try it.

The gully began with an overhang, which I tackled on the left. However, I had been in too much of a hurry, and after three meters had to
jump down again. In the process I got my crampons tangled up and only
avoided a fall thanks to our belay. Over on the right, where at first the
rock had looked too formidable to try, it turned out to be distinctly easier.
The ice proved to be in good condition, and I was able to stab in the blade

After the storm. Fritz Kasparek and Heinrich Harrer follow the exit gullies leading out of the Spider.

of the ice ax with one hand and a stout ice piton with the other, then pull up on them and walk my twelve-pointers up quickly. It was very hard and risky work, but what alternative did I have?

If I had spent time looking for more running belays it would have cost us all the remaining daylight, and the following morning we could scarcely have escaped the terrible avalanches in the gully. It is a principle of mine to accept subjective risks while avoiding objective ones, and the four us held to this on this occasion. The higher we got, the narrower and steeper the gullies grew. In between they built up into overhangs, which we took as they came. Harrer groaned under the weight of his increasingly heavy rucksack. In order to climb more safely at the front we had been passing back the contents of our rucksacks to the others on every possible occasion. Heini and Fritz had relieved us of everything they could in a spirit of evident comradeship, and to this was added the weight of the pitons which accumulated as they took them out. The last man began to look like a porter. The two of them accepted the monstrous effort without once complaining. It was this teamwork that enabled us to win through. Fritz never said a word about his hand although he must have been in great pain; the bandage around the wound was saturated in blood.

We now needed to find a spot in this system of grooves and chimneys where we could be moderately safe from avalanches and stonefall. After climbing an ice bulge I came upon a ledge protected by an overhang. It was outward-sloping and exposed, like everything on the Eigerwand, but at least it was sheltered.

I drove a ring piton into a little crack right up to the ring. To get any other piton into the rock was a work of art, as the rock on this final wall was much looser than elsewhere. With a great deal of patience we eventually managed to hammer in a sufficient quantity to tie our kit and ourselves to. The previous evening had taught us that everything that was not attached could slip from our hands to be lost forever.

In the Exit Cracks

Unfortunately, we could not all sit together. Three meters away there was a second place where it was possible to belay and cut away some of the shelving ice, and Fritz and Heini worked away to install their bivouac there. Between us we stretched a rope along which we could pull a billycan clipped on a carabiner.

As on the previous evening, the good-natured Wiggerl did all the cooking. Kasparek's spirit stove had long since joined my shin of pork on the road into the abyss. We still had no inclination for solid food. All we wanted was to drink, preferably coffee, and of that we had ample supplies. We still had enough food to last us a week, but it remained untouched. I was not anxious to repeat my experience of the night before. None of us was particularly exigent in the matter of space, but this ledge was annoyingly narrow. I could not find a comfortable position. There was no question of lying down. We had already spend the night before sitting up, but this time it could not even be called sitting. With my crampons stamped into the ice (which meant that I had to keep them on) I slumped from a sling around my chest, suspended from the piton.

If only Wiggerl would at least sit still! But he just went on peacefully boiling one can of coffee after another, and in our hearts we could find nothing to say against that. He would take a swig, pass the can on straight away, and immediately set another on the gas stove, the humming of which gave us a feeling of well-being. Apart from that, we felt perfectly calm. We knew what we would have to face the next day, and that the weather would be bad. Only Fritz grumbled, "When I get down again I'm going to light a dry cigarette with a dry match!"

We two had purposely taken neither alcohol nor tobacco with us. Kasparek, however, who could not do without his smoke, had found his cigarettes and matches unusable, hence the complaint. It was only to be expected, as although we were not absolutely soaked to the skin we were nevertheless quite damp.

"Quite apart from that, we felt perfectly calm. We knew what we would have to face next day, and that the weather would be bad. Only Fritz grumbled: 'When I get down again I'm going to light a dry cigarette with a dry match!'"

Harrer and Kasparek at their third bivouac, above the Spider.

For me this latter circumstance had particular significance, as the Thermogene had got wet. This had happened during the course of the day, and the wadding, which was only supposed to be applied to rheumatic spots for a couple of hours at most, now burned my knees and toes horribly. No longer did I feel pampered as at first, but really tortured. "Better to let it burn," we decided. "At least it will prevent any freezing." Unfortunately, we were mistaken.

At last Wiggerl stopped cooking and began to prepare for the night. With indescribable calm he proceeded to change his clothes and draw on his bivouac slippers, whereas we had just settled down as we were. Darkness had long since fallen; it was already after eleven o'clock. Even Fritz had kept on his crampons. I would gladly have taken mine off, but as already mentioned I needed them to stop myself from sliding. Wiggerl's antics took him a good hour, and then at last we could pull the bivouac sack over our heads. His broad back was turned toward me and I could lean against it comfortably. He was so soft and warm that I forgave him the disturbance he had caused. As peace returned, my eyelids closed and I fell asleep.

A violent cold shower woke me up again and set our teeth chattering. I was surprised to see that it was light already. In fact it was 5:00 A.M., and I had slept through the whole night. The others told me that several avalanches had swept over our heads without my noticing.

"Go back to sleep," said Wiggerl settling back into the position that I found so comfortable. I noticed for the first time that it must be extremely uncomfortable for him.

"Have you slept?"

"Of course not. But when I saw how well you were sleeping I kept still, because you are the one who is going to need it most. Go back to sleep, Anderl. It's snowing and we can't do anything for the time being."

However, now that I knew my rest was causing him agony I could not settle down again. On top of that, I was too cold and worried about the weather. The snow was falling dry. We could hear the storm but not feel it, as we were in the lee of the west ridge. But from the ridge and the summit came the sound of its roaring. Every so often, as the weight of snow piled up on the summit ice slopes, it would break away in avalanches. We were able to observe their route and timing exactly. It was lucky for us that we had climbed this far the previous evening, as below us everything falling from the summit slopes was gathered as into a funnel. Only a small side stream fell past us, and on our ledge we received no more than the whirling snow dust.

Wiggerl carefully resumed his task as cook and produced hot chocolate made with canned milk. We knew that this would be our last meal until we got back to the valley, yet we did not throw away the ample provisions we still had. We might need them still.

Our every move was being observed from the valley, and a Munich journalist who had reached Scheidegg at exactly the right time telephoned the following dispatch to his paper, the *Münchner Neueste Nachrichten*, that evening. It was titled "Between Hope and Fear."

"At 12:30 P.M. on Saturday the weather turned bad over the Eiger. A slate-gray wall of cloud, dark and threatening, rolled toward the Lauterbrunnen valley. After a severe, five-hour struggle the four climbers had surmounted the slanting gully, which perhaps contains the hardest pitches on the face, and traversed the snowbank over the yellow cliff on the right of the gully. At one o'clock they stood in a row at the left edge of the snowfield. Heckmair, the mountain guide with the most extensive training and perhaps the greatest experience on ice, was in the lead.

For the next half hour the climbers were hidden in cloud, but at 2:30 P.M. it cleared again. They had just crossed the snowband and the leader was just reaching the overhang before the so-called "Spider." Without stopping, Heckmair— who remained in the lead all day—traversed onto the Spider. We watched him wielding his ice ax powerfully and swiftly forcing a way to the middle of the slope. Immediately, he ran out the whole rope length to reach a snowband running up to the top left-hand end of the Spider. Vörg followed up as second man.

"Heckmair went on again up the steep snowband or, more accurately, gully, until he reached a brown rock where he stopped and belayed Vörg, who came up equally fast. They then sat down on the rock to wait for the others. Their performance, their power ax work, their careful belaying and astonishing speed clearly showed us, as we watched them excitedly through the telescope, that they were in great form and still full of energy.

"Meanwhile Kasparek and Harrer had been resting at the end of the lower snowband. From 3:00 to 3:30 P.M. the face was again veiled in cloud, and as it cleared the watchers crowded around the telescopes. The leader of the second party was just traversing onto the Spider as Heckmair reached the rock in the upper snow gully.

"The second party moved slower than the first, but just as carefully and safely. Heckmair and Vörg were now at 3600 meters. At ten past four the face clouded over again, leaving us alone with our hopes and fears once more. The four climbers still had 350 meters to go before the summit.

"The weather began to look very threatening again. Throughout the day it had been impossible to decide from one hour to the next whether it was finally going to get better or worse. Now the air over the Lauterbrunnen valley was dirty gray and the Jungfrau and Mönch were lost in cloud. The glacier icefalls shimmered pale blue in the failing light. Between the rain clouds was a patch of blue, and over the Grosse Scheidegg the sky was still clear, but the weather was rolling up inexorably. The party must still be in the funnel of the Spider. At 4:25 P.M. it began to drizzle, and five minutes later there was a cloudburst. It must have broken over the face like an ocean wave. Suddenly a cry of horror

*was torn from the throats of the watchers: "The face!" The whole breadth of the
north face was one appalling waterfall. The water cascaded over the rocks in
ten, twelve, fifteen broad, white, foaming bands. A beautiful rainbow arched
above Alpiglen, but who had eyes for it or the marvelous play of its colors? Up
there, the pair on the snow slope were fully exposed to the plunging torrent.
Would they be able to hold on?*

*"At last the cloud cleared and it became possible to see through the telescope.
There was the snowfield and there, yes, there they were. Calmly and deliberately,
they were already moving again. They had come through the deluge! Having
been able to take shelter below the rocks at the side of the gully, Heckmair and
Vörg probably had an easier time of it. But already the face was covered over
again; the last we saw was that one of the upper party had climbed down some
way, presumably to throw a rope to the others and safeguard them.*

*"At 6:15 P.M. we were able to see that they were all together again and head-
ing for the upper end of the snow gully. Heckmair was standing straddled, belaying the others. Then he turned and continued, cutting steps. At seven o'clock
all four were at the top of the snow gully. An hour later they were still climbing, having either found no bivouac site or, more probably, preferring to keep
going as long as daylight should hold out in order to get as near the summit as
possible. They were now at 3700 meters, far above the Spider, and had thus
achieved an outstanding performance in the last fourteen hours. The weather
was looking more hopeful for the time being. Patches of blue showed between
the dirty-looking clouds, which were not getting caught up in the crags, so the
climbers had some visibility.*

*"At 8:30 P.M. it began to rain again,
but in the intervals we could see the party
still underway. After half an hour they
seemed to be preparing a bivouac site. For
Kaspareck and Harrer this will be the
third night on the face, for Heckmair and
Vörg the second. In wet clothes and on
probably exiguous stances it will be a testing experience, although all four are iron-
hard men.*

*"Our last observation was at ten
o'clock. The sky was starry. In the middle
of the face floated a light-colored cloud, and
below it shone the strange light of the
Jungfrau Railway Eigerwand station. Otherwise all was dark. For the four men up
on the face the problem now was to hold out
through the hours of darkness. They had
enough food for five or six days. Probably*

Harrer and
Kasparek spend
an icy-cold night
beneath the tent
sack.

they did not sleep much but passed the night crouched over their cooker making hot food or tea. There could be no more question of retreat; they must get up at all costs. They were at 3750 meters, which left some 200 meters to the summit.

"On Sunday morning we awoke to rain. The windows were blind with cloud. The weather has broken, and there is nothing to be seen of the face. Up there it must be snowing. Kasparek and Harrer have now been on the face for sixty-five hours, Vörg and Heckmair for forty-three. At five o'clock it was raining, at six o'clock it was raining, at seven o'clock it was raining; at eleven o'clock there was still nothing but uninterrupted, pouring rain."

Up on the face, however, we had no inkling of the anxiety that we were arousing. All we knew was that we could count on no outside help.

It became necessary to leave our sheltered place and go out into the storm; a hard thing to do, but after a moment's reflection the decision was not difficult to make. Of course, like Merkl and Welzenbach on the north face of the Charmoz, we could have waited for the weather to improve, but I did not have the nerve, since even after the weather cleared up conditions on the face would not be much better at first. We were all in favor of pushing on.

So it was that, after packing everything again and roping up as a four-some, we stepped out calmly and confidently to tackle the last and most difficult hours on the wall. It was still snowing and snowing, as it had the whole night. The avalanches came down at regular intervals, and each time we had one hour in between to climb farther. The sight of the route we had to follow was appalling. The rocks were coated with ice, on which the treacherous new snow was building up. I used to have the naïve idea that where snow settled there must be a hold underneath, but what I did not know was that in clouds the humidity can be super-cooled to -39°C. Mixed with snow, this humidity in suspension was being swept against the wall, forming a layer of clear ice to which the snow was sticking even below the overhangs. The wretched rock was coated in a smooth film of ice to which the new snow adhered. Splendid to look at, but horrible to climb, especially on a route of this order.

Wiggerl was unable to stop taking photographs even in these circumstances, just as he had during the bivouac. Knowing that I had been against the whole business of photography from the outset, he grinned at me apologetically. In fact, he was right to obtain this record.

I fought my way up to a small projection of rock. When I looked back down at my companions I could not suppress a smile; they were leaning against the wall like a bunch of icicles; an avalanche had just shot past that left us well and truly frosted. Two possible alternative routes remained: a gully line which, according to our observations, caught the main force of the avalanches pouring down the face, or a much safer, but harder, shallow chimney. Since Wiggerl had now joined me I opted for the latter, but in the first few meters alone I needed three rock pitons, and so I went for the gully.

To get to the gully it was necessary to descend a little way, so I left one piton in and rappeled down. Just up onto the top of a little pinnacle, and I would have a splendid and safe belay below the gully. But I was not on top of the pinnacle yet. I had a serviceable hold for my right hand but could find nothing at all for my left on the ice-glazed wall. As I tried to thrust my way up I slipped off and found myself standing two meters below on a little patch of ice; my crampons bit and I stopped dead in my tracks.

Wiggerl, who held me quite securely on the rope, grinned down impertinently. Straightaway I grappled with it again and slipped down again, exactly as before, only this time I did not come to rest on the slab, but swung across into the gully. This time Wiggerl did not grin, he just held me. I had thumped my back-

side, but it had been accustomed to worse pain since my early school-days. Nevertheless, I was now feeling small and humble and detoured modestly around the pinnacle to the opposite side, where things turned out to be easier. Hardly had I chopped the icy crown off with my ax to make a level stance and hammered in a belay peg than an avalanche came sweeping down the face like a thick veil of mist. All of us stood belayed to the ice piton and under cover; it whistled around our ears, but could do us no harm. The real danger was that we might inhale the whirling ice dust and suffocate, so we drew our scarves around our noses. After a time the last vestiges of the avalanche had swept past and I started up the gully very much aware that the mainstream of the next avalanche would pass down it. Before that happened, I wanted to be above its near-vertical top section. It was no place to hang around. The ice was much harder than the previous evening and it took a lot of strength to climb it, without cutting steps and balancing only on the two front points of my crampons. Well, we could not choose the conditions. The degree to which ice climbs vary in difficulty is so great that they cannot be graded.

With the ice hammer I chopped nicks to use as handholds. After about

"Wiggerl was unable to stop taking photographs even in these circumstances, just as he had during the bivouac. Knowing that I had been against the whole business of photography from the outset, he grinned at me apologetically." In the Exit Cracks.

10 meters the angle eased slightly and I could chop out a stance again. From here, I could already see that the gully did lead somewhere, so I dispatched a joyous yodel to my friends. Wiggerl, was soon standing next to me. Then it started again. This time, we had a grandstand view as the white plume appeared first at the right-hand edge of the face. It took three or four minutes before it spread like a curtain across the whole width of the face to a point above the gully in which we stood. It was obvious that we were directly in its path, even though it was only a subsidiary flow. There was just time to hammer a second piton into the rock, then it was upon us. With our rucksacks over our heads and our scarves wound around our faces, we waited for the shock. The pressure wave did not tear us from the belay, however, but merely pressed the points of our crampons more deeply into the ice. We now had to make sure that there was no snow build-up between us and the ice of the gully, since this might have forced us off the stance. There were no stones—we were already too high up for that—and the snow was fine-grained and therefore did not have much force behind it. In addition to which, the main mass of it shot past over our heads. We were soon in high spirits again, happy at the way things had turned out and rejoicing at this new view of the drama of nature, which neither of us had experienced before.

"Another one survived!" we told each other.

We shook ourselves dry like wet poodles, and I climbed another rope-length while Wiggerl brought up Fritz and Heini. Suddenly from the west ridge we heard a long-drawn shout, which was repeated after a pause. It could only be meant for us, but I realized that an answer would be misunderstood. The distance was much too great for communication, and unintelligible cries could too easily be interpreted as appeals for help. I therefore passed down the word, "Keep quiet, don't answer!"

Later we learned that the guide Schlunegger, who had distinguished himself on the rescues in 1935 and 1936, took the trouble in spite of the weather to climb the west face to the summit to discover if there was anything to be seen or heard of us, and if necessary to get a rescue party underway. That we should remain so active and cheerful in such circumstances seemed unimaginable, so he returned to the valley with the report that in these conditions no living creature could possibly survive on the face. At this time we were in the best of spirits, being certain of reaching the top before long.

The gully now reared up steeply again. "Wiggerl," I yelled, "watch me here, it's getting hard again!" The actual snow, which fell continuously, did not bother us much. It was only when the larger flakes came that we knew it was getting warmer. The next avalanche would probably be longer coming, but all the heavier when it hit.

For now, it was snowing wet and heavy. It had been a long time since the last avalanche. I had better climb the overhang quickly. The ice here was no longer thick enough to hold pitons. After the second hammer blow they fell through the hollow ice or bent uselessly on the rock beneath. At the overhang I could only place my crampons one above the other, since the old ice had shrunk to a narrow strip and the new ice covering the rock was much too hard, smooth, and thin. The tip of the ice peg, which I held in one hand like a dagger, only penetrated a little way; it was the same with the pick of the ice ax. Suddenly both skidded off at the same time. Had I been in a bridging position I might have been able to keep my balance, but with my feet in line there was no holding it.

"Wiggerl! Look out!"

And away I went. Wiggerl took in as much slack rope as possible and I shot straight down toward him. It was more of a fast slide than a fall, as I was still below the overhang when I slipped. At the moment of falling I turned face outward to avoid going over backward. After all, we all like to see where we are flying to.

Arranging a belay under difficult conditions on a little rock ledge in the Exit Cracks

Wiggerl dropped the rope and tried to grab me with his hands. In the process, one of my crampon spikes drove into the ball of his thumb, flipping me upside down. As I shot by headfirst I grabbed at the rope. This gave me a jerk so that I completed my somersault, to my own astonishment landing upright some distance below the stance with my crampon points embedded in the ice. The momentum with which I had thudded into Wiggerl had knocked him off, and now I was able to hold him too. Quickly we scrambled back up to the stance. The peg had been torn out, so I put in another one at once. The whole affair had taken only a few seconds; instinctive reaction saved us. Our friends below were blissfully unaware that anything had happened. Had it been otherwise, the rope that bound us together would have plucked them off after us in a great leap down the face.

Meanwhile, Wiggerl had tugged the mitten off his wounded hand. The spike had gone right through, and blood spurted out both sides. It was dark, so not arterial. By way of further diagnosis I suddenly squeezed it as I had Fritz's lower down. He grimaced with pain, but as he did not keel over, I took it that no bones were broken. Only he was so pale, perhaps from shock, that if he had any color left at all it was green.

"Are you going to faint?"

"I'm not sure."

I anchored him again and placed myself so that he could not fall whatever happened.

"Pull yourself together, everything depends on it."

I glanced up at the face. Thank God the avalanche was holding off. Whipping off the rucksack, I bound up the hand. Rummaging around in the medicine bag, my fingers curled around a little vial of heart stimulant drops that a concerned lady doctor in Grindelwald had given me for just such an eventuality with the remark, "If Toni Kurz had had drops like these, he might have survived the crisis." We were only to use them if the situation was really serious. I thought that the moment had come. There was something about 10 drops on the label. I poured about half the bottle into Wiggerl's mouth. The other half I drank myself because I was thirsty. A couple of glucose tablets to chase it down and we were back in business. There was still no sign of the avalanche.

"Wiggerl, I'm going to try the overhang again right away."

"OK, but please don't fall off on me again," he answered in a weak voice.

I concentrated every ounce of nervous energy on getting this delicate and dangerous pitch behind me as quickly as I could, even to the point of doing without any running belays. I ran out almost the full 30 meters of rope before I could get one of the small rock pegs to sit properly. No sooner had I clipped into it than the feared and long-awaited avalanche

"I ran out almost the full 30 meters of rope before I could get one of the small rock pegs to sit properly. No sooner had I clipped into it than the feared and long-awaited avalanche arrived."

arrived. Good fortune had held it back just long enough but now it broke loose with real power. It could not really hit me, since the gully went off to one side, but farther down Fritz and Heini caught the full force of it. Nor could Wiggerl complain that he got too little of it. All I could do was to take in the rope as tightly as possible so as to back up their wobbly peg belays. I also watched the strength of the waves of the avalanche and when they got really close, I shouted, "Now, now . . . hang on . . . it's coming down thick now!"

In fact these were mere cries of despair. Afterward no one mentioned having heard a thing, but at the time I had the feeling that I was being of enormous help. Suddenly everything went dark and my head was smashed against the wall by a mass of falling snow, leaving me with a lump on my forehead. It only lasted a few moments, then I was free again, but the others were still getting a pounding. The avalanche seemed to go on forever, a consequence of the long time it had taken to build up.

"It's getting lighter . . . no . . . watch out! Watch out!" Then the main mass came down, some of which also reached me. Once again I bellowed, "It's nearly over, hold on, h-o-l-d on!"

After what seemed like an eternity to us, it finally began to ease off but we still had to wait a while before the last trickles were over. Wiggerl came up, the others followed, and I could continue climbing. Ouch! My ankle. I must have twisted it during the fall. It could not be broken, or I would have felt it more. It was not important, even if it did hurt like hell.

The gully now became easier-angled, but the possibilities for running belays also grew fewer. Suddenly, we again heard the voice from the west ridge. "Don't answer," we whispered to each other down the line. We were all too familiar with the procedure. First you get one individual who comes along, has a look, and if he hears anything the whole rescue apparatus is set in motion. With the sheer scale of this huge mountain it would take hours before he was back down and the rescue team was up on the top. By then we would have made our own way up. To be sure, we were all the worse for wear, but we were not yet unfit for battle, not by a long shot. We were nevertheless pleased with this sign, which showed that someone was concerned about us, and it gave us a renewed incentive.

Shortly afterward we reached the top of the gully. We had overcome the rocks, but were far from having reached the summit. A steep ice field, where we used up the last of our pegs to avoid being swept away by avalanches, led on upward. It continued to snow steadily, and it was getting thicker and thicker. Avalanches roared down the face uninterrupted, but we were now beyond their reach.

Now for the first time we were exposed to the full fury of the storm. Long before the rope ran out it was impossible to make oneself understood. Our windbreakers iced up to such an extent that we could only move in jerks. I felt like an armored knight, in addition to which the saturated Thermogene burned horribly. Every so often I had to jump up and down to relieve the irritation to which I was helplessly subjected. Wiggerl, who had got rid of his Thermogene long before, remarked that I must be suffering from altitude madness. Resigned to my fate, I stamped on through the storm toward the summit. The straps of our crampons also began to contract, cutting into our feet and making them go numb. However, we were finished with the face and would get through now whatever happened. Now it was all up to us. The dangers and difficulties had been overcome, and even the storm could no longer kill us.

In spite of this, the conditions could not be described as pleasant, and we nearly fell through the cornice. In its upper part, the ridge is nearly horizontal, but in the thick mist I thought it swept up steeply again. We had taken the last snow slope, now swept bare by the wind, in zigzag fashion. I was just about to put in another turn, when the very next step saw me standing out over the cornice. A few meters behind me, Wiggerl did the same thing. Suddenly he roared "Stop! Get back! There's a cliff below you there!"

Very faintly, a distance below us, we could just make out the shimmering outline of the cliffs of the south side of the mountain. It would have been accursed bad luck to have survived the north face, only to plummet over the south side because we had missed the summit.

Somehow we had imagined the experience of standing on the summit, having solved the last and greatest problem in the Alps, as much more solemn. The storm allowed no respite to think of anything else. We shook hands, scratched the ice away from our eyebrows so that we could at least see, and carried on down the west face, into the wind. It was now a great advantage that Fritz and Heini knew the way. Only a few days before, they had climbed the Mittellegi Ridge and down the western flank of the mountain.

Now we could see how much new snow had fallen in the course of this one day. Due to the lesser angle of the west face, it had settled to a depth of half a meter in places where it was neither drifting nor being blown away. It was not pleasant new snow such as one gets

On the summit ice field

in winter, but a heavy, lumpy mass lying on ice slabs. Often the whole lot would slip with us on it, but it almost always stopped at once.

Now that the excitement of immediate danger was gone, a leaden weariness invaded our bones. Probably I was in the worst state, as I had all the pains in the world to keep up with the others. I thought to myself, "I've done my bit, now they can do theirs and get us down." As last man on the face, Heini Harrer had made a gigantic physical effort carrying loads, but had used up less of his nervous energy than the rest of us. Now he took the lead. As for myself, I mostly waited until the others disappeared into the mist and the rope was taut, then sat down and shot past them on the seat of my pants, so that the three of them had their work cut out to hold me. It was not an ideal example, but then what is exemplary on the Eiger? On one of my little slides I burst the elastic on my overtrousers so that they kept falling down. I did not care about that, but the direct contact with the snow was so unpleasant that I carried on a running battle with my nether garments, which consumed the rest of my nervous energy.

All that mattered was losing height. With every meter the storm lost something of its force and the snow fell less thickly. But we were not to get away without one more test of my sorely tried nerves. In the impenetrable fog, Heini had led us too far to the left. Luckily Fritz and Heini soon noticed the mistake, or we could not have avoided a further bivouac. In our condition it would have been fearful, and none of us would have escaped unharmed. In 1957 a German party that had just climbed the north face lost their lives on this very descent.

Nevertheless, at that moment, we almost bivouacked again. A momentary clearing in the cloud showed that we would have to slog our way back up for 200 meters in order to cross a cleft that separated us from the west ridge. To me it seemed worse than the hardest part of the north face. I felt a total disinclination to go back and was all for trying to descend over the overhang. My friends simply dragged me uphill in spite of my protests. I was the only one to kick up a fuss; the others did not utter a word.

A thousand meters of descent lay behind us already, and at 3000 meters the storm was no longer as violent as it had been at the top. Our ice armor began to thaw, with the consequence that we were soon soaked through to the last stitch. Now that we had crossed the cleft we were certain of reaching the valley that same day and began to wonder if we could get a room at the Kleine Scheidegg Hotel without money, and whether they would let us have some dry clothes. Harrer asked me, "Anderl, do you have any money so we can get a room?"

Naturally I had no money, that being about the last thing you require on the Eigerwand, so we decided to make the best of it and go on down to the tents as we were. We had completely forgotten that we had been watched and that people were anxious for our safety. Thus when we got down out of the cloud an hour or so later it came as a surprise to see a seething mass of dots in front of the hotel hundreds of meters below. It did not cross our minds that it had anything to do with us.

We were still on rock, and clambered carefully down amid grunts and groans. Presently a Swiss lad came storming up toward us. Goggling at us as though we had just landed from the moon, he asked hesitantly, "Have you just come off the North Face?"

"Yes, but what's going on down there?"

"That's the mountain rescue. They've come up to look for you."

Suddenly we realized that it was to do with us, and slowly, very slowly, joy began to burgeon inside us at being given back to life. Down below, the crowd become more and more turbulent, then started swarming up the hillside like ants. Soon the swiftest were within 50 meters. For a moment we hesitated, then, all weariness forgotten, bounded toward our friends. They fell around our necks with whoops of joy and whirled us around in war dances. We joined in with a will, and no one thought anymore about all the aches and pains that had been torturing us a few minutes before.

Freissl and Brankovsky, the two Viennese climbers we had met on the face the first day, were there too. Once our success seemed assured they had not withdrawn from the scene in a sulk, but had assumed the job of communications with our friends who kept telephoning from Munich. Now they were the first to welcome us. Freissl held out a flask of brandy and said boisterously, "Drink some of that. It'll do you good."

With our friends had come reporters from all over the world, there was a continual blaze of flashbulbs around us. Among the journalists, whom we climbers generally look on with a good deal of suspicion, were two who became our friends, Guido Tonella from Geneva and Ulrich Link from Munich, author of the account quoted above. Throughout their careers, these two and the late Kurt Maix from Vienna related the doings of mountaineers with accuracy and honesty, certainly no easy task in view of our sensitivity to attempts to manufacture sensations at our expense. However, those— regrettably few—that understood climbers and climbing and gained our confidence not only became friends but finally became members of the circle.

An American reporter asked us to set up a bivouac on the spot for his benefit. That was asking too much, and, escorted by our friends, we literally fought our way through the excited crowd.

Now others took over and did our thinking for us. Warm rooms were waiting and our friends brought dry clothes. We badly needed hot baths. Wiggerl was already standing in the tub as I came into the bathroom. He stared at me with the wide, soulful eyes of a dying calf.

"Poor guy's a bit touched. Why doesn't he sit down?" I thought to myself, and without more ado climbed into the tub. A moment later I shot out again as though I had landed on a spring. Quite apart from first-degree frostbite, my feet were still fiery red from the irritation of the Thermogene. They stung as though pricked with a thousand needles. However, a climber always finds a way out of any situation. We let our feet hang over the edge and lowered ourselves in the hot water up to our necks.

For three days we had eaten next to nothing. Now our hunger was so gigantic as scarcely to be satisfied. One schnitzel after another disappeared before the gaze of our astounded public. A uniformed official from the embassy in Bern turned our dinner at the festively decorated table into a kind of victory feast over which he made a speech full of unpleasant nationalistic phrases, despite the fact that we were in Switzerland. The victory of the Schmid brothers on the North face of the Matterhorn also had been made the occasion of a celebration in Zermatt, but that had been within a restricted circle and was therefore appropriate. The pile of congratulations and invitations that now poured in from all over the place was enough to submerge us. All through the night they continued to arrive, including one from the Reichskanzlei in the name of Hitler, stating that he wished to see us. From this there was no escape. Admittedly, it could be construed as a great honor, but I would have been happier to carry out my plan to travel over to Chamonix to attempt the Walker Spur on the Grandes Jorasses.

Things even went so far as a little reception hosted by the guides of Grindelwald. It had not been easy for them to watch us pick off "their" face. Consoling words were found on both sides.

A week later Riccardo Cassin climbed the Walker Spur. By this time we already had been "received in audience by the Führer." It was the third time I had stood face-to-face with him. Of course, he did not remember having held a long conversation with me about the motivations for mountain climbing. I did not let on for a moment. He showed us the most gracious side of his nature and surprised us with his searching and knowledgeable questions.

"Now you need to recuperate," he announced.

The Reichssportführer was standing by and took over at once. He had us installed on the *Columbus,* which was setting out on a Scandinavian cruise. We were just loaded onboard and our opinion was not asked at all.

Stormy reception at Kleiner Scheidegg. Left to right: Heinrich Harrer, Fritz Kasparek, Anderl Heckmair, and Wiggerl Vörg.

Anderl Heckmair with the army
mountaineering school at Fulpmes,
around 1942

11. Consequences

After our return from the Eigerwand we were no longer masters of our own destiny. We were taken over, monopolized. In full uniform—not very tactful in regard to neutral Switzerland—staff officials from the Sonthofen Ordensburg appeared and swept us "home to the Reich as national heroes." With the benefit of hindsight it is easy to see what we should have done, but at the time we were more or less numbed by the reaction to our success and submitted ourselves to the will of others. A big reception was given for us at Sonthofen, and we were promptly enrolled on the Ordensburg staff as *Bergsportführer* (mountain leaders) at a salary of 300 marks. It was the first time I had received a regular salary, and it represented a step up in the economic scale that I found very pleasant. Less pleasing was a vigorous address by Dr. Robert Ley, head of the Reichsorganization, in which he spoke of us as Party members and expressed his pride in our performance.

We were not Party members. My sole relation to the Party was that I had stood next to Hitler for a couple of hours and had spoken with him. We were drilled, clothed, and forced into line. The fact that for ten years I had had no fixed address, had not reported anywhere, and had spent most of my time wandering around abroad was not questioned, although for someone else such behavior might have entailed trouble, and perhaps worse.

I want to say a few words about the political consequences of the first ascent of the Eigerwand, since I am still questioned about them up to the present day, and in many books the four of us are branded as Nazis who climbed the Eiger as a kind of "National-Socialist Greater German Record." The suggestion was made that climbers from fascist countries were primarily interested in the Eigerwand for reasons of nationalistic ambition. The suggestion is pure nonsense. I and most other climbers of that period had little or no interest in politics. The furor in the papers after the ascent, celebrating us as "heroes," gave the impression that the ascent was inspired by the Nazis. The Italians were guilty of similar nonsense after Riccardo Cassin's conquest of the Walker Spur, yet I am sure that, like ourselves, Cassin and his companions were only interested in success in mountaineering terms.

As to our reception and decoration by Hitler, the truth is that just like anyone else we felt honored to be suddenly plucked out of our anonymous lives and presented to the most powerful man in Germany, and to be decorated by him. The same thing could have happened to a dancing bear. As an apolitical young man, I had no way of foreseeing where the Nazi road would lead. It was only after the outbreak of war that the true political situation became clear. Nevertheless, I do not blame people in other countries for thinking as they did. The Nazis built us into such celebrities that people believed that we had

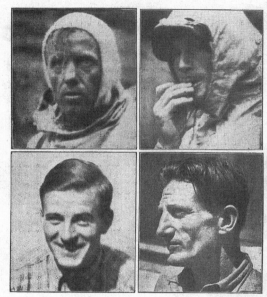

7.
Drittes Nachtlager vom 23. zum 24. Juli. Von hier aus erreichten die vier Bergsteiger den 3975 Meter hohen Gipfel des Eiger und lösten damit das letzte und gewaltigste alpine Problem.

6.
„Die Spinne", ein 300 Meter unter dem Gipfel liegendes Schneefeld, wo die Bezwinger der Eigerwand von einem schweren Unwetter heimgesucht wurden. An dieser Stelle erhaschte unsere Flugzeugaufnahme die Bergsteiger.

5.
Die schwierigste Stelle der ganzen Wand: Ein zehn Meter hoher Ueberhang.

4.
Gemeinsames Biwak der vier Bergsteiger vom 22. zum 23. Juli. Hier sind Mehringer und Sedlmayr, die ersten ernsthaften Bewerber um die gigantische Wand, im August 1935 erfroren. Darüber die „Rampe", die bisher noch keines Menschen Fuß betreten hat.

3.
Zweites Eisfeld, auf dem Kasparek und Harrer, die Donnerstag einstiegen, von Heckmaier und Vörg, die erst Freitag den Durchstieg begannen, eingeholt wurden.

2.
Erstes Biwak der Seilschaft Kasparek-Harrer vom 21. zum 22. Juli 1938.

1.
Hier verunglückten 1936 die Seilschaften Kurz - Hinterstoißer und Rainer-Angerer.

Zum erstenmal

Einzigartige Dokumente
einer einzigartigen Leistung

Die Sieger.

Oben: Die beiden Oesterreicher Fritz Kasparek (links) und Heinrich Harrer. Unten: Die beiden Bayern Ludwig Vörg (links) und Andreas Heckmaier, beide Sportlehrer auf der Ordensburg Sonthofen. Gemeinsam erstiegen diese vier die niebezwungene Nordwand des Eiger.

been supported by and received monies from the Party. However, that is simply not true.

I am glad that since those days mountaineering has freed itself from that type of pressure and has grown into a truly international sport.

I attached a condition to our annexation by the Nazis. I agreed to enrollment on the Ordensburg staff with the understanding that we would be helped with an expedition to the Himalayas. This fit perfectly with the ideas of our then leaders, who were out to advance German prestige abroad by every possible means. We were a godsend. There was nothing modest about our demands. Not wanting to have to beg for every penny, we asked for a round sum of 100,000 marks, which was

Reception in
Lauterbrunnen.
Anderl Heckmair
and Wiggerl Vörg
chat with the
German
Ambassador to
Bern, Dr. Köcher
(middle), his wife
(left), and the wife
of the resort
director (right).

Reception in Lauterbrunnen. Anderl Heckmair and Wiggerl Vörg chat with the German Ambassador to Bern, Dr. Köcher (middle), his wife (left), and the wife of the resort director (right).

granted at once. Thereupon I signed on and suddenly found myself employed as an Ordensburg guide. Wiggerl did likewise.

The only activity we were called upon to perform was as agreeable as anything we could have dreamed up for ourselves: "Get to know the Allgäuer Alps." We did one climb after another for our own pleasure. In between, we made highly amateurish preparations for the expedition to Nanga Parbat. Our first concern was food supplies, and when we had bought 17,000 marks worth we turned to the matter of equipment. At this point our activities were stopped. What had happened? Permission for the expedition to start depended on the Führer's personal consent, pending which all preparations must be shelved.

"How can we obtain this consent?"

"The best thing would be to go to see the Führer in person."

The opportunity presented itself at Christmas. I was detailed to take a picture to Hitler as a Christmas present from the Ordensburg. First of all I had to call on Ley, who had a house at München-Grünwald. He arranged for me to go to the Christmas feast of the "Old Warriors," or Party veterans, in the Löwenbräu beer cellar, where Hitler was to be present. I therefore drove off in my Opel Olympia in the direction of the cellar, only to find that I could get nowhere near it. The Stiglmaierplatz was barricaded to cars and packed with people. How were we to get through? I drove back to the gateway, kept my hand on the horn, and drove flat out at the wall of people. As though by magic a channel opened before me down which I recklessly drove. Even the ranks of SS men flew apart, and I drove up to the portal in an elegant curve. I was immediately surrounded by SS and even saw several drawn pistols.

"Park the car, the Führer is expecting me!"

The car disappeared, along with Wiggerl, and I raced up the steps, the picture under my arm, with the whole SS pack at my heels, who were by no means sure whether it was true or whether they were dealing with a madman. Once inside the hall a lane again opened up before me as I strode toward the Führer, who sat blinking at me in astonishment. Suddenly recognition dawned on his features and he invited me to take the place next to him; whereupon the SS officer who had been occupying it instantly vanished. Hitler had actually recognized me. When I mentioned to him that he had once pumped me on the subject of mountaineering he also remembered that conversation. Now for the first time he began to see how the pieces fit together. This seemed to me the strategic moment to press my claim, after passing him the picture, which he did not even glance at. He frowned and said, "I need you for quite a different task."

What other tasks could we fulfill as mountain climbers? I hinted at the importance of a success in the Himalayas for German prestige, but he was no longer listening to me and was concentrating on his speech to old warriors instead.

Autograph duties in Grindelwald

It was a real Bavarian meal—roast pork, potato dumplings, and beer—as much as you could eat and drink. Hitler ate spaghetti with tomato sauce, an apple, and drank only mineral water. A couple of passages from his speech still remain in my memory.

The first went as follows:

"When there is a row in the home, the crockery starts to fly; when there is a row between people, what flies is highly explosive. Czechoslovakia sticks like a spear into the side of Germany, and must be broken off."

He went on:

"Among German comrades no one can opt out. As soon as they are

Rest and relaxation in Scandinavia, a trip prescribed by Hitler. Left to right: Anderl Heckmair, Fritz Kasparek, Heinrich Harrer, SS Sturmbannführer Felix Rinner (the official escort), and Wiggerl Vörg, summer 1938

out of diapers, their place is in the *Jungvolk* movement, then in the Hitler Youth, and later in the SS or SA, or if we have no use for them there, then as conscripts in the armed forces."

The implication of these words was unmistakable. Deeply disturbed and at one stroke cured of many illusions, I slunk out of the hall before the proceedings were over. It was clear that Hitler would not only risk a war, but probably wanted one. If that happened, it would be the end of freedom in the mountains. There could be no thought of fulfilling our mountaineering plans. It was a profound disappointment, and the certainty of what was to befall us depressed me. I felt like immigrating.

A glimmer of hope that we might still make it flared up again when, after our plans had been dashed, the Himalayan Foundation took up the idea and even requested us to complete our plans. At the last moment, however, everything fell apart again through underhandedness by someone behind the scenes.

Up until that time I had taken pains to avoid any special girl who might pose a danger to my spiritual well-being or threaten my unbound, carefree existence. But then I met a nice girl and she became my wife. From then on, I lived in Oberstdorf.

Thus it was that my participation in the expedition came to an end. But one of us ought to go. The only one who was completely free and independent was Heini Harrer, so I called him and chewed his ear off to the effect that he should go with the members of the Foundation in order to gain their influence and support for the real expedition the following year. So Heini Harrer went off to Nanga Parbat, the war broke out, and he was detained in India. The rest of us were called up and clothed in the "honorable" field gray. Vörg fell on the eastern front on the first day of the Russian campaign. No one attached the slightest value to my mountaineering experience, and I landed in the infantry, also on the eastern front.

In March 1940 I was enrolled in a *Jäger* or mountain regiment at Sonthofen and was sent to France the following month, by which time the campaign was over. One day I was informed that I had been posted UK. Short for *unabkömmlich* it meant "reserved for essential duties." All Ordensburg staff members were needed for a special task on the eastern front, although I was not told what, and were therefore assembled for political indoctrination at Falkensee in Pomerania. We ducked out of an introductory address by Reichsleiter Ley and were caught playing cards in a tent by a lout of an SS man who made a huge disturbance about it and sent in a special report. In the course of all this, a lengthy

"After our return from the Eigerwand we were no longer masters of our own destiny. We were quite simply taken over, monopolized." Reception with Adolf Hitler, summer 1938. The Reichssport-führer and the home affairs minister were also present.

questionnaire had to be filled in, obviously for the purposes of finding out where we stood politically. "How long have you been a Party member?" "What Party honors have you received?" and so on. My questionnaire remained blank, as I could only answer each time with "not applicable." Thereupon, I and a couple of others were taken off UK and posted available for active service again on grounds of political unreliability, and there followed unpleasant months serving in the central sector of the eastern front.

However, at Fulpmes near Innsbruck there was an army school of mountaineering, and I knew that Rudolf Peters, my rival for the Grandes Jorasses, was serving there as an officer. I wrote to him that I too would rather be up in the mountains than in the morass of the eastern front. He replied by return mail that he had requested the High Command to have me posted as an instructor. I was mighty pleased, but heard nothing more for half a year. During this time I might have been killed not just once but umpteen times if my sharpened perceptions had not enabled me to head for cover at the last moment. At long last, however, I found myself on the way home and reported for duty at Fulpmes, where I found all my old climbing pals, among them Hias Rebitsch, Hansei Lucke, and August Vörg, Wiggerl's brother. Rudl Peters, who had the rank of captain, was our boss.

From that time on the war was won as far as I was concerned. Although an order came out stating that no able-bodied man was to serve more than nine months on the home front, none of our regularly changing commanding officers of the High Mountain Regiment let us go. Our Alpine experience was too valuable. Thanks to us there were no accidents during mountain training, whereas elsewhere there were continual fatalities. Cheap as human life might be at the front, obituary reports were frowned upon on the home front. Our commandants thus preferred to hold on to us, and we had nothing against that. And so we lived through those terrible years until one day the dream of empire and final victory was over. I had no desire whatever to be taken prisoner, and so I walked over the mountains to Oberstdorf where I had set up a home.

My first action was to establish a small garden and start growing vegetables. Before long we had a boarder who wanted to be guided in the mountains; this client led to others, and presently I had enough to do and to live off. When the German Alpenverein was reestablished it fell to me to train the mountain guides. I attached great importance to making it clear to aspirant guides that they should not only impart their skills to their clients, but also show them the beauties of the mountains. The basic principle was to stay well within the clients' capabilities in order to foster their desire for more. It was taken for granted that a modern

Anderl Heckmair
(left of center) as
a soldier of the
Wehrmacht, on
his way to the
eastern front,
1941

guide must be a mountaineer through and through and know all about every aspect of the subject taught him during the course of the three-year training.

In the summer of 1947 the newspapers carried the news that the Eigerwand had been repeated. The names of the two climbers were Lionel Terray and Louis Lachenal from Chamonix. Despite the fact that we had been widely accused of nationalistic competition and that our ascent had been linked to German National Socialism, it was a genuine pleasure to me to learn that French mountaineers had made the second ascent. On impulse I sent a telegram of congratulations and was anxious to see how they would react. Their message of thanks was equally spontaneous and included an invitation to Chamonix.

At one stroke, this remarkable second ascent of the North Face made it once again a major objective for climbers from all over the world. Just as during the 1930s, it made the headlines more often than any other mountain in the Alps. We who had made the first ascent in 1938 never for a moment assumed we were the only climbers capable of the feat. Even in 1938 the Italian climber Riccardo Cassin, who made the first ascent of the Walker Spur immediately afterward, had been lying in wait. If we had not done it he certainly would have tried—and succeeded.

We had the most advanced technique, equipment, and clothing for the time; but development never ceases, and all our gear is long out of date. Later climbers of the face have had quite different postulates. The wall has not become any easier or the dangers any less, but climbers have had equipment made of modern, lightweight materials, more highly developed rock and ice pitons, and so on. After many successes and further tragedies and victims, in 1961 this evolution finally made possible a winter ascent of the face, which no one would have dared contemplate in 1938. The climbers who achieved this were Toni Hiebeler, Toni Kinshofer, Anderl Mannhardt, and Walter Almberger. The ascent was planned down to the last detail in every respect, ranging from types of pitons to the choice of companions. After seven demanding days climbing they celebrated success, proving once and for all that the impossible no longer really exists.

It was not long before the inheritors of the tradition appeared on the scene. In thirty days of extreme climbing, in winter conditions, they forced a *direttissima* or direct route up the face. The driving force behind this venture was Peter Hag, and his companions, the Stuttgart climbers Karl Golikow, Siegfried Hupfauer, Jörg Lehne, Rolf Rosenzopf, Günter Schnait, Günther Strobel, Roland Votteler, and Englishman Don Whillans. Teamwork as perfect as they achieved could only come about through total mutual confidence. During the climb they found themselves competing with a party led by the American John Harlin, one of the best extreme mountaineers of his day. His companions were the Scot Dougal Haston and the American Layton Kor. On the twenty-seventh day, Harlin fell to his death when a fixed rope broke. The two groups finally joined forces and reached the summit after being on the face for a month.

Opinions concerning this performance were many and various. I was skeptical, and leaned toward the view that hard labor of this order could be carried out by paid "assistants," who would fix the ropes and who could be regularly replaced. The so-called climbers could then come along, clamber up the ropes, and celebrate their "victory." Time and money would count for nothing. In international climbing circles a real furor developed over the meaning or lack of meaning of such an enterprise, and Riccardo Cassin convened a meeting to discuss the matter at Lecco on Lake Como. Unfortunately, only one of the Eiger Direct climbers was present, the English climber Don Whillans. As no one was keen to discuss the ascent in the absence of the "accused," only the subject of regulations for mountaineering was heatedly discussed—and unanimously rejected.

At another discussion in Trento, the majority of the direttissima team was present. I had to revise my prejudices entirely. The climbers of the Eiger Direct revealed themselves to be genuine mountaineers. My questions were more than just testing, they bored through to the nerve. Gradually I was forced to the view that this manner of mountaineering also represented progress.

It was a development that showed no signs of abating. In 1969 Japanese climbers—five men and a woman—forced a "superdirettissima" up the Rote Fluh, surely the most "impossible" of all the Eigerwand's "impossible" features, with an outlay on equipment that in our day would have been simply unthinkable.

By 1970, Toni Hiebeler had chronicled ninety-six ascents of the Eigerwand. Thirty-nine climbers had lost their lives on the face. Now, the ascents are no longer counted, and hardly anyone speaks of the victims anymore. Since 1938 more than twenty new routes have been recorded and a solo climber has done the face in four hours fifty minutes. One wonders at what point he started and stopped his stopwatch.

Nothing is spared on our North Face. It is described as a "wall of death," although that is the fault of the climbers rather than the climb. On any mountain walk, an oversight or deliberate neglect regarding clothing and equipment can lead to complications and in some circumstances even to death. On the north face of the Eiger an infringement of the unwritten laws of mountaineering or any failure to grasp them can only lead to catastrophe.

In addition to the many victims and the hardly describable tragedies that were played out on the face, there have been grotesque occurrences and even Alpine swindles that had to be cleared up in a court of law. On one occasion, pictures of a new ascent of the Eigerwand were sent to the editors of a newspaper; among them, however, were people who knew something about the subject and their suspicions were aroused. The photos were placed in front of me without comment. My opinion was that they were taken on the Eiger, but certainly not on its north face. Toni Hiebeler followed up on the matter and had the photographers brought to court.

Kurt Diemberger and I were nominated as expert witnesses. The two persons concerned insisted that they had climbed the face in fog, but it was obvious that the pictures could not have been taken at the places claimed, and in any case it is unusual for climbers to peddle their pictures around. The modesty of these two was a sham for the benefit of the court. To initiates it was clear that their ignorance of mountaineering matters was such that they could not possibly have climbed the face. Finally Diemberger, who made the thirteenth ascent, discovered a memorial plaque on one of the negatives. It had been claimed that the picture had been taken on an ice overhang on the ramp, but the plaque is set into the rock at the foot of the face in honor of the Italian climbers Sandri and Menti, who lost their lives on the climb. In the whole history of mountaineering, which extends back more than 100 years, there have been very few dubious ascents, as it is part of the unwritten code of honor that climbers should stick rigorously to the truth regarding their deeds. On the Eiger, however, nothing is impossible.

In 1958, on the occasion of the twentieth anniversary of the first ascent of the Eigerwand, I was particularly honored to receive a specially struck gold medal at the reunion of mountaineers that is always associated with the Trento International Mountain Film Festival. Riccardo Cassin also received one for his first ascent of the Walker Spur of the Grandes Jorasses, and those who had repeated the two routes were given silver medals. There was a great deal of applause and the atmosphere, if highly official, was one of outstandingly friendly camaraderie.

Souvenir photograph of the Trento Mountain Film Festival, 1958. Left to right: Arne R. Heen, Walter Bonatti (collage), Riccardo Cassin, and Anderl Heckmair

I was happy, yet deep inside I reject honors of this sort, since mountaineering is not the kind of sport in which outstanding performances are rewarded with prizes. Sportsmanship is needed in the highest measure, but the performance represented by a great first ascent cannot be precisely measured and evaluated. In the last resort all that counts is the subjective joy, the memories, and the friendship that often arises from a challenge shared and met. Whether one is subsequently glorified or has one's achievements despised as a senseless game leaves me completely cold. I am sure that other mountaineers feel the same way.

The real pleasure on the "Eiger anniversary" was that it provided an opportunity for everyone to meet, so it really developed into a celebration free of all envy and pretension. Each of us knew what the others had achieved and endured, and could evaluate what lay behind these achievements from personal experience. When human beings meet in these circumstances there are no more distinctions according to nationality, East-West geography, or political creed; all that matters is the individual. The fine thing about such a meeting is that climbers from all over the world metaphorically rope up together. For me, this rope had begun to form just after the war with that exchange of telegrams with Lionel Terray and Louis Lachenal and their invitation to Chamonix.

Anderl Heckmair
and Hermann
Köllensperger
after their ascent
of the Walker Spur
in August 1951

12. Grandes Jorasses

t was not possible to accept the invitation to Chamonix right away. In 1947 there was still no chance of getting a visitor's visa for France. Three years went by before I was able to return to the Mont Blanc range. We remained in touch by mail, however. They asked how things were going and what I was doing; jokingly, I replied that as far as food went no one was bursting out of his clothes. They took it literally and started sending a parcel of goodies almost every week. Where was the hereditary enmity between France and Germany that had been drummed into us for so many years? Real climbers feel neither jealousy nor nationalistic hatred. Mountains do not form frontiers to divide us, rather they use frontiers to unite us in the same ideal. I could feel this in the friendship that was growing through this correspondence.

In 1950 the French were the first post-war climbers to visit the Himalayas, and they were the first to climb an 8000-meter peak, Annapurna. Together with Maurice Herzog and Gaston Rébuffat, Lachenal and Terray were the outstanding members of the party, and their names became world famous, but far from growing conceited they repeated their invitation to visit them in Chamonix.

At this time I got to know a young climber named Hermann Köllensperger whom I liked particularly for his openness. His name was well respected on account of several extreme climbs in the Wettersteingebirge. One day as I was going up for a traverse of the Schüsselkarspitze I saw a solo climber descending the slabs from the Leutascher Dreitorspitze. He was much too far to the right, so I shouted up some directions which he gratefully accepted, and before long we met up. It was Hermann Köllensperger. We exchanged a few friendly words and each went on his way. A few weeks later he came over to Oberstdorf, and we agreed to take up the invitation to Chamonix the following summer. If all went well, we would try to fulfill my old dream of climbing the north face of the Grandes Jorasses.

The days of bicycling were over. We sat in the train to Geneva like any other tourist. Leafing through an illustrated magazine, I came upon a full-page advertisement extolling the fragrance of the spicy Swiss Toscanelli cigars. I enjoyed this kind of smoke, and as a stall was already open on the Geneva station when the train rolled in at 4:00 A.M. I treated myself to a packet. They were strange-looking things, just like gnarled roots. Not having eaten, I felt hesitant of trying one immediately. A small café already stood open for the first-shift workers, and one sturdy fellow was downing black coffee with a shot of grappa in it. Although I was less sturdy, I felt strong enough for that and ordered one too. It tasted loathsome on an empty stomach, but as I had to pay for it anyway, I drank it. After that I lit up my Toscanelli and we strolled back to the station. Just as I reached the steps I went pale and had to sit down before I fell down. Though I blamed it for the way I felt, the Toscanelli still tasted good, and to the horror of

Lionel Terray and
Louis Lachenal
(from the right),
with Armand
Charlet. In the
1930s, they were
among the
candidates vying
for the first
ascent of the
north face of the
Grandes Jorasses.

my friends and family I have remained faithful to the brand to this day.

In Chamonix we wandered pleasantly through the well-remembered streets, feeling happy that everything was as it had been and that I had survived the war to see it all again. It is true that there hardly exists another mountain resort to compare to it for ugliness, yet somehow it emanates a special charm compounded out of so much Alpine history. There is nowhere else quite like it.

There was a man sitting outside a café opposite the guides' office. It must be Terray. I went and stood in front of his table without saying a word. We had never met; would he recognize me at first sight? Surprised, he glanced up, and yes, he knew me straight away. We embraced like old friends, and despite the language problem had no difficulty communicating since all we had to do was read each other's expressions. The first errand was to visit Terray's friend Louis Lachenal, who greeted us no less heartily. In reply to their query as to what we had in mind we gestured toward the Walker Spur. Immediately their faces clouded.

"There is too much snow and ice," said Lionel.

We knew that the winter of 1950–51 had been a hard one, and that the rock was not yet clear of snow and ice. Nonetheless, "May as well have a look," we thought, and went up to the Leschaux hut.

The little hut had changed, having been enlarged in the 1930s. It was deserted, but everything was spotless and tidy. From the presence of a number of typically feminine articles we deduced that the custodian was now a woman. Set aside in one corner, a bed was properly made up with sheets turned down neatly over the blankets. We had great difficulty resisting the temptation to climb in, but finally contented ourselves with the usual blankets in the other corner. After all, we wanted to set out at one o'clock.

We woke up punctually, but the night was not to our liking. It was far too warm and the sky was overcast. With an undeniable "certain relief" we rolled ourselves up in our blankets again with the intention of sleeping until noon. We had done right; when hunger finally drove us from our warm nest with bones aching from lying around, it was streaming rain outside.

A weary-looking party of two women and two men were headed toward the hut. As we were already cooking we put tea water for the newcomers on our gas stove, just like in the old days. The newcomers accepted our thoughtfulness with gratitude and duly invited us to join their evening meal. When they inquired about our goal and we simply pointed meaningfully at the north face, which had just cleared for a moment, their expressions became thoughtful but their hospitality warmer than ever. They even conjured up an alarm clock, which woke us punctually at one o'clock out of a deep slumber.

It was Thursday, August 2, 1951. By contrast with the night before, it was cold. We resolved at all costs to go up as far as the foot of the rock pillar at 3010 meters. Having carefully packed our rucksacks with only those things that were strictly necessary the previous evening, it was not long before we stepped out into the dark on the Leschaux Glacier and plodded up toward the start of the climb. The bergschrunds were soon crossed, and our twelve-pointers bit easily into the hard, steep snow-ice. Everything promised rapid progress, and I lulled myself with hopes of reaching the top in a day and a half, perhaps even a day. Seldom have I been so far off in my reckoning.

When we reached the Rébuffat Crack we stared in amazement. It was a pitch that would not have been out of place on the north face of the Cima Grande. Only a few sparse pitons showed where our predecessors had passed. Higher up we found rappel slings, tokens of earlier retreats during which pegs had been hammered in at seemingly impossible places.

After the crack there was an excellent stance, but already we had to strap our crampons on again; the traverse across the ice slopes was too long for us to consider cutting steps across without them. Every so often we had to take the crampons off to climb an awkward section of rock, then repeat the whole process. It all cost a lot of time, but in the prevailing conditions there was no other way of overcoming this steep zone. This was what Terray had predicted about the state of the face when he voiced his concerns. At last we reached the end of the traverse and the foot of

A world of peaks above the Mer de Glace. The Grandes Jorasses (far left), with the Walker Spur rising to the highest point (4208 m); the Aiguille du Géant (4013 m) (far right); the Aiguille du Tacul (3444 m) at the point of intersection of the glaciers; the Aiguille du Grépon (3482 m) on the Grandes Charmoz (right).

the 75-meter corner. The guidebook had it down as Grade 4 to 5, which we thought was undergraded.

We had been looking forward with some trepidation to the pendulum traverse that led across to the right-hand side of the buttress. The supposedly easy traverse turned out to be completely iced up. In the meantime we had come to an agreement that I would keep on my crampons and lead the icy bits, while Hermann would take over the lead on the stretches of bare rock. The continual changeovers from one to the other kept us busy, and we failed to notice how the hours were flying by. In due course the sun rather worryingly sank behind the Chamonix Aiguilles. We looked despairingly for a bivouac site. Shortly before nine o'clock we reached a little ledge where we could at least pass the night half sitting, half standing. It was high time too; it was pitch dark by the time we had hammered in the pitons.

Although we had spent most of the day battling among ice and snow, on the spot where we now sat there was not a trace of snow anywhere and our throats were completely parched. Apart from Ovomaltine and Nescafé our rations consisted of bread and sausage, but without fluid we were unable to choke down so much as a single bite. Being familiar with this state of affairs from the Eigerwand, I had purposely brought a bottle of cognac and some egg powder which I now mixed with plenty of sugar in a shaker. Despite my well-meant entreaties, however, Hermann, who was an absolute teetotaler, refused to let a drop of this agreeable burning and warming energy food even pass his lips. For my part, I felt a pleasant warmth diffuse through my stomach and was glad that I had often trained on

The icy north face of the Grandes Jorasses; the Walker Spur is on the left.

alcohol. At least I was able to get through the night not too disagreeably.

Before leaving the Leschaux hut I naturally had not wasted time pouring the brandy out of a bottle into a small flask. As we were traveling light I had just stuck the bottle into my rucksack with the thought that if it became a nuisance I would simply hurl it away. This turned out to be unnecessary; on the contrary the bottle became so valuable, at least to me, that I remain convinced to this day that it saved our lives. Consumed a swig at a time, like precious medicine, the bottle's contents lasted the whole four days. My companion, who refused to swallow so much as a mouthful, subsequently suffered from frostbite of the hands and feet, whereas thanks to my good blood circulation I escaped entirely. For me it was proof that, taken in moderate doses over a period of time, even considerable quantities of alcohol do no harm.

Toward morning it began to snow and hail, which under our bivouac sack sounded as though someone was pouring peas over us. Suddenly an avalanche shot past, covering our bivouac with hailstones. By shoveling them into our mixing bowl until they melted, we were at last able to obtain some much-desired fluid for our morning coffee.

Our second day on the face began with an extremely severe pitch exiting the black slabs. In fine weather the subsequent climbing up the slabs of the Gray Tower would have been pure pleasure, but in the circumstances, with stiff, cramped fingers, we could only work our way upward with the utmost caution. Once we got out onto the ridge of the tower the difficulties seemed at last to ease, but it proved to be an illusion. The weather grew worse. On this less steep ground the snow was able to settle, so that we could only guess at the whereabouts of the small holds. A broom would have been the ideal instrument for clearing the rock, but unfortunately we did not have one among our luggage.

In the course of climbing a smooth slab I discovered a splendid undercut hold at the bottom of a jutting flake of rock. No sooner had I grabbed it than the whole great flake broke off and went hurtling down. Ten meters down it landed slap on my new nylon rope, slicing clean through the outer sheath. As I had just paid 15,000 old francs for the rope in Chamonix before setting out on the climb, the flake hurt me as much as if it had fallen on my foot. Fortunately, the nylon strands inside the sheath were undamaged, and subsequent events showed that the breaking strength of the rope had not been seriously affected.

After reaching a small knob on the ridge the new snow made it difficult to know whether to climb the snow or take to the rock. Both were so unpleasant that after placing a solid peg ten meters above the knob I decided to go back down to it and sit out the increasingly bad weather.

It was just noon. We hoped that after a few hours we would be able to go on and bivouac higher up. Snow, rain, and hail continued to pour down on us. Thanks to the peg ten meters above we were secure on our ledge, and above all absolutely safe from avalanches. As the storm did not abate we spent the second night at this spot, where we could at least stretch out somewhat under our bivouac sack. This was necessary, as we were racked by cramps alternately in our legs, stomachs, and backs.

We got our Esbit cooker going, but the stink was unbearable under the tent-sack, and outside the storm extinguished it at once. The only solution was to bring the shaker into action again. It worked automatically—we only needed to hold it in our hands and our shivering did the rest. This gave us a nice little pastime through the night. A shakerful of snow mixed with glucose or candy would be reduced to a lump of ice by the shivering action. Then came a moment of deadlock when more violent movement was required; this also helped to warm us up. The lump would fall apart into an ice-broth and finally, if we were patient enough, the broth would turn into water which we could vary with Nescafé or Ovomaltine. So it went on all night. The sausage, bread, and butter in our rucksacks remained untouched.

As morning approached the weather showed no sign of improving. Retreat was out of the question; we were already too high. No one else could help us out

On the "Tour Grise" of the Walker Spur, 1951

of our fix. Fear was no help either. The only solution was to climb on.

Wearing crampons on my feet I first climbed up to the piton, then traversed across to an icy cleft which in turn led to a projecting spike of rock. The ice was exceedingly steep and so hard on account of the cold that when I tried to cut steps whole dinner plates of it broke away. So I decided to do without steps and simply work my way up as best I could. The closer I got to the aforementioned spike, the steeper it got. A little way below the spike there was a hollow space between the rock and the layer of ice, so that I could use the edge of the ice as a handhold. Just as I got within reach of the spike, a snow slide swept down from above and broke over me. This put too much pressure on the ice rim, which broke off. One meter below I had been able to plant a good ice piton, but it was torn out by the shock. Like lightning I spun around facing outward so as not to trip over my crampons and turn a somersault, then shot down the whole pitch and the length of the rope beyond. Hermann reacted with great presence of mind, and as the rope went slack from the fall he swiftly started to let himself down from the anchor piton to the knob on the ridge below. Before he reached it, however, the rope became taut again, dragging him several meters upward. I fetched up hanging just above an overhang; the peg had held. If it had been torn out, Hermann's only remaining chance would have been to jump down the other side of our bivouac ledge. Thank God it had not come to that. The fall was arrested. The astonishing thing about it was that the sack I had been wearing on my back was now on my chest, and that I was holding one mitten in the other hand. I had let nothing drop, but had received a heavy blow in the back that I could still feel two weeks later.

"Are you all right?" Hermann yelled.

"Still in one piece!"

I hauled myself back up the rope to rejoin my companion. Where I got the strength I still do not know.

Nevertheless, a shock has its effect, and suddenly I felt a natural urge coming over me with positively unnatural force. With an understanding grin, my friend held me on the rope while my bottled-up fear found an explosive outlet. After this, morale was restored, but I had no inclination for further icy adventures and gladly let my rubber-soled companion take the lead up the rock. The cloud grew even more impenetrable and the storm more violent. In the conditions, pitches graded 5 in the guidebook seemed harder than normal 6s. At the stances it was only possible to belay hanging on a loop of rope from the piton.

Just to make our misfortune perfect, I found that I had lost my hammer, which must have been torn from its safety carabiner during the fall. We still had a hammer-ax, which Hermann used as he worked his way up the pitch. Suddenly I heard an oath, a ringing sound, and a whirring, whistling sound in the air. The head had broken off the ax and vanished into the depths. All we had left was the second rock-hammer, which would now have to be lowered on the rope after every pitch so that the pitons could be taken out. This meant that we could only clip one rope through the carabiners, which seriously reduced the runner placements on such difficult terrain.

The last 20 meters of the pitch were less steep. They were thus all the more thickly plastered in ice, and this was the cue to bring my crampons into action again. In any case it was high time, as Hermann had reached the end of his strength.

According to the guidebook, an "easy" groove now led to the traverse to the Red Tower. But what did it look like? Not easy, that much was sure.

The rock was coated in hard water-ice with an overlay of loose powder snow covering the few uneven places that could be used as holds. Like the earlier grooves, this one began with an overhang that I had to free-climb. I forgot to take the hammer-ax and I found myself standing despairingly in the ice groove, hesitating before every move at the thought of the fall I had already taken. The idea of retreating to bivouac below the overhangs crossed my mind, yet clearly the pitch would look no different the next day. In desperate rage I lashed out against the bare ice with the hammer—and behold, a great plate of ice broke away, revealing a marvelous hold on which I could stand on one foot and take a breather at last.

For another 20 meters I had to tiptoe my way up the hard, glassy surface like a tightrope walker, then at last I reached a large block that served as a good belay and enabled me to bring up my companion. Twenty meters higher again and out to one side was a big flake of rock under an overhang, which struck me as a suitably sheltered place for a bivouac. Hermann wanted to climb on and escape from the face at all costs, but it was already 7:00 P.M. and we had another 200 meters to go. The cold and the blizzard had increased in fury so that we could see nothing but whirling snowflakes all around. Moreover our garments were soaked inside and out. The net effect was that our flesh crept at the thought of a bivouac, but higher up the ridge or on the summit the conditions would certainly be worse still. In spite of my companion's objections, therefore, I resolved to bivouac at this point.

The damp, stiff-frozen rope served us as an insulation pad from the ice and snow. Things seemed better as soon as we had pulled the tent-sack over our heads, for in such circumstances one's requirements are modest. We could neither lie nor sit properly, but just huddled together. To keep out the piercing cold we drew up our feet and rolled the edge of the sack under us, but this meant that we had to bow our heads, a most uncomfortable position. The moment either of us tried to stretch out even a little the storm would find a gap through which to come blasting in, inflating the sack like a balloon and spraying us with powder snow.

There are many neat theories about how one should conduct oneself on a bivouac, for example putting on dry clothing. And indeed, I still had a reserve pair of dry stockings and a spare pullover in the rucksack, but it was impossible to change. In the tent-sack we were safe from freezing to death, but not from just freezing. The colder it got outside the more the condensation formed on the inner surface of the tent, trickling continuously and disagreeably down our bodies. The shaker was brought into action again, but in the circumstances our enthusiasm for this kind of exercise was very much diminished. I told myself not to grow apathetic, that I must not surrender to the hostile conditions, and continued shaking without pause. In addition, I deliberately bothered my companion by shifting around so that he could not get to sleep, since I feared that if hypothermia were added to exhaustion he would never wake up again.

Everything has an ending, and even this night finally went by. The snow still showered over us without interruption. Resignedly I pulled the bivi sack aside and was astonished to see the opposite peaks bathed in sunlight that was reflected in the snow falling over us. In all seriousness, I thought, "I'm hallucinating. This kind of thing doesn't happen." The snow crystals cascaded past like myriads of glittering diamonds. The sky had cleared, but the gale persisted and was blasting the new snow up the south side of the mountain and over the north face on which we stood. The air was wretchedly cold, causing our saturated clothing and boots to freeze into solid clumps of ice. Well, complaining would serve no useful purpose, so up we go!

Hermann reacted to my call to action, but had stopped speaking. I climbed with extreme care, knowing that I could no longer rely on him to hold me if I fell. Presently I emerged into sunlight on the upper part of the ridge. We noticed little of its warming rays, since the gale continued to lash the powder snow into our faces, building up an icy crust. Our mittens had hardened into solid balls, so that in difficult places I had to take them off to climb with bare fingers. In no time they were numb, white, and hard as wood. I knew what that meant, and sought feverishly to restore the circulation to the tips by rubbing and moving them. The pain was terrible yet comforting. After six hours of struggle I stood under the meter-thick cornice of new snow at the top of the ridge desperately looking for some means of safeguarding myself before dealing with this last obstacle. Once again I struck out at the bare ice in helpless anger with the blunted hammer until a whole flake broke away, revealing a magnificent ring piton, the same one that Cassin had symbolically hammered into the last meter of rock in 1938. It was a lifesaver. With a yell of triumph I clipped into it and swung up over the cornice onto the summit.

Despite the blue sky, the gale that greeted me was so strong that I was unable to stand upright. Communication with my companion was impossible; only by my tugging and pulling on the rope did he realize that he should come. At last his head popped up over the cornice into the sunshine. It was ten o'clock in the morning. We embraced, then let ourselves slither a few meters down the gentle summit slope so as not to be blown back over the north face. In spite of the sunshine it was far too cold and stormy to rest, so we started down immediately in the hope of reaching a warmer level. What looked to us like a harmless ice gully descended on the southern side of the gap between the twin summits, Pointe Whymper and Pointe Walker. Slipping on his rubber soles, Hermann went first, while I kept on my crampons and belayed him over an icy block.

"Don't slide!" I called down to him. "Face outward and stamp in your heels!"

The Walker Spur

At this point I made the mistake of starting down on the taut rope. Suddenly Hermann slipped again and tore me from my steps. With a powerful leap into some deep new snow I tried to restrain him, but in vain. We shot over a couple of ice bulges and plunged into the depths accompanied by an avalanche of snow. Even as we flew through the air I felt furious that this should happened after winning our hard fight. The important thing now was not to let my crampons catch and start me spinning, but I was unable to stop the rear points from punching through my breeches into the knee beneath. The gully was so steep that although I was aware of blows I actually felt nothing in particular, cushioned as they were by the snow. Three hundred meters lower down we shot out onto the glacier. The leading edge of the avalanche disappeared into a crevasse, and we came to a stop sprawled just a few meters before the edge. I jumped up at once and looked around. My only thought was, "Well, at least we don't have to climb down that part."

Ten meters away to one side Hermann lay motionless in the snow. He was only resting, however, and was not pleased at having to get up again. The hole in my knee bled profusely. Luckily it was only a flesh wound and was soon bandaged up. Hobbling rather than walking, we sought the way down and had no further difficulties. We were extremely fortunate that the weather was fine again. It was difficult enough to find a route down the glacier as it was; in weather such as we had had on the north face we wouldn't have made it. Even so, we managed to miss the hut and land ourselves in new hardships when suddenly a form appeared. It was the warden of the Grandes Jorasses hut. He stared at us as though we had fallen from the sky and showed us the way over the last few slabs of rock, where we had the joy of seeing the first flowers and green grass for days.

Not until we reached the hut did the warden grasp where we had come from. Immediately he was eager to help, providing dry clothes and dressing our wounds. In the process it emerged that Hermann had second and third degree frostbite in his fingers and toes as far up as the second joint. Apart from minor cuts and bruises there was nothing the matter with me, which I attributed to the brandy concoction, which, unlike my companion, I had kept swigging away at until I finally committed it to the void, empty, shortly before reaching the summit. Deeply worried about Hermann's frostbite, I was in favor of continuing on down the valley without delay, but had to allow him a night's rest at the hut. I knew that every hour gained in getting him to a doctor might save him from amputations. To get back over to Chamonix became an obsession, so we went straight up from Entrèves to the Torino hut on the Col du Géant. First, however, another little episode occurred.

Just as on the Eiger, in the heart of the battle we completely forgot that others would be worrying about us. It is reassuring to know that people care, but it can lead to the unfortunate consequences of a major rescue party being organized, as in this case. I first became aware of this when I heard a gesticulating bunch of people discussing an accident on the Grandes Jorasses. I made the mistake of telling the group that we were the climbers who were being searched for. My object was to see that the appropriate authorities were immediately notified of our safe return to the valley. This was not understood; they simply saw from our appearance that we must be the climbers described in the press. In a moment we were

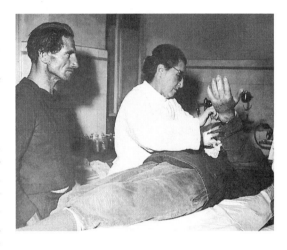

surrounded by a crowd of chattering, gabbling tourists. Cameras were produced, bambini thrust into our arms and perched on our shoulders, photos were taken of us from in front and behind. No one could or would understand our desire to telephone the guides' office in Courmayeur, and not speaking Italian we were unable to do it ourselves. The first to grasp what needed to be done were some guides at the Torino hut, who put the call through at once.

Hermann Köllensperger's frostbite injuries are examined in Chamonix. They healed with no lasting ill-effects.

With the feeling of having done our duty, and in spite of the cloud, we set off down the Mer de Glace. Finding the way through the maze-like icefall to the Requin hut in fog was another challenge, but I was pleased when Hermann said he wanted a bowl of hot soup when we reached the hut, which failed to materialize for a long time. We reached the Leschaux hut at seven o'clock in the evening. After five days we again looked up at the north face of the Grandes Jorasses; it appeared extremely forbidding with its upper part completely plastered with ice. The sight did not make us puff up our chests with success; we felt rather small and insignificant. Thankful for the luck that Fate had dealt us, we gazed up at the mountain that had granted us such a profound experience. That may sound like a platitude; but it is precisely in climbing mountains that a man learns his limitations and becomes humble.

During
preparations for
the 1954
Karakorum
expedition

13. In the Karakorum

lthough the Eiger and the Grandes Jorasses were high points, they were not concluding points in my climbing career. Probably every enthusiastic and active climber longs to see the more distant ranges of the world, and my thoughts and desires were now concentrated on that one aim. As a young climber I had had a faint hope of going on a 1932 Nanga Parbat expedition, for which I helped to pack the kit and transport it to the railway station. The kit went along, but not me.

My second chance was thwarted by the war. Now, however, the time seemed ripe to try for the third time. The Alpenverein was interested in an expedition, but its coffers were empty and I lacked the experience to recruit funds from other sources. I was therefore excited when an invitation from some Scandinavian mountaineers to visit them and their mountains came fluttering through my letter box.

For the first time since the war I climbed aboard an airplane, bound for Stockholm. I was met at the airport by a friendly fellow named Henk Bjerberg, who drove me to his house. In one of the rooms he had set out everything he thought essential for a traverse of Lapland, mainly food. The sight of it made me sit and stare, after which I tentatively broached a question as to whether he had hired porters to transport this mass of kit. That was beyond his financial means, he replied. I had a great deal of sympathy for that argument, so I began to sort things out, reducing especially the

In Lapland. With Henk Bjerberg on the east flank of the Kebnekaise, looking across to the Kiruna foothills, 1952

quantity of food. Even if we reached no supply point for two weeks, it would be enough to take food for only ten days. Better to take in our belts for the last four days than to eat the final salami sausage on arrival. The good Henk could not see this at all, but he was convinced by my experience.

During our march from Kiruna to Abisko, where we elected not to follow the usual route along the King's Trail in favor of passing through valleys rarely visited by tourists and bagging some out-of-the-way summits, even our reduced load proved more than enough to carry. For the final three days, however, we were back on the King's Trail and met plenty of tourists almost crushed under their packs who were only too thankful to unload some of their food onto us, so we did not go hungry. We rounded off our program with some routes in the Narvik region. Among these we climbed the singularly beautiful Stetind, which rises out of the Steffjord like a pillar. During our days at Narvik I received a telegram from Dr. Karl Herrligkoffer asking me to join an expedition to Nanga Parbat in 1953.

Dr. Herrligkoffer was a stepbrother to Willi Merkl, who died on Nanga Parbat before the war, and he was organizing a Willi Merkl Memorial Expedition in his memory. It looked like my life's ambition was to be fulfilled. I threw myself into organizing the expedition, but differences of opinion arose over the choice of members. As we were unable to agree, I withdrew from participating. This was not a hard thing to do, as my old friend Hias Rebitsch invited me join another Himalayan expedition which he had pulled together with the full support of the Alpenverein.

Stetind, a 1300-meter granite monolith in northern Norway

Thanks to Hermann Buhl's incredible solo ascent [of Nanga Parbat], Herrligkoffer's expedition was crowned with success, though there was some distasteful friction afterward. Mountaineers are only human. Nevertheless, I was glad not be have been involved.

That same year Mount Everest was climbed, a feat that ushered in a period of conquest of the Himalayan giants. We, however, had no intention of climbing so high. In order to obtain financing we were obliged to take along a group of scientists whose goal was the still largely unknown Hunza Valley. At the entry to this valley stands Rakaposhi 7788 m, an icy giant that was still unclimbed. We chose this mountain as our objective, but it rebuffed our efforts.

There were twelve expedition participants on the journey out in April 1954—seven climbers, four scientists, and a cameraman. My view was that if we really had to have a photographer then he should be the best we could get. We obtained Eugen Schuhmacher, who brought back the wonderful film *Im Schatten des Karakorum* (In the Shadow of the Karakorum), which enabled us to recoup the major outlays.

We were also lucky with regard to the scientists. Not only did they gather valuable geographical, geological, and botanical data and collections, but they supported our mountaineering activities wherever they could. During the journey I became friendly with one of them in particular, Karl Heckler, a geodetic surveyor from Stuttgart, who tragically met his death in the Hunza River.

And so, at the age of forty-eight, I reached the Himalayas. They were certainly impressive, but I admit that, having seen it all before, in a sense, from pictures and travelers' tales, my expectations were too great. The impression made on me as a boy by the Lalidererwand in the Karwendel was stronger and more overpowering.

Before you can attempt to climb one of the world's highest mountains, you must first reconnoiter it. You cannot just set off with an expedition, including hundreds of porters, without knowing anything about the terrain and the conditions. Two of us, Martin Schliessler and I, were therefore dispatched to reconnoiter Rakaposhi.

We set off from Gilgit with five porters. The Karakorum is a dry, desert range that is only brushed by the end of the monsoons after they break over the Himalayas. Up to a height of 3000 meters, the mountains

The participants of the 1954 Karakorum Expedition pose for the camera in Karachi, including Anderl Heckmair (far left), cameraman Eugen Schumacher (third from left), Karl Heckler (fourth from left), expedition leader Hias Rebitsch (fifth from left, with hat), Martin Schliessler (second from right).

and even the valleys are totally arid unless artificially irrigated, and thus they are all the more beautiful when you reach a high altitude. First gorse begins to sprout from cracks in the rocks, then come tamarisks and even juniper, which grows here to a height of 20 or 30 meters, and finally stretches of green with clumps of wild rhubarb, gooseberry, and numerous other plants that are usually found only in gardens. The most typical plant of the Karakorum is the dog rose, which is found everywhere, even on the glacial moraines.

In the few spots where settlement is possible, farms are on built-up terraces. It was strange to see nut and apricot trees with trunks a meter in diameter. Apricots in particular are the gold of the Hunzas. The fruit is dried and oil is crushed out of the stones, so that supplementary food is available year-round. The very first time we stopped to rest we were offered dried apricots, on which I promptly broke a tooth.

I had heard it said that the Hunzas are the healthiest people on earth, but it proved no more than a saying. We saw men with goiters bigger than their heads and children with all kinds of infectious diseases. In view of

A Hunza farmer

the thousands of flies that swarmed around us up to an altitude of 4000 meters, it seemed no wonder. Swatting and slapping them was pointless. I alone had a defensive weapon in the form of my Swiss Toscanelli cigars, of which I had brought along ample supplies. They drove away not only the flies, but chased my companions from the tent as well.

After two days' march we reached a cirque at a height of about 4000 meters out of which the ice-clad flanks rose for another 3000–4000 meters. Dimensions were deceptive and not easy to grasp. Not until we placed ourselves in relation to them and began to calculate how long an ascent would take did we become fully aware of the enormity of the scale.

Directly in the background, still some kilometers distant, a steep ice gully rose up to a gap in a ridge. Although well furnished with hanging glaciers, it seemed to offer a possible way up. We were just surveying it through binoculars when suddenly some overhanging séracs high up broke off and came down in an avalanche of ice. Ice dust whirled into the air like an atomic mushroom cloud. The strangest thing about it was that apart from the initial boom the whole event took place in silence. The ice dust absorbed the sound entirely. We were spellbound by this drama of nature, but the desire to climb the ice gully was gone. Climbing the face, equally well garnished with hanging glaciers, seemed just as impossible. We therefore returned to Gilgit with a negative report.

Hias reproached us for not having reconnoitered the next parallel valley to see if it offered any better hope. There was no need for him to tell us twice; we set off the next day with the same group of porters. This valley proved to be much longer and higher, and was relatively densely populated. From its broad, U-shaped formation we deduced that there must be a mighty glacier at the end of it. We passed through several bustling villages. The most impressive thing, however, was an intoxicating scent that pervaded the whole valley. It was given off by a blossoming tree that grew everywhere.

We had not been mistaken; there really was a glacier, its snout protruding down into the valley. But what a sight it was! It was a regular trash pile. Glaciers in the Karakorum are mostly fluvial or gorge glaciers formed by the debris of ice avalanches that bring with them all the rubble off the mountainside. In addition, the glacier tongue was so ruptured and rent that even with the donkey we had hired at the last village we could only make progress between the edge and the lateral moraine. The ass dutifully carried the greater part of our food and equipment, but balked at the prospect of climbing a rock step as high as a room. There was no way around it, however, so while one porter mercilessly whipped the beast from behind, another dragged and tugged at each leg until I could not bear to watch such ill-treatment any longer. The donkey seemed quite unconcerned and peacefully bit off a thistle which it continued to chew with pleasure throughout the whole wrestling match.

We trudged along this glacier for at least 15 kilometers. Evening was not far off when we discovered a little track leading up onto the lateral moraine. From this vantage point we could see that the glacier described a huge curve, on the inside of which there was an alluvial island. It looked like a garden of Eden with its wonderful short grass dotted here and there with conifers. No landscape architect could have done a better job laying out a park. We instantly agreed that if a feasible route up Rakaposhi was found from this side, this would be our base camp.

The donkey—Karakorum transport with a mind of its own!

The summit of Rakaposhi, viewed from Surgin Glacier

Unfortunately, it was not to be. As we advanced the following day we again encountered ice avalanches that spread out across the whole width of the glacier. A man may choose to run a risk for himself, but not for an expedition and certainly not for the porters who have to carry supplies. It had already happened once that an entire German expedition (to Nanga Parbat), with the exception of one man who was at the main camp, was wiped out by a single avalanche. There was no option but to turn back hoping to find a safer route on the northern side of the mountain.

Rakaposhi would be climbed from the northwest, but not by us. A British

party accomplished the feat ten years later. Successive expeditions profit from the experience of their predecessors until one day the problem is solved and the goal attained.

Disappointed, we returned with our message that once again we had had no luck. Hias met us halfway with the entire expedition. They had been unable to stand the idleness in Gilgit any longer. There were long faces as we made our report. At this moment a note arrived from our scientists, who were carrying out their tasks in the neighborhood of Batura.

"If Rakaposhi proves too difficult," the message read, "come over here. There are countless unclimbed summits just as high, one or another of which is sure to prove climbable."

It was exactly what we needed at that moment. We reorganized and together with one hundred porters and twenty high-altitude porters marched up the Hunza valley, initially toward Chalt.

This time we went for a mountain that had no name; we did not even know its height. We liked the shape of it, there seemed to be a feasible route, so we wasted no time getting down to work. Once again Martin Schliessler and I formed the scouting party and reconnoitered the route up the mountain as far as a col from which an apparently climbable ridge led to the summit.

At this point I did something stupid that almost cost me my life. Having got back to base from the reconnaissance late in the afternoon, I returned up the Baltar Glacier to Camp I. Normally this took three to four hours, but in my eagerness to report that we were to push on to the col the next day, I raced up in two. In fact the news was not really so important and I could perfectly well have sent a porter, but we were going to need them tomorrow and I did not want any of them to drop from fatigue. It did not occur to me to take it easy myself. As I reached Camp I, new supplies had just arrived, so I lent a hand with the heavy job of unpacking the loads until late at night. When this was finished I returned to base, which I reached at 3:00 A.M. just as the others were getting ready. I joined them without stopping to rest, and on the upper part of the climb even took over the task of breaking trail.

After some twenty-four hours of unremitting effort I was beginning to feel fatigued, but the cornice crowning the col tempted me on to cut a way through. At last I stood before it, soaked inside and out. Now I had had enough. I left the job of sorting out the bivi to my companions and contented myself with belaying them. This was the biggest mistake of all. In addition to the icy wind, a snowstorm blew up. Changing my clothes was out of the question. Two hours went by before the snow cave was big enough for me to crawl inside, and by then it was too late.

Everything I had on was frozen stiff, and so was I. Finally, I could lie back in my sleeping bag, but I did not feel too good. The rarefied air at this

Camp on the
Baltar Glacier

altitude did what it does. Presently I began to shiver violently. The others
now noticed that something was wrong. They put extra covers over me,
gave me plenty of hot tea, and generally did what they could. When morning came I was unable to lift a finger. I had read of cases that began like
this and ended fatally. Knowing that I would not recover if I remained at
this altitude, I entreated my companions to take me down. We had descended no more than a couple of rope lengths when I began to feel so well
that I gladly would have climbed back up to the ridge. However, I had also
heard about euphoria, a sensation of extraordinary well-being that sets in
before the last stage of illness. It might not be that, but I couldn't be sure. I
said to the others, "Look, you can see how much better I am. You go back
up and continue the climb. I'll go down with one porter to help me."

They looked at me anxiously, but I looked and sounded so cheerful
that they finally gave in to my suggestion.

On the way down I hurried so much the porter could hardly keep
up. We passed Hias coming up with his column 100 meters away to one
side. He called out, but I did not reply as I was unable to explain and
the terrain did not lend itself to traversing across.

Down, down; I could think of nothing else. Black spots appeared before my eyes again. At last we reached the level Baltar Glacier along
which the route now lay. I wanted to reach the doctor at Camp I, but was
now incapable of doing so. I lay down on a slab of rock. I wanted to die.

The porter, however, was having none of this. Gesturing with up-
raised arms he begged, "Sahib, sahib, go farther."

Go to hell, I thought. Why wouldn't he leave me in peace? It was so
pleasant to switch off completely. Thereupon, he pulled me up onto his

broad back and tried to carry me. He was soaked in sweat from our head-long descent and did not smell very nice. This had the effect of bringing me back to my senses. Forcibly I freed myself from his back and stumbled along in his tracks, continuously trying to send him away so that I could lie down. He must have known what this implied, as he gave me no peace.

Our strange behavior on the glacier had been observed by our friends at Camp I. Immediately they hurried to meet us. I was vaguely aware of people standing around me, then I fainted. When I came to I was lying in the tent with the worried face of the expedition doctor above me, then I lost consciousness again. The next time I had a glimmering of consciousness I was shivering so violently that the whole tent was shaking. Two men were kneeling on me to hold me down, but I felt very well and found it highly amusing.

Later the doctor told me that I had had a high fever and that he had diagnosed acute pneumonia. Injections and tablets improved my con-dition, but I began to suffer violent headaches. I would never have be-lieved that a head could hurt so much. There was something wrong with my eyes too; I couldn't see out of the right one. Through the other, how-ever, I could distinguish enough to see that it was raining and that the whole expedition was assembled at the camp. I figured they had gath-ered to bury me. Well, things had not gone that far yet; they would just have to wait another couple of days. And in fact it never did get that far. I recovered surprisingly fast, and soon I could stand up and walk.

Now I was granted a fool's license and could do or not do whatever I pleased, but only under the supervision of the doctor, who did not trust me out of his sight.

Those were halcyon days. I could laze around, take photographs, eat to my heart's content, do as I wished. Everyone was nice to me. I was treated like a raw egg until finally it began to seem too silly and I insisted on resuming the push toward the summit, which had been interrupted on account of my illness and the onset of the monsoon.

Everything was prepared the evening before, the loads were shared out and packed. Down in camp, it began to grow dark, while the sum-mits 4000 meters above were still bathed in sunlight. Rapt and reverent we gazed upward. Suddenly a wall of séracs broke off to one side of our peak and went roaring down across the whole width of the glacier up which the morning's route lay. Hias and I looked at each other.

"We going up there?"

"Nah!"

Our desire to climb up that glacier completely evaporated. Once again it was the scientists who helped us out of the mess. The next day we were fiddling around, unable to formulate the magic words that would put an end to all this when a messenger arrived with a slip of paper:

"Highest peak in the whole range definitely accessible from Batura Glacier." And here we were tussling with a mere subsidiary summit!

Now we had a good reason to abandon our efforts here, quit the Baltar Glacier, and head over to the Batura valley, which lay on the other side of the main crest of the range. Nevertheless, this required a march of a week or ten days, the employment of more than 100 porters and all the work of organizing them. Such decisions are not taken lightly.

It was a real release to get going. I walked with a group containing my close friends Hias, Martl, and the doctor. The latter was distrustful of my swift recovery. A ten-hour march is the normal order of the day in the Himalayas. I held out, but in the evening by the campfire I noticed that I was far from being well. Luckily we were in an inhabited area, and the next day somebody found a horse for me to ride.

Now, I am no horseman, but as I was having more and more difficulty walking, there was no alternative. Going along the Hunza valley I found myself alone on my nag on the *Raffig*, a kind of artificial path built up with nothing but dry stones across the cliff face, far above the foaming river. The body of the expedition was ahead, the camera team a day's march behind, and the porter who was supposed to be escorting me had loitered in his home village as we passed through. I hung on to the horse's neck and hoped it would not do anything stupid like stumble over the edge.

In a village called Aliabad—although any connection between it and baths seemed very remote—I noticed a barrack-like building. I knew that during the 1920s the British had built a military sick bay somewhere in the Hunza valley. Perhaps this was it. I pressed the old horse's head around until it was pointing in the right direction. The clever beast seized the point and ambled over. A handsome, intelligent-looking Pakistani emerged from the door. I asked, "Doc?" He nodded. I slid off the horse and knew nothing more for a couple of days. When I came to I was lying in a clean bed. It was twilight, but I had no idea whether it was morning

Camp in the Dianor Valley

or evening. Beside the bed were the Pakistani and our expedition doctor. It is strange how slowly one's thoughts return after a long period of unconsciousness. At first I did not understand anything at all, then I recognized the expedition doctor, and slowly it dawned on me that I was on an expedition and what was wrong. The presence of doctors comforted me so much that with a deep sigh I fell into a wholesome sleep. After two weeks I was able to get up again, but one of my eyes still smarted and watered. The iris was torn. In the doctors' opinion, this had no connection with the pneumonia, but I did not believe them.

At this time I received the following letter from Hias which simultaneously gladdened and saddened me.

28 July, Camp II, 4800 meters

Dear Andreas,

We are stuck into the Batura Glacier and have already dug ourselves an ice cave. However, we shall soon have to move out, as a crevasse that was a modest size at first widens day after day and will soon divide Martl's work of art in half.

After three reconnaissance probes from base camp we made our way up via a difficult ice route. At this point the Captain found a better way around through some flowery pastures. But, like an idiot, I have forgotten to explain first about the nut we are trying to crack. It is the unnamed highest peak (almost 7800 meters) in the Hunza-Batura massif—the one we saw from the other side when we were on the Baltar Glacier. From here it looks easy. Jochen Schneider says he could do it on skis. The lower part of this ski slope appears to be a savage, 2000-meter-high icefall barring the way to the snow corries above. By dint of pitching three camps we overcame this rather dangerous icefall with a good deal of difficulty, and yesterday Dolf and I reached the plateau, from which the way to the summit looks open. Tomorrow we are going to carry supplies up to Camp III at 5400 meters and then push on farther. If nothing goes wrong, the summit should be reached in about 14 days. From one of the cols we ought to be able to climb three easy "7000ers."

In a way I am afraid of disheartening you with my report, but on the other hand I want to keep you regularly informed. The first ascent of this Batura summit, taken together with the work of the scientists, will make a great success of the expedition and we shall be able to celebrate a triumphant campaign in Pakistan. The Captain has already become a great mountaineer and is very helpful, and Wixling is also leading columns of porters on his own. However, I am missing you greatly and have to try all kinds of contrivances to make up in some degree for your absence.

How are you getting on? If you are neither better nor worse it would probably be best for you to go down to Minka with Eugen. Otherwise better to stay at Aliabad and wait for us at Baltit on the way back. It won't be long now before the journey homeward together, and we shall certainly find fine things to see on the way.

An icefall on the Baltar Glacier

I will be needing my Leica now that you are no longer available as an extra photographer. Please send by return together with the lenses (I no longer remember what I loaned you).

We shall be back in Baltit in three to four weeks. In the meantime, keep your fingers crossed for us and stay well.

Everyone sends greetings. Good-bye for now.

Yours,
    Hias

For a lifetime I had looked forward to visiting this distant range, and now, through my own fault, it had beaten me.

My companions did not in fact attain the highest summit, but they climbed a subsidiary peak, and thus achieved a modest mountaineering success. How lucky they were was shown a year later, in 1959, when a British expedition lost their lives in an avalanche in the icefall.

The scientists were already on their walk out, and I looked forward

Ferry on the Hunza River

to a visit from them. Instead, there came the news of Karl Heckler's accident. My diary entries read as follows:

Aliabad, July 26
Today my mood has reached another low point. Pillewitzer and Heckler were due for a visit. I waited the whole day in vain. Not that it is of much importance, but I feel so excluded from everything that a visit from my comrades would have cheered me up.

July 27, noon. The doctor has just broken the news to me as gently as possible that Karl Heckler fell into the Hunza River yesterday on the way from Gulmit to Baltit, and that his body has disappeared. I cannot seem to grasp this news, but now understand why no one was able to spare a thought for me.

Karl Heckler

I now insisted on being discharged from the sick bay and took up an invitation from the mir of Hunza to recuperate at his castle in Baltit, where I ran into the other scientists. Soon I was feeling so well that I would have liked to hurry back and join the climbing party, but I was informed that they too were now on the march out.

This was yet another disappointment. That is how expeditions are; you start out with too many illusions. Expeditions are not pleasure cruises. They bring hard work, renunciation, adversity, and disappointment, one after another. As recompense you still have a great experience and, with good luck, success. If your luck is bad, expeditions can cost you your life. All this should be taken into account, but when adventure beckons it rarely is. Prestige and fame often do not enter into the equation, or they rapidly vanish. Yet the memory remains. With this new insight I journeyed home.

After returning
from the 1954
Karakorum
Expedition

14. New Challenges

At home in Oberstdorf a very kindly, elderly gentleman was waiting to see me. He turned out to be the famous Professor Ernst Enzensperger, who with his brother Josef had been one of the outstanding Alpine pioneers around the turn of the twentieth century. He was an idealist of the purest kind. Together with Richard Schirrmann he was one of the founding fathers of the German Youth Hostels Association.

It was a great pleasure to meet this deserving man, whom I had admired all my life. It proved to be no courtesy visit. He was following a carefully considered course of action that was to give my life a new and significant orientation.

Enzensperger told me how the youth hostel association had hostels scattered all over the country, including the Alpine regions. There were already two in Oberstdorf. Except in schools, youngsters never gathered together in such numbers as in youth hostels, and the hostels therefore offered an opportunity to do something in the educational line. He asked if I would be interested in guiding hostellers in the mountains. In fact I could not imagine myself in this role, but as it is difficult to disappoint someone as nice as old Enzensperger, I agreed. The more I thought about it, the more I believed I could make a contribution, particularly as the assignment included training teachers, educators, and youth organizers in mountaineering matters, and I already had been conducting training courses for German mountain guides under the auspices of the German Alpine Club for many years.

Working as a mountain guide and ski instructor for the German Youth Hostel Association in the Allgäu Alps during the 1960s

My work with young people of all ages became an essential part of my life. It did not bother me at all to go for little strolls and walks with them. My groups ranged in age from as young as six or seven up to eighteen- or twenty-one year-olds, with the majority between fourteen and sixteen. Most of them had never seen mountains before. Sometimes we had children with learning difficulties and other physical challenges.

I had a particularly interesting case one winter. During winter courses I emphasized cross-country touring and using skis as a means to an end. A group of long-haired youths arrived from Hamburg who had hardly seen snow, let alone skis and mountains. The course organizer asked me to deal with this group personally. I was skeptical, but after we outfitted them with skis I decided to test them by taking them for a tour lasting several hours over flat terrain. I was all set to deal with mutiny and found myself speechless with surprise when one of them clapped me on the shoulder and announced that he had never dreamed anything could be so beautiful. After that everything else was small potatoes. They practiced all the exercises, from side slipping to stem turns, with fiery enthusiasm, and after a week I was able take them on proper ski tours. Such experiences are profoundly satisfying, and I am grateful to old Enzensperger and the youth hostel association for giving me the opportunity to work with young people and introduce them to nature. I found that occasional references to my own experiences stood

With Otto-Ernst Flick on the Matterhorn in 1956

me in good stead, since thereafter they believed what I told them and followed me without question.

In the course of my new duties I never forgot my own mountaineering dreams, and my wanderlust was far from being satisfied. Among my private clients was the wealthy industrialist Otto-Ernst Flick, whom I had met while walking the Heilbronner Trail in the Allgäu Mountains. He asked me if I would be willing to guide him. Before committing myself, I wanted to know what he had in mind. The answer came straight back.

"The Matterhorn."

With the exception of the first time, storm and cold was always my fate on the Matterhorn, and I usually had my work cut out to get my clients down off the mountain safe and sound. Flick suggested engaging a second guide. I agreed, since there is nothing to compare with the knowledge of a local person. Yet even that did not satisfy me.

"If necessary, I can get you up and down blindfolded," I said. "Then you will thank me, perhaps pay double the fee, and I'll never see you again. I would rather you climbed the mountain easily, even if things get complicated, and get an appetite for more."

In the Allgaü Alps, c. 1948

Nonplussed at my direct manner, he looked at me.

"What are you proposing?"

My suggestions were carefully noted in his diary. Over the next two years we carried out all these tours, during which he proved himself very strong and possessed of great powers of endurance. Ten-hour walks did not trouble him in the least, even in pouring rain. But difficult climbing was not on the agenda; the man was not a climber, only an exceptionally strong mountain walker.

Before putting the Matterhorn project into action, therefore, I deliberately took him on a few trips, such as the Kopftörlgrat in the Kaisergebirge, which are difficult for a non-climber and were beyond his standard on rock. My aim was to prepare him for the impending difficulties of the Matterhorn. He took it in his stride. The experiment had been worthwhile, and during these training climbs we grew closer to each other as human beings.

A guide has close personal contact with his clients. This can become friendship and even comradeship when the guide offers them something more than merely getting safely up and down and is not only concerned about collecting a fee. I thought to myself that in the circles frequented by my industrialist it must be rare to find someone willing to undergo all the fatigue and hardships of mountaineering and still take pleasure in the natural world. Yet this man had these traits, and the fact helped me develop a special patience.

We soon came to an agreement that he would call be by my first name and I would call him by the initials OE. This was adhered to throughout the adventures we shared. From the beginning I made it plain that mountain climbers are not lackeys and in the interest of safety sometimes even have to be blunt and harsh. In practice, it never came to a scene, as I always took care to keep our undertakings within his abilities—which, moreover, were considerable—in an effort to preserve and nurture his will to effort and his love of the mountains.

Further qualities OE possessed were the ability to remain calm in the worst situations, which partly stemmed from his confidence in me, and to never to lose his ironic sense of humor. He was always able to find a joke about himself and his surroundings, a characteristic that stood us in good stead both in the Alps and on our later journeys to Lapland, Africa, and North and South America. Naturally, such a rich man has, in many respects, quite a different outlook on life from the rest of us, but in the mountains, where money and social distinctions play no part, he showed his true character. Unless guide and client can get along together, it is no good. The latter has to suffer hunger, thirst, cold, heat, and fatigue like his leader, and must not sulk or lose heart—though he has a right to curse vigorously, of course. If, in spite of all this, he loses neither his temper nor his enthusiasm, then that is something exceptional, especially so on the part of anyone coming from such an environment. OE united all these elements. He had always been a brilliant, passionate rider, but mountaineering, that special form of freedom attained through much hardship, and the immediacy of nature, meant even more to him.

But I digress. After some ascents around the Jungfraujoch to acclimatize to altitude, we climbed the Matterhorn in great style. OE was radiant and announced that he would now like to go to the Himalayas.

I was shocked. At great heights every mask falls away and there is no longer any formal politeness. Who knew whether we would be able to stand each other's company for long in such circumstances? I therefore suggested, "How about if we make a journey through Lapland lasting several weeks as a trial run?"

I wanted to see how we got along for a prolonged period in primitive conditions.

"Done!" he said. "You can go ahead and make the preparations."

We carried out our plan in 1957, but before that I had another narrow escape.

In September 1956 I was sought out by Wiggerl Gramminger, my old friend from the Munich mountain rescue team, who wanted to know if I would accompany him to Zermatt where a pair of German climbers were missing on the Matterhorn's west face. Two of their friends who had just returned from an attempt on the Eigerwand wanted to look for them, but the parents of the missing youths wanted experienced mountaineers to go too. I readily agreed, and the next day the four of us were on our way to Zermatt with rescue equipment and stretchers.

Basing ourselves at the Schönbiel hut, we began by searching the avalanche cones at the foot of the face. Because of the danger of stonefall, this had to be done early in the morning while the face still lay in shadow and everything was frozen stone-hard. We found nothing, but at the side of the face an ice gully led upward to the Zmutt ridge. Perhaps we would see something from there.

We roped up to cross the bergschrund. I let one of the youngsters lead off, but only gave him ten meters of rope to play with. This was enough for crossing the crevasse, so I tied on at this point. He was unable to surmount its upper lip, however, and had to climb down. Meanwhile his friend had tied onto the other end of the 40-meter rope, and, having found a better line, got up at once. The party was now underway. Gramminger tied on between me and the one who had failed. Once up into the gully, we all climbed together. In principle, you shouldn't do this, but when everyone trusts one another it is a common practice. After all, these kids had just come from the Eiger, so they ought to be pretty good. The pace was too hot for Wiggerl, and as we had to search on all

Accident on the
Matterhorn.
Badly injured,
Anderl Heckmair
is carried off the
mountain by
Wiggerl
Grammiger,
September,
1956.

sides anyway he untied and pushed off on his own. We carried on, but
had not climbed 20 meters before Wiggerl suddenly shouted out. I
looked at him; he pointed upward, and I saw a body shooting toward
me. The leader had fallen off. I had neither a stance nor a belay. The best
I could do was to plunge in my ice ax and pass the rope over it with a
clove hitch. It was no good. The ax was torn out and away I went as if
shot from a catapult. The third man received such a tug that he shot over
my head. I was pulled one way and then the other. So it went for 200 meters,
until I shot headfirst over the bergschrund and lost consciousness as I
landed on the other side.

A sharp pain in one shoulder brought me back out of the darkness. I
recognized the north face of the Dent d'Hérens, but what had happened
to me and what was I doing here? I began to remember that we were on
a search party, then everything went black again. In the far distance I
heard a voice saying, "Here comes Wiggerl. It'll be all right now, he'll
help us."

After we had shot past him, Wiggerl took three-quarters of an hour
to climb down the 200 meters we had descended so swiftly. With the
calm of a seasoned campaigner he took stock of the situation. The bird
of ill omen who caused the accident was hanging in the bergschrund,
so he was hauled out first. There was nothing wrong with him apart
from a few scratches. The other one had landed on his back and was
wailing horribly, but also only had grazes and bruises. I was lying

The injured Heckmair is transported down the Zmutt Glacier to Zermatt.

crumpled and unconscious, with one arm sticking out in an unnatural position.

Wiggerl immediately put the shoulder back into the joint; he knew how to perform this trick better than anyone. That brought me back to my senses. It was as though the pain had blown away. Together, they helped me to my feet. Something else seemed to be wrong; I could stand, but I was unable to hold up my head. Also the pain in both sides was so bad it was difficult to breathe. Any attempt to carry me hurt still worse, though I am not given to complaining. We seemed to get along best if I held on to Wiggerl's rucksack and leaned my head on his shoulder. Step after step, we reached the Schönbiel hut after seven hours. The next day I was carried down on a stretcher. At the clinic in Zermatt they found that the seventh cervical vertebra was fractured, my shoulder dislocated, and all the ribs in my back broken.

Enveloped in plaster, I was able to travel home in the Volkswagen. Once again I was X-rayed from head to foot, and this time a fractured pelvic vertebra was found. Since I was unable to move anyway, I was spared a plaster jacket. In mid-December they discharged me from the hospital fully cured and by Christmas I was giving ski lessons.

In the hospital I was visited not only by my family, but also by government representatives and friends who traveled a long way to see me. I was touched. Instead of flowers, those who knew me well brought bottles of high-proof liquid to be "taken in medicinal quantities." I already had experience with this type of self-medication, and no doubt it contributed to my rapid recovery. One visit gave me particular pleasure and had far-reaching consequences. This was from Helmut Münch, who was warden of the Kirzschule outdoor-pursuits school at Baad and who was also taking the courses and examinations to become a mountain guide. We got along well and soon became close friends. I welcomed the advent of university graduates into the guiding profession, which was then still a rarity, though it is now a matter of course.

Helmut asked me if I wanted to journey with him to Mount Athos, and instead of bringing flowers or schnapps to the hospital, he brought a bundle of literature on the area. I had plenty of time for study. In May 1957 we drove through Yugoslavia to Salonika, where at times we could only advance in first gear. In the glove compartment we had a personal letter from the Queen of Greece, which opened all doors.

The community of monks in the monasteries of Athos was said to be the oldest republic in the world. Since the year 1000 only monks have lived at Athos, and women are forbidden even to set foot on the peninsula. This is carried so far that even female animals are excluded, so there are no cows or chickens. Only cats shamelessly yowl their love songs, as they are needed to keep down the mice, which also are not an exclusively male community. We wandered from monastery to monastery through a kind of subtropical park landscape, accompanied by the twittering of birds that we rarely saw among the thickets of furze, laurel, and other unusual plants. At each monastery we were welcomed with ouzo—an aniseed-flavored spirit—Turkish coffee, and sweet confections. A room would be readied for us, though when our royal letter was read we were sometimes moved to a "princes' suite." As special guests we were also shown the greatest treasures of the famed libraries, among them a fifth-century Byzantine Bible in which wonderful miniatures were painted on parchment. I regretted not knowing more about it all and being able only to stand and admire. Helmut, who had had a completely different education from mine, was rapt with enthusiasm.

On one occasion our letter had not the slightest effect. In the most southeasterly monastery, which we entered through the back door, a glum-faced fellow advanced toward us. We handed him our letter, but he showed no interest at all; probably he could not read. Addressing us

Departure from Zermatt. In spite of a broken back, Anderl Heckmair (second from right) is able to make the journey home.

A punctured tire,
near Saloniki

in insulting tones and in a language of which we understood not a single word, he conducted us through the building to another door which led back into the open air. The door slammed shut behind us and we heard the bolt being drawn on the inside. Well, not to worry.

As we wanted to climb Mount Athos anyway, we bivouacked under a tree on a spur of the mountain. The sun sank glowing into the western sea just as the full moon rose like a golden ball out of the east. Around us was total silence, and we watched reverently. We reached the summit the next day in cloud. Scorning the disused mule track, we clambered up a rock ridge on the eastern flank. On the top stood a small chapel still half full of snow and containing valuable icons. Athos rises 2100 meters out of the sea. We were greatly admired for this "feat." Of course, from a mountaineering point of view it is no feat at all. The most beautiful part of it was the night out, which we owed to the miserable monk.

At the next monastery, which was on the western side of the mountain, the monks were once again extremely friendly. It was a school of painting, and we were proudly shown the masterpieces they painted in the old style like ancient icons and even sold. We also made a short excursion to see the hermits dwelling in the cliffs just above the sea. Here our climbing abilities came in handy, as we were able to clamber down cracks and grooves to suddenly find ourselves standing before a meditating anchorite. He did not utter a word but made friendly gestures and prepared the usual coffee for us. These hermits were partly supplied from the sea, drawing up their provisions in nets as their predecessors had done for more than a thousand years.

Hermits were the first men of religion to settle on Athos. Subsequently monasteries were founded, the first of which was Lavra, still the most important. Two cypresses dating from the time of its foundation stood in the cloister garden; they were more than one thousand years old. Most of the monasteries were inhabited by only a few monks. At the Russian Panteleimon, for example, which was built to house 3500, there were only 60 monks in 1957. We were told that the republic had survived many such crises in its thousand-year history, and the monks looked to the future full of trust in God.

After Athos we visited the monasteries of Meteora, which are no more than museum pieces. They were built in the Middle Ages perched high on enormous pillars of conglomerate. The monks could retreat there in times of danger. Originally there were about 23 of these discrete monasteries on their rock turrets, but now no more than five remained. Determined to see an abandoned monastery, we circled an outcrop which we suspected of holding a ruin, but without finding any possibility of getting up. The monks must have drilled and bolted their way up, then taken out the equipment and hauled up their supplies by rope. Our latest climbing techniques are not so modern after all! But we had no ironmongery with us and had to give up.

Finally we wanted to climb Olympus, but the gods were ill-disposed to us and opened the floodgates of the heavens so wide that we were literally washed away home.

In the autumn of the same year I made the planned journey to Lapland with OE. We flew to Stockholm, then took the train to Kiruna, from where we climbed Kebnekaise, the highest mountain in Sweden. We also did some nice tours from Abisko. Then there happened what must happen when people spend a lot of time together.

The "elevator" at one of the monasteries in Meteora—the only means of connection to the outside world

A march was planned to Unallakaz and back via Riksgränsen. Owing to the shortcomings of the map, which was on a scale of 1:200,000, my calculations were 10 kilometers off, and in trackless territory in Lapland foot travel is only about 2 kilometers an hour. Because Abisko lies 300 kilometers north of the Arctic Circle, it never grows dark in summer, and we set out at three o'clock in the morning. First we walked for 15 kilometers along the well-marked King's Trail, which I already knew. We polished off this stage in three hours. The remaining 15 kilometers could be done comfortably in ten hours, inclusive of stops. The route lay westward, still along a track, though not a very good one. After a bridge the track petered out, and as foreseen we plodded on through bogs choked with dwarf birch and willow until the calculated ten hours were up, but without any sign of shelter. After checking our position with the compass, I pulled out the map. Suddenly the scales fell from my eyes and I realized what a mistake I had made. We still had five hours to go! Luckily, there was no nightfall, but the weather turned bad and whipped us with mixed rain and snow. In a soggy valley I had to check our course again with the compass. Cloud cover obscured the surrounding summits, but OE, who was more than 6 feet tall, stood out of the dwarf vegetation like a lighthouse.

As we sat down to rest in a clearing he at last said, "I suppose we'll be getting there soon?"

I had been dreading the question for some time, so at last I admitted my mistake. It was an unfortunate confession to have to make, and I feared he would really let me have it. But no, there was not a word of reproach. It wouldn't have changed our situation anyway. Onward!

Toward midnight we reached our objective, which turned out to be a tiny cabin. Two Norwegians were snoring away inside. After we made a fire and changed into dry underclothing, I hauled our ample provisions out of the sack. OE fell on them like a wild man, ravenous with hunger. I knew just how he felt; it had happened to me after my first trip to the Dolomites. It is impossible to control yourself, even with the best will in the world. Anything you can get your teeth into goes straight down. He gobbled things as fast as I could pull them out of the sack, and I had to be careful that he did not swallow the wrappings into the bargain.

The next day OE flatly refused to cross the mountains to Riksgränsen, so we had to turn around and return by the same route, if you could call it that. The weather had now turned fine letting us see something of the

On the south summit of the Kebnekaise in Lappland

strange and marvelous landscape. We took our time, spent the night in a Kota—a Lapp dwelling—and finished the tour on the best of terms.

There was no doubt that OE had the necessary qualities of endurance and self-control for expedition life. We could now go ahead and make real plans.

The first-class passage by sea from Narvik to Rotterdam gave us a chance to relax in comfort. I turned over the question of our next goal in my mind. It was premature to aim for the Himalayas. In accordance with my principle of never exceeding the capabilities of my clients, I therefore suggested Africa as our next objective.

Anderl Heckmair
in the African
bush

15. Travels in Africa

recalled a tip that Heini Harrer had given me after he had become a world traveler. He mentioned that his most interesting mountaineering in Africa had been in the Ruwenzori Mountains, which were relatively easy to reach by air and then various methods of ground transport. From a technical point of view they apparently were not too difficult; what they called for was endurance and a willingness to endure hardship, as it rained there the whole year round. It sounded like just the thing for OE! Cautiously, I began to present this idea to him.

He was not against the proposal, but said that if he was going to visit Africa then he wanted to see Lake Chad, about which he had heard a great deal. I on the other hand knew nothing about it, so I quickly looked it up on the map and duly discovered it on the southern border of the Sahara. The Ruwenzori lie on the equator. For my part, if we were going to travel as far as the Sahara, then I wanted to see the Hoggar Mountains. This time it was OE who had never heard of them. I described to him how in 1932 I had gazed in fascination from the summit of Toubkal out over the endless desert, thinking what a great experience it must be to cross it. In the middle of the desert rise two ranges of mountains, the Tibesti and the Hoggar Mountains, both rise above 3000 meters.

OE told me to work out a time schedule and cost estimates. That was easier said than done. The biggest problem is always to find the right companions, but for this purpose I had a good choice of candidates. During the war I had gotten to know a doctor in Fulpmes who I thought to be thoroughly suitable as a mountain climber, as a doctor, and as a human being. His name was Jochen Singer, and we were still loosely in touch. One telephone call was enough. I told him what a terrific trip I had in mind for him and suggested that he think it over and call me back.

In addition, I knew a scientist with all the necessary qualities for such an undertaking. This was Dr. Achim Schneider, a lecturer in geology at the University of Berlin, a man whose knowledge was to enrich our journey.

Both agreed, though I did not withhold the problems that were to be expected. The preparations took two years, but at last the time came to ship the vehicles—it had transpired that our plans could be accomplished only with the use of cross-country vehicles, which we had to bring with us—and a ton of baggage off to Nairobi.

To climb the Ruwenzori it is necessary to take the rainy season into account when making plans. We therefore settled on mid-September 1960 for our departure, flying to Nairobi along the course of the Nile, which from the air looked like a dribble draining down a gutter. Our vehicles and supplies were waiting for us. We collected them, and the journey began.

To get acclimatized and for specialized training we first headed to Uganda to climb the Virunga volcanoes. We were particularly tempted

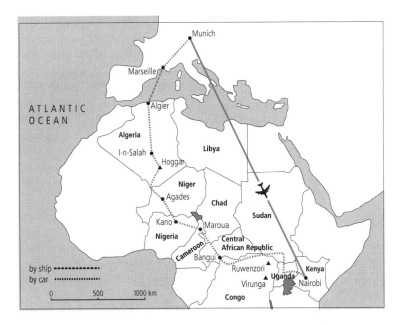

by Nirogongo, which was said to have the most substantial lava flow in the world. Unfortunately, it stood in what was then Congolese territory, and fighting and unrest there prevented us from crossing the border. We had to content ourselves with the 4000-meter Muhawura, the "Father of the Lost."

A belt of bamboo forest provided ideal gorilla habitat around the foot of the mountain. Our local guides were full of advice on to how to behave in the event of an encounter with gorillas. However, though we heard cracklings and rustlings, we never saw so much as a tail. This was not surprising in view of the fact that the bamboo thickets grew so densely that we had to keep in close physical contact with each other to avoid any of the party getting lost. Without the local guides we could not have got through. One of them excitedly showed us a steaming, horribly stinking little heap that he assured us was gorilla droppings, but I was skeptical and by no means sure that the fellow had not laid it there himself for the promotion of the tourist trade.

We were also told to be watchful for snakes. Our doctor had an assortment of antitoxins with him, as different snakes have different venoms, and unfortunately you cannot know in advance which kind is going to bite you. Yet during the whole of our journey through Africa I saw only three snakes, two of them dead and one living. The latter was sunbathing lazily and seemed grateful that I did not do him any harm.

The ascent of Muhawura and the neighboring Mgahinga, which is

"Now our way led northward along relatively good roads through the Elizabeth National Park, where we photographed an enormous elephant from disquietingly close quarters."

almost as high, gave us a foretaste of what the Ruwenzori held in store. There were cloudbursts against which our alpine umbrellas were ineffective, while in plastic capes we soon marinated in our own juices owing to the warm, humid atmosphere. That is typical of mountaineering in Africa. However, no one complained; we were all too enchanted with the change of scene.

After crossing the bamboo belt, throughout which we in vain kept an eye open for gorillas, we wanted to reach the summit of the mountain. Our African guides did not understand this at all. I could see their point of view, as we had to pass through a veritable forest of stinging nettles that were far more painful than our European ones. At last we broke out into the upper zone of groundsel, lobelia, and heather, which continued all the way to the top. The most widespread plant of all was the knee-deep moss, in which it was impossible to find firm footing. There were no views from the summit, as at high altitudes the rain is mixed with thick fog. Nevertheless, we had attained our first goal, Mgahinga.

We now wished to turn our attention to climbing the nearby Muhawura. To reach it, we had to cross a high col about a kilometer wide. Our guides were afraid of this area, claiming that it was infested with dangerous wild animals. To us it seemed more probable that they really wanted to descend and spend the night with their wives in the village before going back up the mountain. We therefore insisted on our plan. During the march through the boggy jungle, however, we could see from their tense features and nervous bearing that they were not pretending. In our ignorance we saw nothing dangerous. We were like beginners in the mountains standing on an avalanche slope with no inkling of the peril they are in. The relief of our Africans was visible as we descended from the saddle onto relatively more open terrain and reached the steep flanks of Muhawura. The keeper of the next shelter assured us that the warning had been fully justified and that incidents involving buffaloes and big cats were frequent and that they would attack if disturbed or frightened.

Proud and exhausted after their ascent of Ruwenzori—Achim Schneider, Anderl Heckmair, Otto-Ernst Flick, Jochen Singer

The summit of Muhawura is 4600 meters above sea level, and the 3000-meter descent was most unpleasant. We all felt the effect of the un-accustomed effort but we were in a cheerful mood at having attained another objective.

Now our way led northward along relatively good roads through Queen Elizabeth National Park, where we photographed an enormous elephant from disquietingly close quarters and also hippopotamuses, a great crocodile that looked a thousand years old, trotting giraffes, and marabou birds. The word "park" implied a reserve where all forms of hunting were forbidden. In general, the animals took no notice of cars. However, it was forbidden to get out and the rules had to be observed; only then was it safe.

At last we reached the Ruwenzori, which, according to our geologist, were not volcanic in origin like almost all other African mountains, but instead were formed from a gigantic slab raised out of the rift valley, 5120 meters high and divided by erosion into five groups. At Fort Portal, a fair-sized town at the foot of the range, local merchants are well used to mountaineers. The process was to go into a particular shop where the owner, an Indian, asked, "How many of you are there?"

"Four."

"Then you need twenty porters who will require this, that, and the other."

There was nothing to say or do but pay up.

"Where will the porters wait for us?"

"They won't be waiting for you at all. You just go down the valley and report to the chief guide. He will do the rest."

It was as easy as that. To think that we had spent so much time worrying and planning! However, it might not always turn out so simple. At Kampala we paid a courtesy visit to the local mountaineering club in the hope of gathering information. It transpired that my name was known in the heart of Africa, and this smoothed our path. The Kenya Club members had sent advance word of our arrival, which no doubt explained why everything went so easily. Climbers look after one another. A non-climber would have run into difficulties.

The walk in was extremely interesting. The route lay through house-high elephant grass. It was in fact the most dangerous part of the expedition, as the region is full of wild animals, though there is no danger to be seen, at least not until it is too late.

Elephant grass is two to three meters high, and without local guides one would never find the way through. On one occasion I dropped behind to change the film in my camera and afterward had no idea how to catch up with the others, who had vanished into the sea of grass. I felt properly afraid, and was relieved to come upon a trampled-down path. Presently the guides emerged from the grass shouting and gesticulating wildly. Noticing my absence, they had come to find me. They explained that my trodden path was not a proper track at all, but had

The Bujuku hut at 3800 meters on Ruwenzori

"Then we came to a forest of giant groundsels, so strange that we would hardly have been surprised to find a brontosaurus peering at us around the corner."

been made by wild animals. If I had gone much farther I might have found myself face to face with an elephant, and there's no telling how they will react. After that I never lagged more than one meter behind the others.

The second part of the approach march led through primeval forest where apes swung through the tree tops some 40 to 50 meters above the ground. We crossed innumerable rushing streams without bridges, and trudged through swampy valleys. Then we came to a groundsel forest so strange that we half expected to see a brontosaurus peering at us around the corner. There was nothing new about wading in knee-deep moss, however, as we had already had plenty of that on the Virunga volcanoes.

At the end of each day's march we were accommodated in a corrugated iron hut. The last of these was the Bujuku hut at 3800 meters, which even boasted a stove. Despite all our efforts to light it, it would only give off smoke but not burn. Our scientist then had the idea of filling the ash scuttle with paraffin and setting fire to it. The result was a hot moment not only for the stove but for us too, as we briefly thought we were being blown up. After that everything was all right again.

Our porters found shelter in a cave and were wretchedly cold, yet they remained cheerful. I was not too proud to sit down in their circle and share the gruel from their pot. This inspired feelings of intimacy that we never again experienced with our local guides.

The mentality of the Africans had been described to us quite poorly. We had been told that they were lazy, lying, and furtive. Our experience was exactly the opposite. Three days before reaching the Ruwenzori valley I lost my Rolex wristwatch. It was sent after me by relay runners carrying it from village to village. At the Bujuku hut rain drummed on the tin roof in the morning, and we thought that we could comfortably sleep in, as our Africans would not venture out of their cave. On the contrary, our guides and porters got us out of bed and insisted on allocating the loads. They were right, too; a couple of hours later it was fine again.

The higher we got, the stranger the vegetation became. Vertical crags were thickly clothed in moss, and had not Hubert Mumelter once written in the *Mountaineer's Primer*, "Overhanging moss and slime, that's no place for you to climb"? Luckily, we did not need to climb through the overhangs. We always managed to find a way through, and at last we happened upon two bivouac huts at 4400 meters on Point Helana. Here our porters deposited their loads and hastened back to their cave, as no African would set foot on the glacier.

It was just midday, and once again I made a stupid mistake. I knew well enough from the literature that in the Ruwenzori the temperature reaches 15°C by day and drops to -15°C by night, yet somehow I did not believe it, or at least not the second part. The first part I was forced to believe by the state of the snow on the glacier, which had a consistency like porridge. It seemed that it could do no harm to slog on and break trail, so that in the morning we would have ready-made frozen steps. Thus we reached the summit icefalls, all garnished with fantastic icicles. We could have gone to the top, but we would have been caught out by darkness with sopping wet feet and no bivouac equipment. So we returned to the bivouac hut, where we had dry things to change into.

The next day the weather was bad again, but the snow was frozen so hard that we strapped on our crampons and were able to plod up our track without any trouble.

Suddenly a violent snowstorm blew up. It was a real blizzard, or so it seemed to me. Clearly, the warm, humid air masses from the Congo river basin are cooled as they strike the mountains, and even at the equator it does not rain at 5000 meters but snows. Now it snowed with an intensity and thickness greater than I had ever experienced. The snow must have been mixed with supercooled moist air, as a great ice bulge under which we found shelter grew a coat of rime half a meter thick. We were completely sheathed in ice, so that after half an hour, by which time the storm had begun to abate and the air to grow lighter, we decided not to bother about Point Margherita, the highest summit, but to head for Mobius, the third highest, the summit of which we reached successfully.

Although we were right on the equator, we fought our way back down the giant Stanley Glacier through cloud and snowstorm to our bivouac box, where our porters were waiting for us practically frozen. Hastily we continued on down to the warmer climate of the Bujuku hut, where whisky and Toscanelli cigars helped us forget our earlier discomfort. Despite our failure to reach the highest summit we were in excellent humor, and the good doctor expressed our feelings perfectly by noting, "We didn't come on this trip to be admired; we wanted to admire the sights and experience things ourselves."

There was still plenty to experience: downpours so copious that it was like walking under a shower-head turned on full force, and the hospitable receptions as we marched back down the valley. The wives and children of our porters rushed out of every village with cries of delight, bringing us pineapples and bananas as tokens of welcome. These kindnesses on the part of the Africans, who were shy of strangers, touched us, and we were correspondingly generous when the time came to pay them. This gave rise to further celebrations, culminating in much dancing and drunkenness.

As we were only at the beginning of our journey, we imagined that we

In the "snow bog" during the ascent of Alexander Peak

would often experience this kind of thing, but we never again made such friendly contact as we did with our porters in the Ruwenzori.

Now our great journey across Africa really began. As the political unrest made it impossible to go through the Congo, we headed toward the Sudan and then northwest through the Central African Republic to Cameroon, across Cameroon to Nigeria, and from there to Niger and on up into the desert.

Although the journey was long and hard to make, it does not take long to write about it. In places, however, there were no roads and it was beneficial that we had two cars, so that if one got stuck the other could haul it out. Wild animals made it dangerous to sleep out, but we always found lodges reserved for Europeans or else were put up by European farmers.

Our trip in the Ruwenzori was at the beginning of the rainy season. Now we had to pass through the rain zone as it moved southward across Africa. Rivers burst their banks and flooded wide areas. As we had to cross many tributaries of the Congo, we were apprehensive about whether we would get through or not.

At Mboku we found a stranded Englishman with an American car. Although it was only the beginning of October, he would be stuck there until January at the earliest. We were advised to wait also, and the hospitable farmers gladly would have taken us in. With our Jeeps, however, we plowed our way across the flooded landscape. A couple of local boys went ahead of us as pilots. The roads were often flooded knee-deep, and nothing could be seen but water. We would creep along in low gear behind the African boys. At the river itself a whole crowd of them waited to shove us onto the ferry with shouts of joy and then to guide us across the flooded areas many kilometers broad on the other side.

We certainly learned some geography in the process. The Mboki flowed into the Mbomu, the Mbomu into the Ubangi, the Ubangi, after which the country was named, into the Congo. No one ever taught me that at school!

We had 700 kilometers to go from the Sudan border to Bangassou, where the next hotel and fuel were to be found. Getting gasoline had proven to be difficult, as we only had traveler's checks which no one would cash. Fortunately, an American missionary appeared out of the bush like an angel of mercy. He had heard of our predicament and came to cash the checks for us.

Shortly before reaching Bangassou we encountered the first car we had seen for many days going the other way. Everyone jumped out and shook hands all round, asking where from, where to, what the conditions were like, and so on. Such behavior would have seemed completely crazy back home in Europe.

A memorable event in the African bush was our meeting with a big-game hunter. We were running short of fuel and somehow managed to reach a French airstrip. It had not been marked on any map, but we were directed to it when we inquired without much hope for gas at a village. Finding it was pure luck. The commanding officer was away hunting elephants and the sergeant was unable to help us, as everything was military property.

"When will he be back?" we asked

"Maybe in a couple of hours, maybe not for a week," came the reply. It was a fine outlook on life.

Waiting seemed pointless. One jeep carrying all our fuel reserves might be able to cover the 600 kilometers to Bangassou. The drive fell to OE and Achim, who was indirectly responsible for the state of affairs. The latter was our cashier, and being short of Sudanese money he had not filled up at the last stop, hoping to find more fuel at every village in the Central African Republic. Unfortunately, there were no villages and no gas either.

We parted with mixed feelings and came to terms with the possibility of not seeing each other again for a couple of weeks. Jochen and I sat in the canteen with every ground for rejoicing at our comfortable circumstances, but we were too worried about our companions to enjoy the beer. After two hours we were startled out of our brooding by a loud honking. Grinning ear to ear, OE and Achim swung the jeep around to the gate in an elegant turn. We ran out, calling, "What happened?"

"Shortly before reching Bangassou we encountered the first car we had seen for many days going the other way. Everybody jumped out and shook hands all around, asking where from, where to, what the conditions were like, and so on. Anybody who carried on like that in Europe would be taken straight off to a home."

They had met the elephant-hunting commanding officer who had had a successful safari. He had as much gasoline as we wanted. Before long the hunters also appeared and their success was duly toasted. Late in the afternoon the now well-oiled Great White Hunter conceived a desire to go back and inspect his bag. We were to come along; no need to change, it was only half an hour from the road.

If hunters should be believed only with strict reservations, big-game hunters should not be believed at all. The half hour drew into several hours through genuine African bush and bog. OE lost his shoes and as I only had sandals I preferred to go barefoot. The hunter led at such a pace that OE could not keep up, and before long the two of us stood alone together in the bush. Suddenly a brush fire flared up nearby and we fled into a stream. I spotted a clump of trees in the direction in which we had been going and headed for them. As we drew closer we heard a general uproar, and found our friends in the midst of a band of Africans who were in the midst of a meat orgy.

The body of the elephant, big as a room, was entirely skinned. A whole gang of native people were scrapping over the flesh, which they devoured like wolves. Men, women, and children were a gruesome sight with blood smeared all over their naked bodies. Suddenly the mountain of flesh shook. I jumped back, surprised.

"Surely the elephant can't still be alive!"

The hunter laughed and took me around to the other side of the corpse, where I saw there were two men in its belly, tearing out shreds of meat and throwing them to the others who, when they did not swallow them on the spot, roasted them on grills of interwoven branches arched high over several fires, around which they danced. The rain began to patter down again, but could only wash part of the blood from their bodies. We were glad to have a few soldiers with us, for our fear of inadvertently forming part of the feast might not have been entirely groundless.

"This was Africa as no travel agency could offer it!"

The tusks weighed 70 kilos each. Once they had been cut out, we and the soldiers withdrew into the dusk. The feast was still in full swing, and we were assured that it could go on for another week or two. This was Africa as no travel agency could offer it!

The journey continued. Out of the bush into the savannah, out of the savannah into arid plains, and out of the plains into the desert. In the south we saw Arab Negroes and then, as we went farther north, Negroid Arabs. Everything fluidly intermingled at the edges, both vegetation and ethnicity.

We were unable to reach Lake Chad as the land was

so flooded from the rainy season. In fact we were happy to get through to Kano in Nigeria, after which we left the rain zone behind. The closer we got to the desert, the bluer the sky stretched over our heads. Agades was the next big town on our itinerary. Although it is only on the southern edge of the Sahara, it seemed to us to be the middle of the desert already. In former times the place existed mainly for the slave trade, but during our visit it was thronged with tourists and oil prospectors who flew in by airplane. After all, who would be so crazy as to drive across the Sahara?

The vast emptiness of the desert makes a real physical impact, and the nights spent sleeping out under the unbelievably clear starry sky count among the most beautiful bivouacs of my life. We never had to pitch a tent, though it was now November. It was enough to spread a groundsheet on the sand and crawl into our sleeping bags.

Our objective was now the Hoggar Mountains. Acknowledging our inexperience as Saharan travelers, we had eliminated the Tibesti from our plans. Anyone who imagines as I did that a journey across the desert is going to be a matter of monotonous, stubborn endurance will find that the experience is quite the opposite.

Just as we had done in the jungle and the bush, we took turns at the wheel, changing drivers every 50 kilometers. However, the passenger had to keep just as sharp a lookout as the driver to ensure that the vehicle did not leave the track and run into soft, windblown sand at full speed. Nevertheless, it happened regularly. Then it became a matter of strenuous digging, pushing, and pulling, all at a temperature of 40°C "in the shade," which unfortunately did not exist. In the middle of the desert Achim even succeeded in finding a nail to drive over, thus producing a flat tire. This feat must be even more difficult than finding the proverbial needle in the haystack, but Achim just would not give up trying. Tamanrasset was a much-visited place with an airfield and a hotel to go with it, but unfortunately the latter was full. Unwashed and filthy, we resigned ourselves to another desert bivouac. First of all, however, we reported our arrival in the regular way to the police. As we were doing so a man in civilian clothes came into the office. From the way the clerks immediately got down to work it was clear that he must be of some importance. Ignoring us completely, he went over to an official, took our papers from him and studied them. Suddenly he spun around and shot a question at me, "Are you the Anderl Heckmair who climbed the Eigerwand?"

I admitted that I was. He was delighted and introduced himself as the commanding officer. Being from Alsace, he spoke fluent German. Not only that, but he was a climber and well-acquainted with alpine literature. OE remarked dryly, "With you, it doesn't matter where we travel, you're a big celebrity."

But what could I do about it?

On camel back through the Algerian desert

The Hoggar range is of pure volcanic origin, formed, according to contemporary theory, out of plugs forced up as out of a tube. The basalt towers rise here and there out of the landscape, all of them difficult to climb. During the 1950s, Maurice Herzog, who was Minister of Youth and Sport in France, encouraged the best French climbers to go there. Therefore, all the accessible summits had been climbed already.

Anyone with the skill to tackle severe climbs will find fulfillment here. There are no weather problems, and in November, when we were there, the heat was quite bearable. The only preconditions, as in any mountain range, are sufficient technical skill and willingness to face effort and hardship. We did a number of fine routes, among them the highest summit, 3000-meter Mount Tahat, which in fact is no more than a mountain walk, albeit over trackless scree, among which lay great lumps of petrified wood proving that the region was once forested. There are many such curiosities in the Hoggar. Among the basalt gorges are rock pools which, so I was informed, date from prehistoric ages. We were warned not to bathe in them, as some contain crocodiles which, although very degenerate and no more than 50 or 60 centimeters long, are still very aggressive.

Nevertheless, the typical Hoggar basalt towers interested us, and we wished to climb at least one of them, the not too difficult Issekrem. Naturally, we didn't travel across the desert merely to climb, since we could do that both better and much more simply in our home ranges. Still, when you have the ability and find yourself in front of such an obelisk, you feel a certain itching in the hands and feet. It is a special kind of fun to climb such an unusual peak and gaze out across the endless expanses on which mountains lay like the lost toys of giants.

We did not want to leave Africa without having ridden on camelback. Our idea of joining a caravan for a couple of days was promptly discouraged. I could understand that, just as I would not have been keen to take absolute beginners on a serious climb. Nonetheless, we arranged for camels at Tamanrasset. Some Tuaregs helped us into the saddle. It was not easy. The camel lies on the ground. You creep up on it from behind—the front end bites—and swing up onto the wooden saddle. Instantly the back end rises into the air. If not prepared, you plow headfirst back into the sand. Finally we were all in a saddle with our shoes hanging on a convenient peg in front of us. Bare feet are pressed into the camel's neck and the toes twiddled powerfully. The camel then

In the Hoggar Range: "Still, when you have the ability and find yourself in front of such an obelisk, you feel a certain itching in the hands and feet. It is a special kind of fun to climb such an unusual peak and gaze out across the endless expanses on which mountains lie around like the lost toys of giants."

begins to move. The more you twiddle the faster it goes, but if you doze off it stops. We rode 18 kilometers to a Tuareg colony where tea was ceremoniously prepared for us. Unveiled women were in charge while the heavily veiled men had nothing to say. In our jeeps we could have covered the distance easily in 30 minutes. By camel it took a good six hours, since camels walk no faster than 3 kilometers per hour. We felt a certain grudging respect for the caravans, though they were already being supplanted by motorized transport.

Finally we set out from Tamanrasset for the journey home. Comfortable hotels were available at the oases of I-n-Salah, El Golea, and Ghardaia, and the settlements were linked by asphalt roads. The charm of the primitive and untrodden now behind us, we headed for Algiers as fast as possible. It was still 2000 kilometers from Tamanrasset, but on good roads passable by anyone with an ordinary car. Although the spell of the unknown was gone, we had enjoyed plenty of it on our journey through Africa.

An excursion in
the Cordillera
Negra

16. Peru—Cordillera Blanca

Climbers are lucky to have intriguing objectives all over the world to justify journeys across the continents. Even while we were traveling through Africa I began planting the idea in OE's mind that there were a lot of worthwhile and easily accessible peaks in South America, notably in the Cordillera Blanca in Peru. As everything went exceptionally well in Africa, it was not difficult to kindle his enthusiasm for this new plan. Preparations began anew. They took two years, and we set off in mid-April 1963.

This time OE brought along his son Rudolf and the latter's friend Henno. Besides our African team we had a very valuable addition to the party in the form of my old friend Dr. Fritz März, who could speak Spanish and already knew Peru from an earlier expedition. There were seven of us, which is really too many for an expedition, but each had a job to do, and we were all compatible so there was no friction.

These days you don't actually "travel." Instead you fly. You go to sleep and wake up in another world. Airports, hotels, and stations—and soon even cities—all look the same. The thing that makes you aware of being on another continent is the sight of human beings of a different race. In Lima, where our expedition began, the old Spanish colonial houses seemed not unlike home, so not until we got out into the country did we sense the difference, the strangeness.

To reach the Santa valley we had to travel 200 kilometers and cross a pass 4000 meters above sea level. We hired an ancient truck for the trip that wheezed its way up from sea level and often gave us the opportunity to stretch our legs a little. As we breasted the top of the pass, the icy giants of the Andes rose before us.

The view up the Santa valley is dominated by the 6800-meter bulk of Huascarán. A month or so before we set out, the international press had been full of reports about an ice avalanche from Huascarán that had overwhelmed a whole valley, wiping out ten villages and killing 4000 people.

Such news is soon forgotten in the hectic pace of modern life. Only OE thought to ask whether we should be traveling to such a dangerous spot. I did not completely believe the reports about the scale of the disaster, and replied that now that the avalanche had fallen there would not be another for a long time. I was wrong about this—six years later, in 1971, a violent earthquake caused another avalanche to break loose, almost totally annihilating Yungai and the neighboring villages. This time the death toll was 40,000.

On reaching the quake area, we were shocked. An entire glacier had in fact split away from the northern summit of Huascarán, poured over a rock face 1000 meters high, burst through a moraine, and roared down the 20-kilometer length of the valley, rebounding from wall to

wall like a toboggan and destroying everything in its path. Corpses were still being fished out of the Pacific, 400 kilometers away. Two months later, as we stood on the avalanche debris, it was already beginning to sprout green shoots, for Peru is so fertile that they have a saying: "Plant your walking stick in the ground, water it, and it will start to grow and flower."

Even if the proverb is not quite literally true, we saw a grain of its truth in that ruined valley, where life already bloomed between the wooden crosses that had been placed everywhere on the avalanche rubble in memory of the victims.

The main town of the Santa valley is Huaras, which lies above 3000 meters. We checked in at the Monterrey Quarter Hotel, a little outside the built-up area. It had a swimming pool in which the water was heated to 32°C. That was enough for us; we immediately booked rooms for a month so that we could use the hotel as a base camp for our forays.

As usual, acclimatization and training tours came first. The Cordillera Negra was suitable for the purpose, and we hoped to get a fine view of the crest of the Cordillera Blanca across the valley. However, the weather

"Some of the mules were still half wild and had a habit of leaping into the air and lashing out with all four feet as soon as the loads were placed on their backs and before the saddle-girths could be tightened up, so that bits and pieces flew in all directions."

decided otherwise. This did not matter to us, and it gave us a good reason to do some training expeditions in the main range itself. Our first trip, undertaken with the object of getting used to the height, the porters, and the animals, lay past Huascarán into the Ulta valley.

The march of our porters with their beasts of burden past the front of our hotel was observed with curiosity by the other guests. Mountain climbers are rare enough in our part of the world, where they are gaped at by the rest of humanity. Elsewhere the contrast is greater still. Among the porters was an elderly man whom we pointedly told to go home because of his advanced age. The other porters asked us to take the old guy along, even if only at half pay. We agreed to this, and noticed that they all seemed much relieved. Some of the mules were half wild and had a habit of leaping into the air and lashing out with all four feet as soon as loads were placed on their backs and before the saddle girths could be tightened up, so that bits and pieces flew in all directions. No one could do anything with them except the old man, who only had to go near them and they would fall quiet again. This phenomenon was not an isolated occurrence; it happened every day, and in the end we gave the old man not half the normal rate, but double.

We rode down to the floor of the valley and then along it for several days to the *lagunas*, small lakes formed against frontal moraines. On one side, the glacier tongue reached into the water, on the other were thickets of rose bushes. I had never imagined that such a spectacle existed.

The silence was broken only by occasional beautiful birdsong. Yet, however peaceful and marvelous these *lagunas* might seem, they were treacherous and much feared because of their tendency to break through the moraine and flood the whole valley as though a dam had burst. We decided that we were satisfied enough with this first gentle ride of several days duration. We had wonderful impressions of flora and fauna, and the main purpose of establishing working relationships with the porters and animals had been achieved.

The valley was full of white and blue lupines, while in boggy places trumpet lilies grew as thick as daisies at home. There were also masses of yellow slipperwort and plants unknown to me, shrubs with red blossoms, and most amazing of all, orchids and bromeliads growing on box and rose trees. Only the fauna were not particularly forthcoming. We could hear birds twittering jubilantly, but could not see them. Pumas were said to be numerous, but they remained equally invisible. The porters had a terror of pumas, though, and kept a fire going throughout the night.

The complete team of the 1963 South American Expedition

The ascent of
Palcaraju

Once we had soaked away the effects of this first tour in warm baths and the hotel bar at Monterrey we felt ready for new and more serious exploits. In high good humor and full of enterprise and resolution we rode off into the Ishinka valley, as full of flowers and blossoms as the last. This time we immediately found a goal that was within the powers of the party, a fine trapezoidal ice giant dominating a lateral valley.

"That one's ours!" we agreed.

We were surprised to find a trail leading into this side valley so well trodden that we could have ridden up it. It ended before a stone house at the foot of the glacier. True, the door and window frames were empty, but it boasted a roof. There was also another *laguna,* this one artificially drained to avert flooding. As this task had taken several years, the engineers had built themselves the house which now stood abandoned and available for our use. We made ourselves as comfortable as possible and climbed several 5000–6000 meter peaks. After this we felt fit enough to tackle our chosen mountain.

It snowed thickly all night long, yet in the morning the snow was only ankle deep. After such a snowfall in the Alps, the accumulation would have been up to our waists, but in the dry air of that altitude the snow evaporated as fast as it came down. Only in the rainy season, which is summer, is there enough snowfall to build up the snow cover and glaciers. This is no wonder, since the moist air masses out of the Amazon Basin break against the ramparts of the Andes, which rise up to 7000 meters in places. The mighty storms that result cause the formation of cornices that have been the undoing of many a mountain climber, among them Fritz Kasparek, our companion on the Eiger, who fell through one on Salcantay. Despite the mist we found our way through the chaotic maze of crevasses as though we had been this way often. But we grew apprehensive about cornices as we neared the crest. Just below the top, I no longer trusted the ridge and instead climbed a much harder rock buttress. Meanwhile Jochen, who had Rudolf and Henno on his rope, strolled up the crest of the snow arête to the summit. He had heard much less about the danger of cornices and therefore worried less about them.

Presumably we were the first to climb this mountain, though it made no difference to me. I was much more interested in the flight of two majestic condors that sailed past us close enough to touch.

We arrived back at our hut in darkness and saw the summit from which we had just returned glowing in the last light. It was snowing again as we headed down the next morning, and we found the warmth of the valley very pleasant, though we bivouacked again at 4400 meters.

It would be narrow-minded to travel around the world as a climber and nothing else. The mountaineering objectives serve as focal points for the journey, and the experience grows from contact with unsullied

Glaciated lake below Palcaraju

nature and lonely places. These are found above all in the mountains and we enjoy them as a recompense for the innumerable hardships we undergo. Moreover, there is so much to see and hear when you consider the world with an open mind. While still at home I made it my business to learn something about Inca culture and had read a couple of books about Pizarro's conquest of Peru. Now that we were on the spot we were not going to miss the chance of seeing at least a couple of the renowned cultural sites. As it was impossible to see everything, we decided to split up. Five of us were interested in the Chavin civilization in the neighborhood of Huarás, while Dr. Schneider, the geologist, and I agreed to make an excursion to Cuzco.

Before leaving Huarás, however, we unexpectedly found ourselves involved in a fiesta. We were sought out at the hotel by a Peruvian whose son was studying in Germany and who wanted to meet us. He asked whether we knew a place called Bad Aibling, where his son was at the Goethe Institute. It happened that Jochen Singer lived just nearby and that I had spent half my childhood there. Señor Alfonso Vega was so overjoyed at this coincidence that he immediately placed his house at our disposal. We would have preferred to stay on at the hotel with the heated swimming pool, but refusing the invitation would have been an insult. Four of us, therefore, moved over to his house, where Señor Vega enjoined us to wear a white shirt and a tie that evening, as there was going to be a little celebration. We imagined a dinner party in our honor.

Together with some señoritas we were loaded into a VW bus and driven bumpily over to Huarás. As we made the tour of the town, the young women disappeared into various houses, but we drove on through the inky night. Why we did not stop anywhere remained a mystery. Presently it began to rain, but the drive continued. A fine old celebration, we thought. At last, after a good hour, Señor Vega drew up in front of a house where one of the girls had vanished earlier. Now she emerged all dressed and made up and climbed in beside us. One after another we picked them up again in all their finery.

Finally he deposited us under a projecting roof where we could shelter from the pouring rain and drove off into the night. "What now?" we wondered. Pressing our backs against the wall we waited for someone to come. Someone turned out to be Señor Vega again, this time on foot, and we trotted behind him in single file around to the left and through a door. Inside there was a patio where many people were already standing or slouching around wearing festive decorations, which were now placed on us also by a young mulatto girl as pretty as a picture. Thereupon we were led into a room decorated with paper flowers and illuminated with green and pink neon tubes. The ladies sat on one side, while the men stood on the other.

We were introduced to our hostess and now we learned that it was the christening feast of a child, to which the highest official in the town had been invited. What we were doing there was still unclear. The others, who knew a few words of Spanish, made more or less tortured conversation. I sidled away into the doorway where two local men were standing. Despite their elegant suits, they seemed out of place too.

Some guitar players marched out, took their places, and the fiesta began with a dance. Between dances young girls brought around drinks and a veritable buffet spitted on toothpicks. This went on for two or three hours, during

The old porter who was able to clam the wild animals

which I cursed my social awkwardness and longed for the party to end.

Eventually I was spotted by Señor Vega as he danced by. He came and led me to an adjoining room where there was a bar. He could have shown me that right at the beginning! After a couple of piscos and sangrias I began to thaw out and made my way over to the two men in the doorway. I brought them back to the bar, where we toasted each other eagerly. At this point the musicians decided to have a rest. My friends took their guitars from them and serenaded me. I always thought that it only happened like this in dreams or films, but here it was in reality— Spanish music, Spanish singing, and with a Peruvian rhythm that went straight to my legs. I could not resist it, and began to dance. Whether it was the pisco or the rhythm, despite the fact that I had never danced a solo in my life, the others assured me that it looked skillful and not at all ridiculous. The spell was broken; we were wallflowers no longer. Now the fiesta really got underway, and so it went on until daybreak. As we bade our farewells we were showered with invitations, all of which we unfortunately had to turn down as our private bus to Lima stood waiting.

Achim and I were taking the expedition's baggage to Lima, for which we needed the whole bus. Neither the driver nor the bus looked especially trustworthy. We ground our way very slowly up to the top of the 4000-meter pass, but down the other side he drove like a wild man, flashing past other vehicles always exactly at the passing lanes. In reply to our entreaty to drive a little slower he admitted that he would be happy to do so, but that we were going so fast because the brakes were out of order.

We did not stop long in Lima, but flew 1000 kilometers southward to Cuzco, passing Salcantay on the way. I got a close-up view of the icy giant on which Kasparek had fallen to his death.

Out of necessity to get seats on the plane, we turned to a travel agency. It was cheaper to be part of a group and all formalities were taken care of by the airline representative. We were met at the airport in Cuzco by a guide with a taxi waiting to whisk us off to the feudal Grand Hotel. A whole tourist program was available to us. We did not want it all, but it had its amenities. The other tourists followed it to the letter and obediently took the recommended rest while we strolled on over to the marketplace.

Apart from gringos there seemed to be no one but native Indians, and the market scene was correspondingly bright and scented. Strangers were ignored. Everything was authentic, both the colorful llama-wool ponchos and the restaurant that an Indian woman had set up in the street. As I am always ready to try anything, I sat down on the curb and had a bowl of the brew she was offering for sale. I was thoughtfully passed a battered spoon, which was first wiped on a not very clean-looking skirt, but I denied myself this achievement of civilization and ate with my

The railway through the Urubamba Valley to Machu Picchu

fingers like the Indians. The stuff I shoveled into my mouth was so spicy that tears practically spurted sideways out of my eyes. Beside me a two-year-old child was cramming the same concoction into his mouth as fast as he could. I passed him my bowl and he devoured its contents as well without changing his expression. Shaking my head, I abandoned the restaurant and returned to the hotel, where we were collected by our guide for a tour of the town and the Inca sites.

The crowning glory of our sightseeing tour was our trip to Machu Picchu the next day. There were only eight of us in the party, and we did not have to take the usual overcrowded transportation as a special coach had been arranged for us. We set off punctually at 6:30 A.M., ascending to a pass in a series of hairpin bends. The pass was the watershed between the Atlantic and the Pacific Oceans. Next the route went down, down into a beautiful broad valley that soon deepened and narrowed into a gorge leading into the main valley of the Río Vilcanota. The little stream up on the pass had now developed into a torrential tributary of the Amazon, flowing into the Atlantic 6000 kilometers away.

Our little bus rattled and jolted along. The view was breathtaking. Now and again there would be an unplanned stop because of Indians driving their beasts along the track; obviously there was no road. Whenever this happened a mulatto boy who was hired for the purpose would jump down and clear the Indians and their herds out of the way. Suddenly we found ourselves passing through gloomy primeval forest and presently arrived at the "town" of Machu Picchu, which consisted of a few miserable wooden shacks and a bus that waits to take tourists up to the holy sanctuary of Machu Picchu.

In 1911 an American archaeologist who was riding through the Urumbamba valley heard from an Indian that there were ruins up on the mountains. The existence of this city had been suspected for a long time, but its location was unknown. What must his feelings have been upon first seeing this mysterious ruined city, now one of the wonders of the world?

The Incas, masters in the art of dry-stone wall construction, built the city walls on extraordinarily steep slopes, thus gaining one terrace after another on which they laid soil for agriculture. No irrigation was required, as Machu Picchu is in the jungle zone where it rains practically every day. In the center are the holy temples, on which the guide gave a very thorough commentary. However, as I understood no Spanish and my companion had soon heard enough, we set off to make our own discoveries and let the strange atmosphere work on us. In this way an experience is more intense even if it later turns out that something interesting was missed. A short visit to such a place is always much too cursory; it would be necessary to spend at least a week there. We always allow too little time, and then regret it for the rest of our lives. We did attempt to reach the absolute summit, on which there were more terraces and a temple, but we ran out of time.

At one point I nearly had an accident. An orchid the size of a man's fist was growing on the steep flank of the hill, and I wanted to photograph it. I was not exactly a climbing novice, but rarely have I been so mistaken in estimating difficulty. I could see that the ground was very steep, but that neither impressed me nor prevented me from traversing across the hillside toward the flower. The layer of light humus that lay only finger-thick over the bedrock was so dry and dusty that it crumbled away at the touch. There was no question of finding firm hand- or footholds; only some thorny shrubs offered a little purchase. I got to within a couple of meters of the orchid when suddenly a branch rose up and hissed at me. It was a snake. All of a sudden I did not care anymore for the orchid, but crabbed my way back with extreme concentration. When I reached level ground once more my knees were shaking and I felt quite

The Inca city of Machu Picchu nestled at the foot of the holy mountain Huayna Picchu

pale. From then on I humbly enjoyed the wild begonias that grew every-where in an abundance such as you would scarcely find in a botanical garden in Europe.

Nature and culture could not be more closely associated than they were here. With this impression we returned to Cuzco and on to Lima, where we met up again with our companions who extolled the Chavin culture to us with equal enthusiasm.

Our undramatic yet thrilling "expedition" was over. Now that we had poked our noses into South America, we began to dream of the north. I therefore asked OE, "What about a trip along the 'dream road of the world' from Canada to Mexico, striking off left and right to tackle some of the mountain objectives along the way? There are plenty of them."

Arriving in New
York on the MS
Bremen

17. The Dream Trip— Canada, the United States, and Mexico

O nce again two years went by before our "expedition" was ready
to go, naturally under the patronage of OE, who this time brought
his younger son Frederick so that he too should undergo the test
afforded by the joys and hardships of such a journey. A new member of
the party was Alois Deiss, my friend and mountain guide colleague, who
was to lose his life in an avalanche in the Ötztal in 1970. Once again
Jochen Singer accompanied us as doctor. We had learned in Africa and
South America that his presence was a guarantee of good medical care.

Like innocent schoolboys, we looked for a mountaineering objective
in Canada and hit upon Mount Waddington, north of Vancouver. It
might have been any other four thousander, of which there were plenty
in the neighborhood, but we had picked out not only the most difficult
but also the most inaccessible of them all. After that we wanted to climb
a few peaks in the Rocky Mountains, visit Yellowstone National Park,
take a look at the Grand Canyon, and then climb Popocatapetl and possibly Orizaba, the highest mountain in Mexico, while also taking in any
other sights we could manage on the way. However, things generally
work out differently than you expect.

With our previous experience, the financial means at OE's disposal,
and the ample time for preparation, the whole trip went like clockwork.
In any case, it was no longer the great step into the unknown—there
was no time to spare for improvisation, we were constantly dependent
on the timetable and our objectives. There are only two ways to travel,
with plenty of money or, better, with plenty of time; best of all with both.
At least we had the first on our side.

To recuperate from the wear and tear of preparations, Alois Deiss and
I set off in advance by sea on August 18, 1965, to New York, where we
were to tie up the final loose ends. The others were to follow by air. Our
ulterior motive was to taste the pleasures of a first-class sea voyage just
once in our lives and to see something of New York. Although the lazy
life on board was marvelous, the six days from Cherbourg to New York
were enough to grow weary of it. You can even have enough of stuffing
yourself to bursting in a valiant effort to store fat for lean times to come.
Even at breakfast, in addition to the usual menu, I would polish off a leg
of lamb, a veal fillet, or some goulash, greatly to the disgust of Alois, who
suffered from seasickness. After he was more or less back on his feet he
still would go suddenly pale over the breakfast table and rush outside to
the rail. There has to be balance in nature—one eats, another throws up.

In New York I was duly impressed by the skyscrapers. The Natural
Science Museum with its unique mineral collections was surprisingly
interesting, as was a visit to a bar in Harlem. There had just been a bout
of racial disturbances, and we were warned away from the neighborhood. In fact, we saw nothing that seemed dangerous.

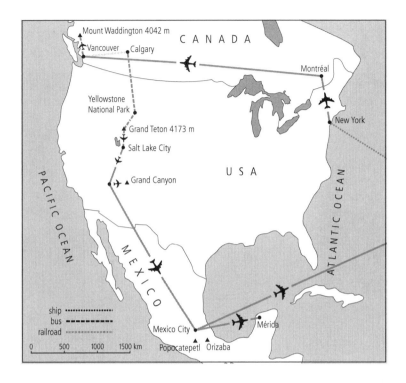

The next day we almost missed the airplane. We got in at 3:00 A.M. and had to get up again two hours later in order to be at the airport by seven o'clock. It was exactly seven o'clock when we woke up! Unwashed and unshaven, we caught the flight to Montreal at the very last moment. There we were met by the celebrated climber Fritz Wiessner. He had been the first to climb Mount Waddington and gave us precise information as well as contacts that greatly facilitated our undertaking. Indeed, he made the whole thing possible.

From Stowe, his home in Vermont, he telephoned God and the world on our behalf. If friendship is international, mountaineering friendship is particularly so. We all hold to the same ideals, and in the case of some-one whose reputation is known beyond his own home turf everyone is aware of what he has done and—more importantly—what kind of a person he is. Recognition and esteem go hand in hand, friendship is immediate, and each one does what he can for the other.

Thus, Canadian climbers were waiting for us at the Vancouver airport, accommodations had been arranged for us, and we were shown, with justified pride, around the wonderful Pacific city, ringed with mountains and with the most beautifully landscaped parks I had ever seen.

Fips Broda, president of the Vancouver Mountaineers, had been born

in Salzburg and he introduced us to every climber in the city. Some had been to Mount Waddington and showed us slides, concentrating on the mountain's special and unique character. For the first time we began to understand something of the difficulties of our project. There was no reason to fear the technical difficulties, although they were around grades 5 and 6. The difficulties of access had diminished since Wiessner's day. He had to fight his way for weeks and months through pathless terrain just to reach the mountain. These days you take an airplane and a helicopter flight and are simply set down at the point of departure for the peak. This was only one aspect of the arrangements in which we received every kind of help and support. No one would fly a non-climber to the departure point. It was necessary to have a firm recommendation from well-known people, of whom we were not in short supply. The great danger was that if the weather broke the thermometer could plummet in an hour from zero to -40°C. Supercooled humid air masses move in from the ocean and condense on the mountain as ice. This phenomenon occurs in the Western Alps, too, as I had experienced on the Eiger and the Grandes Jorasses, but whereas there the layer of verglas

The team and their baggage are set down at the foot of Mount Waddington

may be 10 to 20 centimeters thick at the most, on Mount Waddington it can form more than a meter thick.

The summit of Mount Waddington is just over 4000 meters high, while the spot where the helicopter set us down to begin our climb was at about 2000 meters. It was already September, rather late in the season and the month in which these sudden storms occur most frequently. We had to promise solemnly to remain where we were even if it snowed for weeks. Good weather was bound to come in the end, and then they would get us out. We therefore purchased enough food for three weeks and an equivalent amount of fuel for melting snow; after all, we did not have to carry it all. Our doctor had explained to us that theoretically humans can go a whole month without solid food, but only three days without fluids. Two seaplanes carried us and our baggage to Ghost Lake, a little mountain lake, where we were picked up by the helicopter and transported in relays to our starting point amid ice and snow. Here we set up a base camp.

As the helicopter chugged away after bringing in the last loads we began to appreciate the remoteness in which we had had ourselves set down. There was no way back under our own steam, and if things came to the worst we would just have to dig into the snow and wait. For the time being, however, the weather was fine. Before long the tents were up and the cookers purring. After an ample meal and a healthy swig of Canadian whiskey my Toscanelli tasted as good as it ever did. Everything is relative, and no Grand Hotel comfort could replace the romantic scene around us. The following day we made a timid attempt to reconnoiter the notorious Bravo Glacier.

Some Japanese climbers had been there shortly before us. Owing to bad weather they had failed to reach the summit, returning with reports of very rotten ice. And in fact the glacier did not look particularly inviting. It was seamed with crevasses and séracs apparently ready to fall at any moment. On the right of the glacier was a rocky spur that we thought

An ice edge on the ascent of Mount Waddington

would go and up which we made our way for a couple of pitches. The only question we kept asking ourselves was how we were going to get into the upper glacier basin.

Despite this uncertainty, the following day the whole party climbed the spur, which turned out to be not so simple. Our fears proved groundless, as we were able to reach the upper glacier easily and without any great loss of height. Thus, we circumvented the Bravo Glacier, where a whole expedition had once come to grief.

The way forward was clear to see. Less clear was how we were going to get across an almost horizontal ice ridge. There was no other solution but to sit astride it and work our way along *à cheval* for an hour and a half, which is not a very agreeable pastime on ice. I knew how suddenly such a thin rind of ice can crack off, and took good care to keep the pressure of my thighs equal on both sides for the entire time—no doubt under the influence of a healthy fear—so that as a result I had cramps in my legs throughout the following night. Next came a steep but compact stretch of glacier up which we also climbed despite signs of growing fatigue occasioned by our heavy sacks. Just as dusk fell we reached a level place where we could pitch our high-altitude tents.

We were supposed to go back down the following day to fetch further food supplies, but somehow the idea gave us horrors. We therefore hit on the excuse that not a single day of fine weather should be wasted and decided to go straight for the summit. It was true that we had no food, but hadn't the good doctor told us it was possible to go without for thirty days? While it was still dark the next morning, we kicked our way for some hours up breakable crust to the upper rock buttresses. It was a real treat to lay a hand on the warm, dry rock.

From a notch on the ridge we could see the summit above us. Now we were sure of bagging the summit. I wanted to enjoy the climbing to the full (as if I could not get any amount of it back home!) and jettisoned all unnecessary ballast. Even my two cameras remained in the sack which I left in the notch, an action that I regret to this day, as nowhere have I seen stranger ice formations on a vertical face. We had been told that in these parts ice could form meters thick on perpendicular rock walls, but I hadn't really believed it. This layer is then eroded by the warm air, so that transparent, tattered banners of ice are left projecting out as much as five meters, looking as though they have been attacked with a pair of scissors. Beautiful as they are when illuminated by the sun, in reality they are extremely dangerous, since they were poised ready to fall at any moment and a single one might weigh several hundred tons. On this occasion I was climbing last on the rope and would have had ample time to take photographs, but the cameras were back in that gap, for which I have never forgiven myself. The technical difficulties were considerable, but gave us pleasure rather than trouble. We stepped up onto the summit with genuine Bavarian whoops of joy.

The descent consisted of rappels as far as the glacier, and we stormed down this toward the tents. On arrival a shock coursed through our limbs. The level surface on which the tents were pitched now formed part of a bridge over a vast crevasse. We shuddered to think this might have happened during the night. Since it was now necessary to strike camp anyway, we continued to descend while the daylight lasted, and so reached the narrow ice ridge.

We had no desire whatever to ride our way along it again, so I investigated the edge of rock on which it rested 50 or 100 meters below. Lo and behold, it went without any difficulty at all, and we came upon an ideal little bivouac site.

The sun had set and the full moon was rising over the glacier as we spread our bivouac gear on a granite slab. There was not a breath of wind; we had plenty of warm, dry things; only there was nothing to eat, so we made do without. We knew that the pots of meat stew were waiting for us in base camp, from which no serious obstacle now separated us. The nylon high-altitude tent served as a groundsheet, and before long I was blissfully asleep.

In the middle of the night I awoke from a deep sleep. For no good reason that I could think of I was wide awake and admired the fantastic view. The full moon stood above a splendid icy giant that shone with

"No helicopter appeared. The shadows grew longer and so did our faces, but we sat where we were and were not picked up."

reflected light. Entranced with the sight, I wondered why I had not noticed this mountain before going to sleep. Suddenly the realization shot through me that I had gradually slid down the smooth nylon surface until my head had passed the flat block that had previously obscured the view. My feet were already dangling in space. Cautiously I wriggled back until I could sit up and anchor myself with piton and rope. Then I lay down again behind the block and went back to dreaming of the beautiful view.

The remainder of the descent the next day was protracted but not too difficult, and we reached our well-stocked base camp toward evening. Only someone who has experienced such a healthy hunger can imagine how wonderful the meal, though primitively cooked, really tasted. We called up Vancouver on the radio transmitter that we had been provided for all eventualities, duly obtaining a connection and an answer; we would be picked up the next day. The following morning we joyously struck camp, crated all the expedition kit, gobbled up all the food that we liked the taste of, sat down on the crates and waited. Every time there was a noise we jumped up, but it always turned out to be a distant icefall thundering down. No helicopter appeared. The shadows grew longer and so did our faces, but we sat where we were and were not picked up. Twilight gathered and it grew cold. We sullenly unpacked again, pitched the tents and crawled inside.

During the night the Canadian wind began to howl and soon hail started to fall. Presently its drumming changed to the rustle of snow. A thrill of fear ran through me. Could this be the great snowfall that might last three weeks? No one could sleep, yet as day dawned we all lay where we were. No one spoke a word. At about ten o'clock there was a sudden humming in the air; it could not be another avalanche. We tore out of the tents, and there was a helicopter sweeping toward us like a hornet. The evacuation and the liaison between the helicopter and the seaplane that picked us up at Ghost Lake went like clockwork. The press and a television crew were there, but we were feeling too happy to be upset by that and just let it all flow over our heads.

The real jubilation took place in Vancouver, where our mountain friends were waiting for us. We had to tell our story over and over again, and I think that if we had failed to climb the mountain our friends would have been far more disappointed than ourselves. We were fully aware of how lucky we had been with regard to the weather and conditions and of how much we owed to all those who helped us in our adventure. And now it was off to our next objective!

There are many fine mountains in British Columbia's Glacier National Park, and we picked Eagle Peak as our next goal. It is neither particularly high nor particularly difficult. What it does call for is endurance, a quality it shares with most of the peaks in the Rocky Mountains. The trek takes ten or twelve hours and the place is swarming with bears. Though very strong, brown bears are not particularly aggressive, but grizzlies are irritable and dangerous. The park warden told us some real horror stories. It is no good carrying a gun, as you do not get a chance to shoot when you are having a run-in with a bear. The best thing is to make a lot of noise as you go along, shouting and banging, which we did with our pitons and carabiners. The ideal solution would have been a cow bell to hang around our necks, but unfortunately we had neglected to pack one among the expedition baggage. Thus forewarned, the animals have time to move out of the way before you reach the danger zone. At high altitude we saw a lot of fresh bear tracks in the new snow. The bears withdraw to high altitudes to hibernate, but luckily for us, we never encountered a single bear.

After our ascent of Eagle Peak, a park ranger took me in his car to a garbage dump, which was carefully fenced off, and where there were bears busily rooting around. They are omnivorous, and will devour cartons, packing and all, if they find nothing tastier. We hardly had been there a minute when he suddenly stopped and listened.

"That's a grizzly growling!" he said.

I could hear nothing and wanted to get out of the car to photograph the black bears, but the ranger hauled me back at once. Apparently the beasts move so fast that I would not have had time to jump back in. When one is completely new to a thing one really should just rely on the experience of others, and so I missed seeing one of these fearsome bears.

We now traveled by Canadian Pacific Express across the Rocky Mountains to Calgary passing through such famous places as Golden, Lake Louise, and Banff. The Rocky Mountains resemble the Central Alps but are not so excessively developed, and are unlikely to become so in a hurry, since mountaineering is much less popular in North America than in Europe. Anyone who goes climbing has to be self-sufficient, as there are no villages and huts to depend on. Many mountain ranges encompass national parks. The park rangers, who are responsible for seeing that the regulations are observed, take good care that no one undertakes mountain adventures if not qualified to do so. A special permit may be required for mountaineering, and this is only issued to those who can show credentials from a recognized mountaineering club or a well-known climber. We had such a certificate, and as the rangers were mainly Austrian, Swiss, or German they nearly all knew my name, which often helped to clear obstacles from our path.

We were not hell-bent on *only* climbing mountains, of course. Yellowstone National Park lay on our route and who could possibly drive past such a wonder of nature? We therefore traveled by Greyhound bus from Calgary to Livingston, where we hired a car to continue the journey via Gardiner to the park. Nowhere in the world are there so many natural marvels all gathered together in one place and easily accessible. The ground steams and puffs; there are not just hundreds but thousands of geysers, big and small, whole valleys full of them.

Only a few miles south of Yellowstone, however, Grand Teton National Park offered several worthwhile climbing objectives. Furthermore, at Trail Creek Ranch near Jackson Hole lived Mrs. Woolsey, captain of the American women's ski team at the 1936 Olympic Games and an internationally renowned mountain climber into the bargain. She had been with Fritz Wiessner on the first ascent of Mount Waddington in 1937, so we were welcome guests at the ranch. Fritz Wiessner had also promised to join us in an ascent of the 3800-meter Grand Teton.

While waiting for him to appear, we made a few excursions in the area. There were seventy horses on the ranch, and for the first time I enjoyed riding. Up to now I had sat astride old nags, but never a real horse.

Wiessner turned up then, and we packed our sacks for the ascent of the Grand Teton. It was possible to drive up to the foot of the mountain in a car. We were expected and had no difficulties at the park entrance, which had a building and a barrier just like a customs post. One of the rangers joined our party, which was a great advantage as he had access to a hut reserved for park rangers and situated just below the steep summit rocks.

O-E in cowboy garb at Mrs. Woolsey's ranch

A path led up through the woodland zone and ended at the point where the terrain became more difficult. Half a meter of new snow had fallen, filling in the gaps between the blocks in the boulder field. We had to be hellish careful not to break a leg. It took us a full eight hours to reach the hut, which was just a corrugated iron box, although a roomy one. We undressed and lay down in our sleeping bags, covering up with damp hut blankets. The saddle on which the hut was built was at 3500 meters, so it got quite cold. In the night a storm of such violence blew in that I expected the whole box of tricks to blow away at any moment. The thought of standing roofless in the fresh air, clad in nothing but a shirt, was not pleasant. The next morning everything was deeply buried in snow and the rocks were completely iced up. We were not obsessed with fighting our way to the top at any price, so we decided to renounce our summit bid and descend.

Despite not bagging the summit, we were entirely satisfied with this adventure. Breaking trail downhill in thigh-deep snow is no problem. The American park ranger slid down most of the snow gullies on the seat of his pants at the speed of an express train. In Germany this method of descent is strongly disapproved of, as it has led to too many accidents, but I was finally unable to resist the temptation and ended up doing likewise. Back on the woodland path we rambled along at our pleasure, enjoying the wonderful atmosphere of the place through the intermittent fog as we strode back down to the valley, passing elk at close quarters. If the weather had broken like that while we were on Mount Waddington we would have been in a fine mess. This thought lent wings to our happy mood, despite having had to back out before reaching the summit. We handed back the rental car at the Jackson Hole airport and flew off over Salt Lake City toward the Grand Canyon.

There were places to climb in this, the greatest gorge on earth, but they were not the main attraction for us, though we did want to take a cursory look at them if everything went well. Everything did not go well.

Near the southern edge of the canyon there was a regular city of hotels populated with troops of tourists from all over the world who were content simply to take a look into the abyss. It is in fact impossible to see all the way down to the bed of the canyon, but most tourists did not care about that as there were postcards of it in the hotel. Anyone who wanted to penetrate into the gorge had to go to the "Indian Garden," which was generally done on muleback and took a whole day. Only a few descended right down to the bottom. We climbers went on foot. The mule track was broad and well trodden, so there was little need to take care and one could devote one's full attention to the strange, impressive landscape.

The plateau lies at over 2000 meters and is covered with pine and juniper. The deeper you go, the more the vegetation changes; in fact one passes through practically all zones of vegetation from conifers to cacti. The Colorado River was far from being the poor little trickle that had been described to me; it is a full-grown river more than 2000 kilometers long, quite powerful enough to perform the mighty work of erosion.

An iron bridge spanned the river. The poor mules that carried down the materials for it deserve a monument in their honor. A few kilometers farther on, on the opposite bank, stood Phantom Ranch, swimming pool and all. We were there in the off-season, however, and the ranch was closed and the pool, unhappily, was empty of water. A notice hung on the door, "Open at 6:00 P.M."

It was noon. We had set off much too early, although the eight-hour march was only half as hard as it would have been later in the day. Nevertheless, the tropical heat on the valley floor was such that our tongues stuck to the roofs of our mouths, and the sight of the empty pool did little to cheer us up. Everyone looked for a patch of shade, but I was seized with a desire to reconnoiter one of the peaks that we might be able to climb the next day.

"Peaks" was a funny word to use for these cones formed by erosion. They also had strange names such as Shiva's Temple, the Pyramid of Cheops, Zoroaster's Temple, and so on. The latter attracted me and I wanted to climb it.

As soon as I took one step off the beaten track I was in virgin wilderness. Carefully making my way around the cactus bushes, I sought out the rocky steps, which made some exciting climbing. In between them were flatter terraces covered with thorny scrub. Everything had spines, not only the cacti. There was a little wall about four meters high and I enjoyed the bright red rock and the plentiful holds. Just as I was about to mantelshelf over the top there was such a dreadful rattling noise that I let go in fright and dropped to the bottom. We had been warned about rattlesnakes everywhere we went. Probably this was one, but I didn't get a chance to see it. The fall wouldn't have been so bad if I had not landed seat first in a cactus. After that I made my way down, finding the descent quite a thorny problem. It was a full three days before the doctor succeeded in extracting all the prickles.

Following this adventure, for which everyone naturally had a laugh at my expense, I was a lot less enthusiastic to climb another such peak. We therefore decided to go back via the Kaibab Trail. By contrast with the luxury hotels on the southern edge of the canyon, Phantom Ranch turned out to be a simple place where the service was personal and friendly.

The next day we set off early, well supplied with cans of beer. Naïvely, the Americans only quoted the distance of 6.8 miles without a word about the height difference of 1600 meters, which must have caused trouble to many a hiker inexperienced in mountain matters. We were able to work out for ourselves how long it would take and proceeded accordingly. The trail was a real walkers' path, and the rock scenery almost more impressive than the descent along the Angel Trail.

Quite unexpectedly, we encountered a group of youngsters, the fresh and cheery ones in the lead, then the ones with red faces, then the ones with their tongues hanging out, and last of all two guides, probably teachers, one of whom should have been in front setting the pace. At least, that is how it is done where I come from. But I should report another little episode that also showed how differently things are done in the United States. A chewing-gum wrapper lay on the path. I merely glanced at it, but one of the kids picked it up, put it in his pocket, and walked on. I pondered whether we could ever educate European children on this point of conscientiousness.

View of the Grand
Canyon from the
south rim

Higher up I began to suffer from thirst and remembered the beer in the rucksack. After enjoying every delicious drop I hurled the empty can in a high arc into a gully below. At that moment a group on horseback came around the corner and heard the noise of the can rattling downhill. They all looked at me indignantly and accusingly, while the accursed can clattered on. In nature reserves it is taboo to throw away any kind of trash, but somehow this had not occurred to me until I received that annihilating stare. The damned can rattled down and down unable to find any rest, as though wanting to accuse me in its turn. To think that I had to travel to America to learn this lesson!

At the Flagstaff airport we turned in our rental car and took a direct flight to Mexico, the terminus of our dream journey. What mountaineer would not wish to stand just once on the 5300-meter summit of Popocatepetl? Orizaba, which at 5700 meters is the highest mountain in Mexico, is equally tempting. Naturally we also wanted to see Mexico City and centers of Aztec and perhaps Mayan culture. It was a big program for one visit, but none of us knew if he would ever get a chance to return.

It is said that Popocatepetl can be seen from the city, and that may be true, but I did not see it. Even the approach to the mountain is not easy. Mexican roads were good, but as soon as we got off them—and mountains are never on them—there were only rough tracks. Signposts were found only on the main roads. Therefore, it was hardly surprising that we immediately got lost in the fields of maize. The Mexicans we asked were friendly and indicated the way with voluble gestures, which, however, were wrong. Finally we succeeded in finding the right road, and that brought us up to a parklike landscape at 4000 meters, where we found a lodging house. It was none too clean and definitely primitive, but the owners were friendly. Anyone who is hypersensitive in regard to cleanliness would do better to stay at home. A little dirt does no harm, especially in the pure air at high altitudes.

We set off before dawn, following an indefinite path rising steeply through a gigantic lava field. Our lungs suffered from an irritating, constricting pressure that made us want to cough. Later I read that this was caused by the volcanic dust, but it was too dark to see it at the time. By daybreak we were already up on the snow slopes, which ascended at a steady angle of about forty degrees to the edge of the crater. It was a case of drawing our heads in and kicking our way upward step by step.

The crater lake of Popocatepetl

The important thing was to avoid hurried movements. The rarer air at 5000 meters makes itself felt, but only if you break the most elementary rules of mountaineering and go too fast. There is nothing more boring than trudging up a featureless, giant snowfield. You ask yourself what pleasure there is in it. In the last resort it is not a question of pleasure but of gritting your teeth and getting on with it.

It looked as though we could reach out and touch the edge of the crater, and yet we never seemed to draw any nearer. The air was so thin and crystal clear that it was impossible to judge distance. It is not always like that; it depends on the air pressure, the time of year, and other factors. Anyway, though I had often felt more tired and worn out on climbs, rarely had I felt so sour. My mood changed abruptly as we reached the crater.

The edge was decorated with two crosses fashioned out of iron cable that had benevolently been placed here rather than on the true summit another two hours away, which few bother to visit. We saw no reason to do otherwise. The distant view was enormous in its expanse, while the view straight down, not only toward the valley but into the mountains, was fascinating. Steam issued out of every crack, just like at Yellowstone. In the bottom of the crater, 400 meters below, lay a small, emerald-green lake that sparkled like a jewel when not obscured by a cloud of vapor.

When our hunger and thirst had been satisfied and Toscanelli smoke mingled with the puffs of steam from the crater, my happiness knew no bounds. It was not the first time that the feeling of achievement had produced this sense of rapture, but on Popocatepetl, perhaps on account of these vapor clouds, I felt it particularly strongly. That feeling is a sufficient reward for a mountaineer's pains, and I felt ashamed of my momentary bout of peevishness.

Meanwhile, the snow had softened more than ankle deep; too deep already for glissading down in comfort. Thinking of my sliding exploits on the Grand Teton I sat down on the seat of my smooth nylon outerwear and whizzed downhill at breakneck speed for well over 1000 meters. Although my companions were all appreciably younger they were no longer childish enough to get so much pleasure from sliding on their bottoms, so they dutifully stamped their way down as one should. I was well aware of the danger and somersaulted to a stop before shooting onto the lava slopes. Everything went well, and there was even time to spread out my clothes to dry before the others arrived. The track that I had scooped out with my *popo* led like a ruled line to the summit of Popocatepetl.

After this it was child's play to run down through the whirling lava dust to the lodging house. On the way we collected some specimens of volcanic glass, which lay all around.

The car that had brought us was waiting to whisk us back to the city,

Glissading down
the snow slopes
of Popocatepetl

only 50 kilometers away. The luxuries of civilized life—after our efforts everything around us felt luxurious, even a hot bath—were now restored to their proper perspective, and we enjoyed them to the full. An evening with a mariachi band, where the mescal flowed freely, left our memories of the mountain somewhat hazier but no less beautiful.

After a rest day, needed not so much because of our efforts on the mountain as on account of the victory celebrations that had followed, we felt fit again for the next adventure. Our final objective was Orizaba. This time we had to travel a little farther, eastward past Pueblo. In one little town it was market day, and buses were parked anywhere, anyhow. It looked as though we would never get through. One of our party was seized with panic and insisted that we should reach our objective via a short detour. As no one had a better suggestion, we did just that; but instead of 35 kilometers the detour turned out to be 200. It gave us a chance to see something of the country—yucca woods, lonely pueblos, and a pool that had spread out into an extensive lake. It was the time of transition from the rains to the dry season, the best time for our purpose.

The point of departure for Orizaba was a village with the strange-sounding name of Tlaquichuga, where they were set up to cope with the needs of those wanting to climb the mountain. There was only one store, but it had everything from bootlaces to a cross-country vehicle. The latter had just left to work in the fields and we had to wait until it got back in the evening. It turned out to be an ancient four-wheel-drive Dodge that groaned and rattled its way up the fearful tracks leading toward the mountain. We thought it would fall apart at any moment. The driver's name was Primitivo, but the man could certainly drive. It was dark by the time we reached the hut, a simple corrugated-iron shack once again, but roomy and relatively clean.

We were up and away before 3:00 A.M. The wind was howling and the snowflakes whirled so thickly around us that we could not tell which way to go. Uphill, of course, that much was clear, but nothing else was. In the course of a lifetime of mountain climbing you develop a kind of sixth sense. I had often relied on it when there was nothing else to go on, but it is important that it not be called into question; when there's no way to be certain, it's easy to be led astray from what intuition says is right. It was not challenged on this occasion, as no one could see and no one knew any better than I did. Yet we hit the glacier at precisely the right point. The Mexicans are very proud of the Orizaba Glacier, and we had been warned about the danger of crevasses. However, we had no intention of dropping into a letter-box of that kind in Mexico of all places, so we gave them a wide berth by keeping to the right.

The snowstorm had increased rather than decreased. It was bitterly cold into the bargain, and I had to pull on extra clothes, almost freezing

In the bivouac hut
on the Pico de
Orizaba (left to
right) Anderl
Heckmair,
Friedrich Flick,
Jochen Singer, the
driver Primitivo

my fingers in the process. In the few minutes without my mittens my hands turned as white as a linen sheet and my fingers a yellowy hue, but I brought them back to life through immediate friction with a woolen garment. Next I wanted to make up for lost time by setting a faster pace, which I hoped would also enable us to warm up. I might have saved myself the trouble, as the net effect was to make me out of breath. Not until I had settled back into my usual rhythm did I recover. The wind drove away the cloud and the sun began to warm us, although it remained cold all the way to the summit.

By contrast with Popocatepetl, Orizaba had a proper summit, not just a high point on the rim of a crater. The crater itself was even deeper and wider, but extinct. It would not have been difficult to climb down into it, but what would we do down there? The summit was much more interesting. It's possible to see two oceans from there, the Atlantic in the east and the Pacific away to the west. All we saw were two silvery lines but almost persuaded ourselves that they were the sea. The summit cross was only lengths of pipe screwed together, some of which was missing. In spite of the cold it was beautiful, but we did not hang around for long.

This time there was no opportunity for glissading down as on Popocatepetl, though I had been looking forward to it. We had to stamp our way step by step down the icy, wind-blasted slope with crampons on our feet, giving the "terrible" crevasses a very wide berth. The slopes were less monotonous than on other volcanoes. It seemed that Orizaba had been extinct long enough for erosion to take effect.

By the time we returned, Primitivo was waiting for us, frozen. In Tlaquichuga the merchant solemnly decorated us with medals for our successful ascent of Orizaba.

Although we regretted that the ascent marked the end of our mountaineering program, it left us free to concentrate on the nightlife of Mexico City. This was something special, as the mariachis were incomparable. Two bands played us into the car as we said good-bye, one on each side, both playing different tunes and trying to drown each other out.

In the course of this journey we had been hugely impressed, overcome the inevitable tensions, and enriched our lives with indelible experiences.

This is the essence of mountaineering, so often misunderstood. It enabled us to travel away from the normal tourist track and find satisfactions unsuspected by or simply unavailable to a nonclimber.

What followed was the more typical kind of traveling in high style— a flight to the Yucatán, visits to the Mayan sites of Chichén Itzá and Uxmal, and finally a swim in the Caribbean Ocean. Warm as a bath, there were scarcely any breakers, just a smooth swell as high as a room on which I drifted far out, rising and falling, turning over in my mind all the wonderful experiences we had been through. It was such a perfect pleasure that I was pervaded with a sense of peace with the whole beautiful world.

Yet such a vision of peace was only fantasy. Barely ten meters away from me a huge fish broke the surface, and I remembered we had been warned that this bay was infested with sharks. After that the green waves, blue sky, and deceptive silence no longer entranced me, and I made for shore as fast as I could.

On the shore stood a pair of refreshment stalls, almost incomparably hideous corrugated-iron shacks. In each of them a jukebox was turned up to full volume. The full moon was beginning to climb out of the sea behind the wind-ruffled palms; it was a true farewell picture.

Each of us bought a huge coconut from a peddler. The man peeled the fruit, punched a hole in the shell and stuck a drinking straw in it. We sucked up the ice-cold milk, some with expressions of bliss, others with a grimace. Then we had the nuts split open; some were marvelous, white and delicious, the others brown and stinking. No difference had been visible from the outside.

So it is with life and with journeys: outwardly the same for all, yet all so very different.

Uxmal.
Detail on the
"Cuadrangulo de
las monjas."

With Trudl in the
Allgäu Alps, 1970

18. The Journey Continues

My wife died and our two sons had long since moved out of the family home. I was alone again and a little out of sorts. For me life has always been like being in the mountains, full of ups and downs. I was in the bottom of a deep valley when the prospect of another of OE's expeditions lifted my spirits again. We had decided on a trekking trip to the Himalayas and it was my job to employ an interpreter who would deal with all the correspondence in various languages and keep the expedition accounts during the preparatory phase. This was also the time that the German Mountain Guides and Ski Instructors Association (Verband Deutscher Berg- und Skiführer) was founded and I was kept busy as its first chairman. The association joined the International Federation of Mountain Guides Associations, which meant that I was obliged to attend meetings abroad. Our expedition interpreter, Trudl, accompanied me and our relationship grew close. When we married, tongues wagged and it was remarked that I had married her because she had become too expensive to employ. An Italian newspaper report about my unsettled lifestyle even closed with the comment that after the Eiger my second greatest conquest was my wife.

In my experience, preparing for an expedition takes longer if you are not engaging the services of a travel agent and it was Christmas 1973 before everything was arranged. Wishing to inform OE of the fact, I placed a call to Düsseldorf, but was told, "You didn't know? OE died last night." The job of "unraveling" an expedition that is already organized, even if it is just a matter of a straightforward trekking trip, is like trying to catch a flying arrow. The airline tickets were booked and could not be refunded, only transferred.

An interest in the cultural sites of the Aztecs had been awakened during my Mexico trip with OE in 1965. Furthermore, we had climbed only two of the country's three interesting mountaineering objectives; Ixtaccihuatl was still on my wish list. The opportunity of traveling to Mexico with my wife Trudl and realizing that dream now presented itself. The nighttime ascent of Ixtaccihuatl with the lights of Mexico City and Puebla twinkling in the background was an unforgettable experience. No less impressive were our visits to the many ancient Mexican cultural heritage sites, which we took our time over and enjoyed to the full.

We spent a considerable portion of the following years on our travels. A trekking trip to the Lamjung-Himal was followed in 1977 by a visit to friends in Australia and the year after saw us attending a mountain guides conference in western Canada. In 1979 we visited my boyhood friend Hans Ertl, who for many years had been living the quiet life as a cattle breeder in the Bolivian jungle. The visit was combined with a trip to Cuzco and Machu Picchu, which gave me an opportunity to study the mysterious Inca ruins at leisure, and we also had enough time for a

detour to Huayna Picchu, the holy mountain near Machu Picchu. In 1980
we guided some friends on another trek in Nepal, this time to the
Helambu, where we were once more impressed with the ever-friendly
Nepalese people and their culture.

My wife Trudl also expressed a desire to see the north face of the Eiger.
Since the best view of the face is from the west flank of the mountain,
we climbed this route with two friends in 1981. It was late in the year
and the rocks were heavily verglassed. One hundred meters short of the
summit I insisted that we turn back, since we still had to make a cautious descent of the icy flank, which would take as long as the ascent.
At the spot where we turned back we were overtaken by three young
climbers who, we later learned, fell to their deaths on the descent.

I stood on the summit of the Eiger again in 1988. This time I did not get
there on foot but was flown up the line of "my route" by helicopter.
During the flight I was to provide a commentary on the climb for a television program commemorating the fiftieth anniversary of our first ascent
of the North Face, but the plan was shelved due to the wind noise and the
crew interviewed me on the summit instead. To mark the occasion, the
Grindelwald guides organized their own jubilee celebrations. In Alpiglen,
at the foot of the face, two local clergymen held a short service in the pouring rain. Heini Harrer and I then had the honor of unveiling a memorial
to the climbers lost on the Eigerwand, a table-sized chunk of rock from the
North Face inscribed by the guides. In 1998 our first ascent was celebrated
anew when stone plaques bearing our names were placed in the Eiger
Tunnel of the Jungfrau Railway to commemorate the sixty-year-old event.

Every sporting world record is broken sooner or later, but the first
ascent of a mountain or mountain face remains the first ascent. Only
much later did I learn that our first ascent of the north face of the Eiger

was considered to represent the final milestone in the classical period of alpine exploration.

I am often asked whether I would climb that route again. I cannot think of any reason why I would do so. I did not climb the North Face for prestige or glory, but for the experience it gave me. The record-breaking ascents of recent years do not interest me at all. There is an old poachers' saying that states "Freedom is to be found in the mountains." The sentiment is equally applicable to mountain climbing. We should all be free to do as we please and to find personal pleasure as we see fit. Some climb because of their need for recognition; they overestimate their abilities, underestimate the dangers, and perish as a result. People ask me what I think about the future of mountaineering. I remain convinced that extreme developments, like the present sport climbing trend, will always peter out into nothing. In the 1960s the trend was toward use of artificial aids, an approach that fell into disrepute when "red pointing" and "free-climbing" were suddenly "discovered"—climbing styles that were the accepted norm in the 1920s!

New developments can not be suppressed; this applies to mountaineering too. What are young climbers to do with their extreme dreams and ambitions when all the summits, ridges, and walls in their mountains have been climbed? Well, they then turn to other ranges and objectives, climbing frozen waterfalls in winter and doing acrobatic new routes on virgin rock in summer. If they are only active on low-lying "training crags" they are a long way from being mountaineers, but they may well develop into such, applying skill and fitness to the most difficult climbs around. In my view, someone who only climbs extreme routes or is active only for a short period of time is not a mountaineer, but someone who remains close to the ideal of the mountains as a way of life and sees them as an integral part of life in the broadest sense may justly lay claim to be.

Arthur Schopenhauer once said, *"Wer nicht den Geist seiner Zeit hat, hat nur die Not seiner Zeit"* (He who does not embrace the spirit of the age, merely has the troubles and anguish of the age.) I concur with this assessment; I gave up extreme mountaineering and turned my attention toward gentle climbing at the right time. In this, my apprenticeship as a landscape gardener

Anderl Heckmair, summer 1998

proved to be a great help and my interest in geology opened up further possibilities. More than thirty years ago, the Tourist Association of Oberstdorf invited me to lead geological and botanical walks for visitors to the region. I did this job with much pleasure for more than 25 years, ably supported by my wife, whose knowledge of botany is copious. The participants were always very interested in our tours, with the exception of one individual who introduced himself with the words, "I am not interested in botany or geology. I just wanted to meet you."

The 1990s passed more quietly for me as a natural result of my advanced age. They nevertheless brought much traveling, including trips to Canada and to Spain, where I was asked to give my Eiger lecture again. Although this event now lies more than 60 years in the past, my Eiger report still provokes great interest, primarily among young alpinists, many of whom are unable to imagine how we managed, with primitive equipment and no money, to climb routes in the Alps that still attract the ambitions of many modern-day climbers. For my part, I too admired the achievements of the generation of climbers before me who, without cars and railways (and even without paths and mountain huts), succeeded in making the most remarkable ascents.

In April 1991 a dream I had harbored for many years was finally fulfilled—a trip to Japan. We had friends in Tokyo with whom we could stay but we did not stay long because we wanted to get to know something of the land and the people. A friend of ours, Dr. Michiko Imai, who is famous in mountaineering circles throughout the world and who, in 1969, was part of the team that climbed the Japanese direttissima on the Rote Fluh of the Eigerwand, had learned of our visit and adjusted her busy schedule to accommodate our plans. As a result, we were literally passed from one hospitable Japanese climber to another. Everywhere we went we were greeted with a "Welcome Party for Mr. and Mrs. Heckmair," which gave us interesting insights into the Japanese way of life.

To our delight, we were invited to accompany Michiko Imai to Sapporo, where she was due to give a lecture on the Eiger. Joining her on stage, I was obliged to say a few words, which were translated into Japanese. The evening meal that followed was held in a beer cellar—after Milwaukee and Munich, Sapporo is the third largest beer town in the world. Since I do not speak Japanese, when called upon to propose a toast the only thing that occurred to me was to revert to my Bavarian dialect and say *"Oans, zwoa, drei . . . gsuffa!"* (One, two, three . . . drink!) Everyone was delighted and drained their half-liter bierkrugs with due ceremony.

How often have I returned from such travels with the fondest memories only to have the question come up, "Will such a thing ever happen again?" Should I, at the age of 90-plus, close with "Well, that was it"? Who knows? But at least it ends with a question mark.

THE MOUNTAINEERS, founded in 1906, is a nonprofit outdoor activity and conservation club, whose mission is "to explore, study, preserve, and enjoy the natural beauty of the outdoors. . . . " Based in Seattle, Washington, the club is now the third-largest such organization in the United States, with 15,000 members and five branches throughout Washington State.

The Mountaineers sponsors both classes and year-round outdoor activities in the Pacific Northwest, which include hiking, mountain climbing, ski-touring, snowshoeing, bicycling, camping, kayaking and canoeing, nature study, sailing, and adventure travel. The club's conservation division supports environmental causes through educational activities, sponsoring legislation, and presenting informational programs. All club activities are led by skilled, experienced volunteers, who are dedicated to promoting safe and responsible enjoyment and preservation of the outdoors.

If you would like to participate in these organized outdoor activities or the club's programs, consider a membership in The Mountaineers. For information and an application, write or call The Mountaineers, Club Headquarters, 300 Third Avenue West, Seattle, WA 98119; 206-284-6310.

The Mountaineers Books, an active, nonprofit publishing program of the club, produces guidebooks, instructional texts, historical works, natural history guides, and works on environmental conservation. All books produced by The Mountaineers Books fulfill the club's mission.

Send or call for our catalog of more than 500 outdoor titles:

The Mountaineers Books
1001 SW Klickitat Way, Suite 201
Seattle, WA 98134
800-553-4453
mbooks@mountaineersbooks.org
www.mountaineersbooks.org

The Mountaineers Books is proud to be a corporate sponsor of Leave No Trace, whose mission is to promote and inspire responsible outdoor recreation through education, research, and partnerships. The Leave No Trace program is focused specifically on human-powered (nonmotorized) recreation.

Leave No Trace strives to educate visitors about the nature of their recreational impacts, as well as offer techniques to prevent and minimize such impacts. Leave No Trace is best understood as an educational and ethical program, not as a set of rules and regulations.

For more information, visit *www.LNT.org*, or call 800-332-4100.

Other titles you might enjoy from The Mountaineers Books
Available at fine bookstores and outdoor stores, by phone at 800-553-4453, or on the World Wide Web at www.mountaineersbooks.org

Reinhold Messner, Free Spirit: A Climber's Life by Reinhold Messner. $19.95 paperbound. 0-89886-573-5.

High Achiever: The Life and Climbs of Chris Bonington by Jim Curran. $26.95 hardbound. 0-89886-713-4.

Conquistadors of the Useless: From the Alps to Annapurna by Lionel Terray. $18.95 paperbound. 0-89886-778-9.

Nanga Parabat Pilgrimage: The Lonely Challenge by Hermann Buhl. $16.95 paperbound. 0-89886-610-3.

The Hard Years by Joe Brown. $16.95 paperbound. 0-89886-845-9.

The Last Hero—Bill Tilman: A Biography of the Explorer by Tim Madge. $24.95 hardbound. 0-89886-452-6.

Ghosts of Everest: The Search for Mallory and Irvine by Jochen Hemmleb, Larry A. Johnson, and Eric R. Simonson. $24.95 paperbound. 0-89886-850-5.

The Wildest Dream: The Biography of George Mallory by Peter and Leni Gillman. $18.95 paperbound. 0-89886-751-7.

A Life on the Edge: Memoirs of Everest and Beyond by Jim Whittaker. $16.95 paperbound. 0-89886-754-1.

Kiss or Kill: Confessions of a Serial Climber by Mark Twight. $22.95 hardbound, 0-89886-763-0. $16.95 paperbound, 0-89886-887-4.

In the Zone: Epic Survival Stories From the Mountaineering World by Peter Potterfield. $16.95 paperbound. 0-89886-568-9.

Fifty Favorite Climbs: The Ultimate North American Tick List by Mark Kroese. $32.95 paperbound. 0-89886-728-2.

Everest: Eighty Years of Triumph and Tragedy, 2nd Edition by Peter and Leni Gillman. $35.00 hardbound. 0-89886-780-0.

The Mountaineers Anthology Series: Glorious Failures, Volume I edited by The Mountaineers Books Staff. $16.95 paperbound. 0-89886-825-4.

The Mountaineers Anthology Series: Courage and Misfortune, Volume II edited by The Mountaineers Books Staff. $16.95 paperbound. 0-89886-826-2.